THE ENGAGED READER

Issues and Conversations for Composition

Editorial Committee

William Breeze
Melanie Gagich
Jessica Schantz
Emilie Zickel

Second Edition

VAN-GRINER

The Engaged Reader

Issues and Conversations for Composition
Second Edition
Cleveland State University

Printed in the United States of America
10 9 8 7 6 5
ISBN: 978-1-61740-343-9

Van-Griner Publishing
Cincinnati, Ohio
www.van-griner.com

CEO: Mike Griner
President: Dreis Van Landuyt
Project Manager: Maria Walterbusch
Customer Care Lead: Julie Reichert

Breeze 343-9 Su16
163822-194338
Copyright © 2017

Table of Contents

Unit 1 | Media and the New Millennium

3   Wires and Lights in a Box
Edward R. Murrow

13   The Culture of Shut Up
Jon Lovett

21   Re–Thinking Objectivity:
Columbia Journalism Review
Brent Cunningham

37   Good News for the Future?
Young People, Internet Use,
and Political Participation
Tom P. Bakker and Claes H. de Vreese

Unit 2 | Ethics and Education

59   Who Are You and What Are You
Doing Here?
Mark Edmundson

71   Marketization of Education:
An Ethical Dilemma
Samuel M. Natale and Caroline Doran

89   A Question of Honor
William M. Chace

103   The Shame of College Sports
Taylor Branch

Unit 3 | Urban Growth and Renewal

137   Engaging the City: Civic
Participation and Teaching
Urban History
Amy L. Howard

155   Cities Mobilize to Help Those
Threatened by Gentrification
Timothy Williams

159   Is Gentrification All Bad?
Justin Davidson

167   Gentrification's Insidious Violence:
The Truth about American Cities
Daniel José Older

173   Go Forth and Gentrify?
Dashka Slater

Unit 4 | Cultures and Identities

179   What Happened to Post-Racial
America?
Ward Connerly

181   When Race Disappears
David Theo Goldberg

195   Facts and Fallacies about Paycheck
Fairness
Phyllis Schlafly

199   Why I Want Women to Lean In
Sheryl Sandberg

203   (Rethinking) Gender
Debra Rosenberg

211   Standing Up for the Rights of
New Fathers
Tara Siegel Bernard

Table of Contents

Unit 5 | Science and Nature

217   The Plight of the Honeybee
      Bryan Walsh

225   Our Oceans Are Turning into
      Plastic ... Are You?
      Susan Casey

241   Building Baby from the Genes Up
      Ronald M. Green

245   Genetically Modified Humans?
      No Thanks.
      Richard Hayes

249   Creating "Companions" for
      Children: The Ethics of Designing
      Esthetic Features for Robots
      Yvette Pearson and Jason Borenstein

Introduction

Imagine that you enter a parlor. You come late. When you arrive, others have long preceded you, and they are engaged in a heated discussion, too heated for them to pause and tell you exactly what it is about. In fact, the discussion had already begun long before any of them got there, so that no one present is qualified to retrace for you all the steps that had gone before. You listen for a while, until you decide that you have caught the tenor of the argument; then you put in your oar. Someone answers; you answer him; another comes to your defense; another aligns himself against you, to either the embarrassment or gratification of your opponent, depending on the quality of your ally's assistance. However, the discussion is interminable. The hour grows late, you must depart. And you do depart, with the discussion still vigorously in progress.

—Kenneth Burke, from *The Philosophy of Literary Form: Studies in Symbolic Action*

ଔଔଔଔ

The text you are now holding in your hands derives from one basic, but important, premise: that an educated person must be engaged in the important issues of his or her time. In a world that has become increasingly information-driven, we must take time to consider our lives more closely and with thoughtful scrutiny. In short, our knowledge-seeking selves depend on a willingness to participate in conversations about those topics that most affect us. If you are holding this book, you have already made a choice to undertake the difficult challenge of pursuing a college education. That choice is the beginning of a transformative journey that will see you conversing with classmates, professors and other educators, the authors you read, and even yourself as you grapple with complex issues and ideas.

The time you spend at this university will find you in a great number of conversations on many different subjects. You will be asked to immerse yourself not only in the disciplinary knowledge of your major, but also in many other fields that make up what we call a "liberal education," defined by the Association of American Colleges and Universities as:

> an approach to learning that empowers individuals and prepares them to deal with complexity, diversity, and change. It provides students with broad knowledge of the wider world (e.g. science, culture, and society) as well as in-depth study in a specific area of interest. A liberal education helps students develop a sense of social responsibility, as well as strong and transferable intellectual and practical skills such as communication, analytical and problem-solving skills, and a demonstrated ability to apply knowledge and skills in real-world settings.

The writing class you are now enrolled in will be one of many classes you take at Cleveland State University that focuses on those intellectual and practical skills, all of which are integral to the academic reading and writing experience. In this class you will read essays on a number of topics, organized in the following units: Media and the New Millennium; Ethics and Education; Urban Growth and Renewal; Cultures and Identities; and Science and Nature. These topics encapsulate a wide range of issues encouraging the kind of academic conversations Kenneth Burke illustrates in the metaphor that begins this introduction. To open this book is to enter a parlor where you will find yourself participating in a number of heated discussions, all of which began before you entered and will continue after you have left. Now, however, it is up to you to help shape the discussion—to listen and to speak. As you read the essays here, as you compose your written assignments, and as you discuss these topics with your teacher and your classmates, you are doing just that: joining the conversation.

What role do we have to play, then, in shaping the world in which we live? That is our guiding question. Joining the conversation is just the first step toward a greater understanding of the world in which we live. We leave traces of ourselves on our world without even trying. Imagine what we might leave if we are motivated to engage fully with the society in which we live and the planet on which we depend. The many diverse works in this textbook offer a starting point for exploring the place we inhabit as individuals within a population quickly approaching 8 billion people. You are asked here to consider serious and complex questions about how we live and thrive in our community, in our country, and in our world. The essays in Unit 1 of this book ask you to reconsider something very familiar to you: the pervasive role the media plays in our everyday lives. In Unit 2 you will read a range of essays that focus on the ethical dimensions of the place you now inhabit: higher education. Urban life—specifically, life in Cleveland—is the focus of the readings in Unit 3, while Unit 4 asks you to consider how race, class, and gender impact our lives and the roles we must play in society. Finally, Unit 5 explores the connection between science and nature in our quickly-changing world—a world where more and more we must expand our understanding of what is natural, what is human, and what is safe.

In this class you will read and write about, and discuss with diverse classmates, a range of topics that will affect the future of you all. So enter these readings in the spirit that Kenneth Burke invokes—as a participant in a rich, complex (and sometimes heated) conversation. Our hope is that this will be the beginning of a long engagement you have with the issues that are raised here.

Unit 1

Media and the New Millennium

The 21st century has given rise to many astounding changes in the way that we access and utilize media as a culture. As the media landscape has evolved in the new millennium, the confluence of pre-internet industries and digital technologies has resulted in a culture obsessed with—and perplexed by—public media movements and the discourses that stem from them. More than at any previous point in history, common citizens today—students, activists, consumers, artists, workers—can influence not only the information and viewpoints they are exposed to, but also the way in which this information presents itself in their lives.

With these dynamic and groundbreaking changes in technology, access, and even meaning, we find ourselves challenged at every turn to locate and discern new values in both our private and our public lives. In the early 1990s, conversations about the future of media began to turn towards what we now call "the electronic frontier," a digital space both feared and celebrated for allowing an essentially lawless and unrestricted flow of information from and to all corners of civilization.

As the Internet has grown into the ubiquitous cultural force it is today, we have begun to learn to both utilize its benefits and recognize its pitfalls for engaged and conscientious citizens. It is our immense and solemn responsibility, regardless of personal philosophies, political affiliations, or activist impulses, to remain informed and literate as this electronic frontier grows to envelop and encompass more and more moments of our waking, working lives. "Our history," Edward R. Murrow contended in his famous address to the RTNDA in 1958, "will be what we make it." Never before have we had such great power over our media and its reach in our society. Never before has our media had such great power over us. The future of media is up to us, whether it will provide a grand, experimental forum where we can grow, live, and collaborate, or will become a cell in which we entertain, distract, and isolate ourselves.

1

Wires and Lights in a Box

Edward R. Murrow

Edward R. Murrow was a long-time American broadcast journalist who rose to fame as a radio correspondent during World War II. He later went on to pioneer television journalism, and his critical See It Now *reports led to the censure of Senator Joseph McCarthy. In "Wires and Lights in a Box," originally given as a speech to the Radio-Television News Directors Association on October 15, 1958, Murrow warns that radio and television, both media with tremendous positive possibility, too often broadcast content that distracts us from the more important realities of our world. He argues that, in their relentless quest for increased profit from advertisers, broadcast corporations have largely relinquished their responsibility for the public good and have jeopardized the wellbeing of American democracy.*

CR80CR80CR80

*On October 15, 1958, veteran broadcaster **Edward R. Murrow** delivered this speech before attendees at the convention of the Radio-Television News Directors Association.*

CR80CR80CR80

This just might do nobody any good. At the end of this discourse a few people may accuse this reporter of fouling his own comfortable nest, and your organization may be accused of having given hospitality to heretical and even dangerous thoughts. But the elaborate structure of networks, advertising agencies, and sponsors will not be shaken or altered. It is my desire, if not my duty, to try to talk to you journeymen with some candor about what is happening to radio and television. I have no technical advice or counsel to offer those of you who labor in this vineyard that produces words and pictures. You will forgive me for not telling you that instruments with which you work are miraculous, that your responsibility is unprecedented, or that your aspirations are frequently frustrated. It is not necessary to remind you that the fact that your voice is amplified to the degree where it reaches from one end of the country to the other does not confer upon you greater wisdom or understanding than you possessed when your voice reached only from one end of the bar to the other. All of these things you know.

You should also know at the outset that, in the manner of witnesses before Congressional committees, I appear here voluntarily—by invitation—that I am an employee of the Columbia Broadcasting System, that I am neither an officer nor a director of that corporation, and that these remarks are of a "do-it-yourself" nature. If what I have to say is responsible, then I alone am responsible for the saying of it. Seeking neither approbation from my employers, nor new sponsors, nor acclaim from the critics of radio and television, I cannot well be disappointed. Believing that potentially the commercial system of broadcasting as practiced in this country is the best and freest yet devised, I have decided to express my concern about what I believe to be happening to radio and television. These instruments have been good to me beyond my due. There exists in mind no reasonable grounds for personal complaint. I have no feud, either with my employers, any sponsors, or with the professional critics of radio and television. But I am seized with an abiding fear regarding what these two instruments are doing to our society, our culture, and our heritage.

Our history will be what we make it. And if there are any historians about fifty or a hundred years from now, and there should be preserved the kinescopes for one week of all three networks, they will there find recorded in black and white, or color, evidence of decadence, escapism, and insulation from the realities of the world in which we live. I invite your attention to the television schedules of all networks between the hours of 8 and 11 p.m., Eastern Time. Here you will find only fleeting and spasmodic reference to the fact that this nation is in mortal danger. There are, it is true, occasional informative programs presented in that intellectual ghetto on Sunday afternoons. But during the daily peak viewing periods, television in the main insulates us from the realities of the world in which we live. If this state of affairs continues, we may alter an advertising slogan to read: LOOK NOW, PAY LATER.

For surely we shall pay for using this most powerful instrument of communication to insulate the citizenry from the hard and demanding realities which must be faced if we are to survive. I mean the word survive literally. If there were to be a competition in indifference, or perhaps in insulation from reality, then Nero and his fiddle, Chamberlain and his umbrella, could not find a place on an early afternoon sustaining show. If Hollywood were to run out of Indians, the program schedules would be mangled beyond all recognition. Then some courageous soul with a small budget might be able to do a documentary telling what, in fact, we have done—and are still doing—to the Indians in this country. But that would be unpleasant. And we must at all costs shield the sensitive citizens from anything that is unpleasant.

I am entirely persuaded that the American public is more reasonable, restrained, and more mature than most of our industry's program planners believe. Their fear of controversy is not warranted by the evidence. I have reason to know, as do many of you, that when the evidence on a controversial subject is fairly and calmly presented, the public recognizes it for what it is—an effort to illuminate rather than to agitate.

Several years ago, when we undertook to do a program on Egypt and Israel, well-meaning, experienced, and intelligent friends shook their heads and said, "This you cannot do—you will be handed your head. It is an emotion-packed controversy, and there is no room for reason in it." We did the program. Zionists, anti-Zionists, the friends of the Middle East, Egyptian and Israeli officials said, with a faint tone of surprise, "It was a fair account. The information was there. We have no complaints."

Our experience was similar with two half-hour programs dealing with cigarette smoking and lung cancer. Both the medical profession and the tobacco industry cooperated in a rather wary fashion. But in the end of the day they were both reasonably content. The subject of radioactive fall-out and the banning of nuclear tests was, and is, highly controversial. But according to what little evidence there is, viewers were prepared to listen to both sides with reason and restraint. This is not said to claim any special or unusual competence in the presentation of controversial subjects, but rather to indicate that timidity in these areas is not warranted by the evidence.

Recently, network spokesmen have been disposed to complain that the professional critics of television have been "rather beastly." There have been hints that somehow competition for the advertising dollar has caused the critics of print to gang up on television and radio. This reporter has no desire to defend the critics. They have space in which to do that on their own behalf. But it remains a fact that the newspapers and magazines are the only instruments of mass communication which remain free from sustained and regular critical comment. If the network spokesmen are so anguished about what appears in print, let them come forth and engage in a little sustained and regular comment regarding newspapers and magazines. It is an ancient and sad fact that most people in network television, and radio, have an exaggerated regard for what appears in print. And there have been cases where executives have refused to make even private comment on a program for which they were responsible until they heard the reviews in print. This is hardly an exhibition of confidence.

The oldest excuse of the networks for their timidity is their youth. Their spokesmen say, "We are young; we have not developed the traditions nor acquired the experience of the older media." If they but knew it, they are building those traditions, creating those precedents everyday. Each time they yield to a voice from Washington or any political pressure, each time they eliminate something that might offend some section of the community, they are creating their own body of precedent and tradition. They are, in fact, not content to be "half safe."

Nowhere is this better illustrated than by the fact that the chairman of the Federal Communications Commission publicly prods broadcasters to engage in their legal right to editorialize. Of course, to undertake an editorial policy, overt and clearly labeled, and obviously unsponsored, requires a station or a network to be responsible. Most stations today probably do not have the manpower to assume this responsibility, but the manpower could be recruited. Editorials would not be profitable; if they had a cutting edge, they might even offend. It is much easier, much less troublesome, to use the money-making machine of television and radio merely as a conduit through which to channel anything that is not libelous, obscene, or defamatory. In that way one has the illusion of power without responsibility.

So far as radio—that most satisfying and rewarding instrument—is concerned, the diagnosis of its difficulties is rather easy. And obviously I speak only of news and information. In order to progress, it need only go backward. To the time when singing commercials were not allowed on news reports, when there was no middle commercial in a 15-minute news report, when radio was rather proud, alert, and fast. I recently asked a network official, "Why this great rash of five-minute news reports (including three commercials) on weekends?" He replied, "Because that seems to be the only thing we can sell."

In this kind of complex and confusing world, you can't tell very much about the why of the news in broadcasts where only three minutes is available for news. The only man who could do that was Elmer Davis, and his kind aren't about any more. If radio news is to be regarded as a commodity, only acceptable when saleable, then I don't care what you call it—I say it isn't news.

My memory also goes back to the time when the fear of a slight reduction in business did not result in an immediate cutback in bodies in the news and public affairs department, at a time when network profits had just reached an all-time high. We would all agree, I think, that whether on a station or a network, the stapling machine is a poor substitute for a newsroom typewriter.

One of the minor tragedies of television news and information is that the networks will not even defend their vital interests. When my employer, CBS, through a combination of enterprise and good luck, did an interview with Nikita Khrushchev, the President uttered a few ill-chosen, uninformed words on the subject, and the network practically apologized. This produced a rarity. Many newspapers defended the CBS right to produce the program and commended it for initiative. But the other networks remained silent.

Likewise, when John Foster Dulles, by personal decree, banned American journalists from going to Communist China, and subsequently offered contradictory explanations, for his fiat the networks entered only a mild protest. Then they apparently forgot the unpleasantness. Can it be that this national industry is content to serve the public interest only with the trickle of news that comes out of Hong Kong, to leave its viewers in ignorance of the cataclysmic changes that are occurring in a nation of six hundred million people? I have no illusions about the difficulties reporting from a dictatorship, but our British and French allies have been better served—in their public interest—with some very useful information from their reporters in Communist China.

One of the basic troubles with radio and television news is that both instruments have grown up as an incompatible combination of show business, advertising, and news. Each of the three is a rather bizarre and demanding profession. And when you get all three under one roof, the dust never settles. The top management of the networks with a few notable exceptions, has been trained in advertising, research, sales, or show business. But by the nature of the corporate structure, they also make the final and crucial decisions having to do with news and public affairs. Frequently they have neither the time nor the competence to do this. It is not easy for the same small group of men to decide whether to buy a new station for millions of dollars, build a new building, alter the rate card, buy a new Western, sell a soap opera, decide what defensive line to take in connection with the latest Congressional inquiry, how much money to spend on promoting a new program, what additions or deletions should be made in the existing covey or clutch of vice-presidents, and at the same time—frequently on the same long day—to give mature, thoughtful consideration to the manifold problems that confront those who are charged with the responsibility for news and public affairs.

Sometimes there is a clash between the public interest and the corporate interest. A telephone call or a letter from the proper quarter in Washington is treated rather more seriously than a communication from an irate but not politically potent viewer. It is tempting enough to give away a little air time for frequently irresponsible and unwarranted utterances in an effort to temper the wind of criticism.

Upon occasion, economics and editorial judgment are in conflict. And there is no law which says that dollars will be defeated by duty. Not so long ago the President of the United States delivered a television address to the nation. He was discoursing on the possibility or probability of war between this nation and the Soviet Union and Communist China—a reasonably compelling subject. Two networks, CBS and NBC, delayed that broadcast for an hour and fifteen minutes. If this decision was dictated by anything other than financial reasons, the networks didn't deign to explain those reasons. That hour-and-fifteen-minute delay, by the way, is about twice the time required for an ICBM to travel from the Soviet Union to major targets in the United States. It is difficult to believe that this decision was made by men who love, respect, and understand news.

So far, I have been dealing largely with the deficit side of the ledger, and the items could be expanded. But I have said, and I believe, that potentially we have in this country a free enterprise system of radio and television which is superior to any other. But to achieve its promise, it must be both free and enterprising. There is no suggestion here that networks or individual stations should operate as philanthropies. But I can find nothing in the Bill of Rights or the Communications Act which says that they must increase their net profits each year, lest the Republic collapse. I do not suggest that news and information should be subsidized by foundations or private subscriptions. I am aware that the networks have expended, and are expending, very considerable sums of money on public affairs programs from which they cannot hope to receive any financial reward. I have had the privilege at CBS of presiding over a considerable number of such programs. I testify, and am able to stand here and say, that I have never had a program turned down by my superiors because of the money it would cost.

But we all know that you cannot reach the potential maximum audience in marginal time with a sustaining program. This is so because so many stations on the network—any network—will decline to carry it. Every licensee who applies for a grant to operate in the public interest, convenience and necessity makes certain promises as to what he will do in terms of program content. Many recipients of licenses have, in blunt language, welshed on those promises. The money-making machine somehow blunts their memories. The only remedy for this is closer inspection and punitive action by the FCC. But in the view of many this would come perilously close to supervision of program content by a federal agency.

So it seems that we cannot rely on philanthropic support or foundation subsidies; we cannot follow the "sustaining route"—the networks cannot pay all the freight—and the FCC cannot or will not discipline those who abuse the facilities that belong to the public. What, then, is the answer? Do we merely stay in our comfortable nests, concluding that the obligation of these instruments has been discharged when we work at the job of informing the public for a minimum of time? Or do we believe that the preservation of the Republic is a seven-day-a-week job, demanding more awareness, better skills, and more perseverance than we have yet contemplated.

I am frightened by the imbalance, the constant striving to reach the largest possible audience for everything: by the absence of a sustained study of the state of the nation. Heywood Broun once said, "No body politic is healthy until it begins to itch." I would like television to produce some itching pills rather than this endless outpouring of tranquilizers. It can be done. Maybe it won't be, but it could. Let us not shoot the wrong piano player. Do not be deluded into believing that the titular heads of the networks control what appears on their networks. They all have better taste. All are responsible to stockholders, and in my experience all are honorable men. But they must schedule what they can sell in the public market.

And this brings us to the nub of the question. In one sense it rather revolves around the phrase heard frequently along Madison Avenue: The Corporate Image. I am not precisely sure what this phrase means, but I would imagine that it reflects a desire on the part of the corporations who pay the advertising bills to have the public image, or believe that they are not merely bodies with no souls, panting in pursuit of elusive dollars. They would like us to believe that they can distinguish between the public good and the private or corporate gain. So the question is this: Are the big corporations who pay the freight for radio and television programs wise to use that time exclusively for the sale of goods and services? Is it in their own interest and that of the stockholders so to do? The sponsor of an hour's television program is not buying merely the six minutes devoted to commercial message. He is determining, within broad limits, the sum total of the impact of the entire hour. If he always, invariably, reaches for the largest possible audience, then this process of insulation, of escape from reality, will continue to be massively financed, and its apologist will continue to make winsome speeches about giving the public what it wants, or "letting the public decide."

I refuse to believe that the presidents and chairmen of the boards of these big corporations want their corporate image to consist exclusively of a solemn voice in an echo chamber, or a pretty girl opening the door of a refrigerator, or a horse that talks. They want something better, and on occasion some of them have demonstrated it. But most of the men whose legal and moral responsibility it is to spend the stockholders' money for advertising are removed from the realities of the mass media by five, six, or a dozen contraceptive layers of vice-presidents, public relations counsel, and advertising agencies. Their business is to sell goods, and the competition is pretty tough.

But this nation is now in competition with malignant forces of evil who are using every instrument at their command to empty the minds of their subjects and fill those minds with slogans, determination and faith in the future. If we go on as we are, we are protecting the mind of the American public from any real contact with the menacing world that squeezes in upon us. We are engaged in a great experiment to discover whether a free public opinion can devise and direct methods of managing the affairs of the nation. We may fail. But we are handicapping ourselves needlessly.

Let us have a little competition. Not only in selling soap, cigarettes, and automobiles, but in informing a troubled, apprehensive, but receptive public. Why should not each of the 20 or 30 big corporations which dominate radio and television decide that they will give up one or two of their regularly scheduled programs each year, turn the time over to the networks and say in effect: "This is a tiny tithe, just a little bit of our profits. On this particular night we aren't going to try to sell cigarettes or automobiles; this is merely a gesture to indicate our belief in the importance of ideas." The networks should, and I think would, pay for the cost of producing the program. The advertiser, the sponsor, would get name credit but would have nothing to do with the content of the program. Would this blemish the corporate image? Would the stockholders object? I think not. For if the premise upon which our pluralistic society rests, which as I understand it is that if the people are given sufficient undiluted information, they will then somehow, even after long, sober second thoughts, reach the right decision—if that premise is wrong, then not only the corporate image but the corporations are done for.

There used to be an old phrase in this country, employed when someone talked too much. It was: "Go hire a hall." Under this proposal the sponsor would have hired the hall; he has bought the time; the local station operator, no matter how indifferent, is going to carry the program—he has to. Then it's up to the networks to fill the hall. I am not here talking about editorializing but about straightaway exposition as direct, unadorned, and impartial as fallible human beings can make it. Just once in a while let us exalt the importance of ideas and information. Let us dream to the extent of saying that on a given Sunday night the time normally occupied by Ed Sullivan is given over to a clinical survey of the state of American education, and a week or two later the time normally used by Steve Allen is devoted to a thorough-going study of American policy in the Middle East. Would the corporate image of their respective sponsors be damaged? Would the stockholders rise up in their wrath and complain? Would anything happen other than that a few million people would have received a little illumination on subjects that may well determine the future of this country, and therefore the future of the corporations? This method would also provide real competition between the networks as to which could outdo the others in the palatable presentation of information. It would provide an outlet for the young men of skill, and there are some even of dedication, who would like to do something other than devise methods of insulating while selling.

There may be other and simpler methods of utilizing these instruments of radio and television in the interests of a free society. But I know of none that could be so easily accomplished inside the framework of the existing commercial system. I don't know how you would measure the success or failure of a given program. And it would be hard to prove the magnitude of the benefit accruing to the corporation which gave up one night of a variety or quiz show in order that the network might marshal its skills to do a thorough-going job on the present status of NATO, or plans for controlling nuclear tests. But I would reckon that the president, and indeed the majority of shareholders of the corporation who sponsored such a venture, would feel just a little bit better about the corporation and the country.

It may be that the present system, with no modifications and no experiments, can survive. Perhaps the money-making machine has some kind of built-in perpetual motion, but I do not think so. To a very considerable extent the media of mass communications in a given country reflect the political, economic, and social climate in which they flourish. That is the reason ours differ from the British and French, or the Russian and Chinese. We are currently wealthy, fat, comfortable, and complacent. We have currently a built-in allergy to unpleasant or disturbing information. Our mass media reflect this. But unless we get up off our fat surpluses and recognize that television in the main is being used to distract, delude, amuse, and insulate us, then television and those who finance it, those who look at it and those who work at it, may see a totally different picture too late.

I do not advocate that we turn television into a 27-inch wailing wall, where longhairs constantly moan about the state of our culture and our defense. But I would just like to see it reflect occasionally the hard, unyielding realities of the world in which we live. I would like to see it done inside the existing framework, and I would like to see the doing of it redound to the credit of those who finance and program it. Measure the results by Nielsen, Trendex, or Silex—it doesn't matter. The main thing is to try. The responsibility can be easily placed, in spite of all the mouthings about giving the public what it wants. It rests on big business and on big television, and it rests at the top. Responsibility is not something that can be assigned or delegated. And it promises its own reward: good business and good television.

Perhaps no one will do anything about it. I have ventured to outline it against a background of criticism that may have been too harsh only because I could think of nothing better. Someone once said—I think it was Max Eastman—that "that publisher serves his advertiser best who best serves his readers." I cannot believe that radio and television, or the corporations that finance the programs, are serving well or truly their viewers or listeners, or themselves.

I began by saying that our history will be what we make it. If we go on as we are, then history will take its revenge, and retribution will not limp in catching up with us.

We are to a large extent an imitative society. If one or two or three corporations would undertake to devote just a small fraction of their advertising appropriation along the lines that I have suggested, the procedure would grow by contagion; the economic burden would be bearable, and there might ensue a most exciting adventure— exposure to ideas and the bringing of reality into the homes of the nation.

To those who say people wouldn't look; they wouldn't be interested; they're too complacent, indifferent, and insulated, I can only reply: There is, in one reporter's opinion, considerable evidence against that contention. But even if they are right, what have they got to lose? Because if they are right, and this instrument is good for nothing but to entertain, amuse, and insulate, then the tube is flickering now and we will soon see that the whole struggle is lost.

This instrument can teach, it can illuminate; yes, and it can even inspire. But it can do so only to the extent that humans are determined to use it to those ends. Otherwise it's nothing but wires and lights in a box. There is a great and perhaps decisive battle to be fought against ignorance, intolerance, and indifference. This weapon of television could be useful.

Stonewall Jackson, who knew something about the use of weapons, is reported to have said, "When war comes, you must draw the sword and throw away the scabbard." The trouble with television is that it is rusting in the scabbard during a battle for survival.

Credit _____

Speech by Edward R. Murrow to the 1958 Radio Television News Directors Association national convention, Chicago, Ill., October 15, 1958.

The Culture of Shut Up

Jon Lovett

Jon Lovett is a Los Angeles-based writer and frequent contributor to The Atlantic Monthly, *as well as a former speechwriter for President Barack Obama. He has also written and produced for television, most notably for "1600 Penn" and "The Newsroom." In "The Culture of Shut Up," originally published in* The Atlantic *in 2014, Lovett ponders the current state of public dialogue in the age of the Internet. He suggests that the Internet, which provides for unprecedented access to diverse public speech, will inevitably include speech that is unpalatable or offensive. However, we must resist the urge to "police" or punish such speech if we hope to allow a range of voices to be heard.*

CR£0CR£0CR£0

This essay is adapted from a speech given at Loyola Marymount University on February 11, 2014, during its annual First Amendment Week.

CR£0CR£0CR£0

Too many debates about important issues degenerate into manufactured and misplaced outrage—and it's chilling free speech.

There once was a remote village deep in the rainforest that had no contact with the outside world. And in this small village there were only three village elders who had the ability to speak. So they were in charge. And they'd have arguments. One would say, "I support a woman's right to choose." Another would say, "I oppose a woman's right to choose." And then the third would say, "A real debate here on a woman's right to choose. When we come back, Justin Bieber arrested!"

Now if you were one of the many villagers who didn't have a way to speak, you just hoped that one of the three elders who could speak would make the argument you wanted to make. Sometimes they did, sometimes they didn't. And it was okay, but it bothered you that these three voices didn't really speak for everybody. They were, after all, pretty rich and all one color. (Green. These were green people.) And they didn't really understand what it was like to be aqua or purple or gay or poor like you were. You're a gay poor purple person. They tried to cover the whole world, but generally they focused on what was on the minds of green people from the big cities who watched *Mad Men* and went to Middlebury.

And even as the elders spoke with confidence and seriousness, it felt like they kept getting it wrong. They invaded neighboring villages, occasionally the wrong village altogether. They trusted the CEOs of the village banks even after they plunged the village into a Great Village Recession and then went right back to village business as usual as if it never happened. They built a massive village prison system that punished non-violent village offenders at higher rates than anywhere else in the rainforest. They rigged the village economy against the interests of ordinary villagers in favor of those with close ties to the three elders, those who had donated money to their village campaigns, lobbied their village offices.

Then one day you found this rock and you realized that you could use the rock to write on a leaf. And so you developed a written language and taught it to everyone. And at the big village meetings, when the three elders at the front would have their arguments, villagers could participate. People would write things like, "I agree with you and appreciate your position." Or "I hope you get cancer and die." Or "Here's a picture of what I ate for lunch." Or "Please stop drawing pictures of food, no one cares what you ate for lunch." Or "Check out this cat in a shoebox because adorable."

But it turned out by the time we finally had this great way to communicate in our hands, we were already so angry and suspicious that the rock and leaf became a way to vent our frustrations not just at the elders but at each other.

Bill says, "I support single-payer village healthcare."

And then Mary writes, "Bill is a faggot communist."

And then Ted says, "I won't shop at Mary's boutique until Mary apologizes to Bill."

Then Angela says, "Stand with Mary against the assault on her freedom of speech!"

And then Bill says, "Angela is a racist."

And Jeff says, "Anyone who shops at Mary's boutique is a racist."

And Ted says, "Check your privilege."

And Mary says, "I don't remember who I am in this story but I'm furious."

And then someone writes, "FUCKK YOU TED!!1!" in all caps with a bunch of typos.

Soon there were really only two kinds of messages people would write—either vicious personal attacks, or self-righteous calls for apology—until eventually the villagers, angry and exhausted and sick of the noise and rancor just started pelting each other with the rocks until all the rocks were broken and all the leaves were shredded and finally in the silence, after the dust had settled, the villagers shrugged their shoulders, and turned back toward the smug and satisfied village elders who were just waiting for their chance to regain supremacy—just waiting for the moment when the villagers would come crawling back, desperate to be led, desperate for the reassuring simplicity of the old order, of the establishment, of the way things used to be.

☙❦☙❦☙❦☙

And that's the story of that village.

Anyway, I was thinking about the First Amendment and the freedom of speech, and what lessons I could draw on my time in politics, working for then-Senator Hillary Clinton and our first foreign-born president, Barack Obama, and I kept coming back to a quote by Homer Simpson. Now when I Googled this quote it turned out to be from 1997, which made me realize I am reaching the age when my references stop at a certain year in the culture, and that while you know the *Simpsons*, that episode aired just after today's college freshmen were born and the fact is eventually we all return to the earth.

Anyway, Homer Simpson once said that alcohol is the cause of, and solution to, all of life's problems. And I kept thinking: That's actually a pretty good description of the Internet and how it's changing our discourse. It's basically the cause of, and solution to, everything that plagues our culture.

That's an exaggeration, of course. The Internet didn't cause Donald Trump, and it certainly can't solve Donald Trump. The way you defeat Donald Trump is by getting the ring of power into the hands of a pure soul, a hobbit, say, and that hobbit must journey to Mount Doom and release the ring into its fires. But the Internet: Did you know that every single day, the Internet produces more speech than was created between the dawn of civilization and the year 2006? You didn't know that, because I just made it up. But it feels true. We are all bombarded. We are drowning in information. It's no longer thrown on our doorstep each sunrise, or even just broadcast into our living rooms; it's in our hands every waking hour; the endless stream of talking, as we spend all day moving our eyes from screen to screen to screen; it's the first thing we see each morning and the last thing we see before we go to bed. The shower is the last safe space, which is why it's the only place where we have decent ideas anymore.

In many ways this is good and getting better: We have unlocked the gates and we are removing the gatekeepers. We aren't beholden to the views of the three green elders in the village. (See, I tied it back.) But what happens next—how we face the downside of so much connectedness—will determine whether or not this revolution empowers us, or once again empowers those gatekeepers. And I don't want that to happen, because those gatekeepers suck. They're arrogant and easily swayed by big, nice-sounding dangerous ideas; they're ambitious and careerist and forgetful and unimaginative and shortsighted; they're subject to groupthink, beholden to corporate interests, and enamored of fame and power.

I don't want those voices to drown out the diverse and compelling voices that now have a better chance of making it in front of us than ever before—even as we still have a ways to go. And what I think we have to do, then, to protect this new wonderful thing of "a good idea can come from anyone anywhere"—is we need to stop telling each other to shut up. We need to get comfortable with the reality that no one is going to shut up. You aren't going to shut up. I'm not going to shut up. The idiots aren't going to shut up.

We need to learn to live with the noise and tolerate the noise even when the noise is stupid, even when the noise is offensive, even when the noise is at times dangerous. Because no matter how noble the intent, it's a demand for conformity that encourages people on all sides of a debate to police each other instead of argue and convince each other. And, ultimately, the cycle of attack and apology, of disagreement and boycott, will leave us with fewer and fewer people talking more and more about less and less.

In the past week, the CEO of Mozilla, Brendan Eich, one of the company's co-founders, was forced to resign over his support for Proposition 8, the anti-gay marriage law that passed in a 2008 California referendum before it was later struck down by the courts. But this is only the most recent example.

Here's a list of some other people who were told to shut up, off the top of my head:

The Chick-fil-A guy was told to shut up[1] about gay people.

Martin Bashir was told to shut up about Sarah Palin.

Paula Deen was told to shut up by everyone because her stuff was racist and crazy.

A columnist in the *Guardian* told a woman to shut up[2] about her cancer.

Dylan Farrow was told to shut up about Woody Allen.

Stephen Colbert was told to shut up about satire, I think?

The *Duck Dynasty*[3] guy was told to shut up about gay people.

Alex Wagner was told to shut up about needlepoint[4].

Natasha Legerro[5] was told to shut up about veterans.

Alec Baldwin was also told to shut up about gay people. This one comes up a lot.

Mike Huckabee was told to shut up about women.

The Whole Foods CEO was told to shut up about Obamacare.

Richard Sherman was told to shut up about winning while being black, I guess.

I am not comparing what these people were told to shut up about, or saying some of these examples aren't offensive or stupid or vicious or wrong, often combinations of any or all of those things. And the truth is, these cycles of pearl-clutching followed by either abject sorrow or banishment are of course driven by news outlets looking to score a few hits or viewers by drumming up controversy.

But they're also driven by us, as viewers and readers, all of us part of the culture of shut up. It plays out in the defining down of "hate speech" on liberal college campuses and in the defining down of "anti-American" at conservative conferences. And for every public example there are countless private ones, playing out on Facebook pages and Twitter feeds and I guess Pinterest? I don't get Pinterest.

Yes, it's in some ways a natural response to being more connected to one another; we're just in each other's faces. But it's also dangerous. It narrows the visible spectrum of ideas. It encourages people to be safe and cautious and circumspect when we don't want people to be safe. We don't want people to be afraid of saying something interesting on the off chance it's taken the wrong way.

When the *Duck* person said his crazy thing about the sins of the gays and how nice things were during Jim Crow—which was just wild[6]—Sarah Palin (who maybe didn't know better) and Governor Bobby Jindal (who definitely knew better) said it was a violation of his First Amendment rights. And it wasn't, obviously. The government wasn't removing anyone from the air. A&E under pressure from GLAAD and others considered removing a reality-show persona from the air. So it wasn't a First Amendment issue and the fact that that has to be said out loud should make all of us sad. But that doesn't mean there aren't speech issues at stake here, which is at the heart of conservatives' complaint.

The right to free speech may begin and end with the First Amendment, but there is a vast middle where our freedom of speech is protected by us—by our capacity to listen and accept that people disagree, often strongly, that there are fools, some of them columnists and elected officials and, yes, even reality-show patriarchs, that there are people who believe stupid, irrational, hateful things about other people and it's okay to let those words in our ears sometimes without rolling out the guillotines.

Look, obviously there's an important counter-argument here. It is natural and healthy that as a society we have deemed certain ideas off-limits. While in this country the government can't stop you from saying these things, or punish you for having said those things, it's often good that the personal, financial, and social costs of saying the unsayable are prohibitively high. We all can name examples: hardcore racism and anti-Semitism and misogyny, *Breaking Bad* spoilers, that kind of thing. And it's also true that hurtful words about, say, gay people have a disproportionate impact on the vulnerable; it's easy for me to say *bring on the homophobia,* but what about the kid in the closet in a conservative neighborhood worried his mom will stumble onto his browser history?

The trouble, I think, is when ostracizing a viewpoint as "beyond the pale" becomes not an end but a means to an end; that by declaring something unsayable, we make it so. It makes me uncomfortable, even as I see the value of it. I for one would love homophobia to fully make it on that list, to get to the point where being against gay marriage is as vulgar and shameful as being against interracial marriage. But it isn't. Maybe it will be. But it isn't. And kicking a reality-show star off his reality show doesn't make that less true. Win the argument; don't declare the argument too offensive to be won. And that's true whether it's GLAAD making demands of A&E or the head of the Republican National Committee making demands of MSNBC.

The bottom line is, you don't beat an idea by beating a person. You beat an idea by beating an idea. Not only is it counter-productive—nobody likes the kid who complains to the teacher even when the kid is right—it replaces a competition of arguments with a competition to delegitimize arguments. And what's left is the pressure to sand down the corners of your speech while looking for the rough edges in the speech of your adversaries. Everyone is offended. Everyone is offensive. Nothing is close to the line because close to the line is over the line because over the line is better for clicks and retweets and fundraising and ad revenue.

It's like a financial bubble. It's a bubble of subprime outrage and subprime apologies. I just hope we can rationalize the market before this chilling effect leaves us with a discourse more boring and monotone than it already is—a discourse that suits the cable networks and the politicians but not the many disparate voices who occasionally need to say outrageous things because there are outrageous things to say.

And there are real consequences to the outrage bubble. When Congress was debating the debt ceiling, one of the sticking points was a set of changes to the military-pension system. You don't even have to take a position on these changes to say that it's a reasonable debate: whether we should save money in the defense budget by reducing the rate of increase in pension benefits received by veterans who are younger than retirement age.

The bottom line is, you don't beat an idea by beating a person. You beat an idea by beating an idea.

Agree, disagree, you're not crossing the line, right? Wrong: Supporting this proposal is described, over and over again, as "sick" and "obscene"[7] and "offensive."[8] Do we really want to make policy this way? Do we want our already timid and craven elected officials to have even more to fear?

I'll be honest: In my own small way I feel the chilling effect. I'm in a fortunate position that nobody really cares what I say, but even so, occasionally I'll make a dumb joke on Twitter and the next thing I know it's on a whole bunch of conservative websites that exist to catch liberals crossing the line. As much as I can pretend otherwise, I'd be lying if I said it didn't make me hold back just a little, doubt myself a little, on occasion. And while it's hard to measure the absence of speech, measure the things unsaid, I have little doubt that others on all sides are feeling the same chilling effect, only more so because people do care what they have to say.

The First Amendment's protections have always put a great deal of responsibility in our hands: not only to respect the power of our own speech, but also to respect that same power in the hands of people we despise. We all have more of that power now. And I for one think that's great. Yes, there are those who would say otherwise. David Brooks says we have a "followership problem,"[9] that our lack of trust in institutions is less caused by their poor performance than by the fact we are "cynical and like to pretend that [we're] better than everything else around [us.]" "Vanity," he says, "has more to do with rising distrust than anything else." Maureen Dowd talks[10] about the "nightmare" of an America that "runs on clicks."

I should go beyond the *New York Times* op-ed page but those were just the most annoying examples I remembered. But there are many others—big platforms all—who would tell us to fear the future, to fear the havoc the Internet is wreaking on journalism, to fear a world in which every event, every public utterance must face the gauntlet of Twitter and Facebook. They'd suggest the cacophony of links and hits and likes and retweets, the triumph of the buzzworthy and the Upworthy, are no replacement for a few trusted outlets—the nightly news, major newspapers, weekly magazines, etc.—that everyone experienced together.

I reject this argument. And I reject it for the simple reason that all the chaos and competition is worth it—for all its many downsides, for all the garbage and gossip—if a few loud voices no longer control the story. But that only works if we don't try to replace one tyranny with another, one narrow band of views with another narrow band of views, if we can live with the noise, even embrace the noise, without trying to drown each other out.

Notes

[1] Jonathan Merritt, "In Defense of Eating at Chick-fil-A," *The Atlantic*, July 20, 2012, http://www.theatlantic.com/politics/archive/2012/07/in-defense-of-eating-at-chick-fil-a/260139/

[2] Megan Garber, "On Live-Tweeting One's Suffering," *The Atlantic*, January 13, 2014, http://www.theatlantic.com/technology/archive/2014/01/on-live-tweeting-ones-suffering/283013/

[3] Conor Friedersdorf, "A *Duck Dynasty* Solution for A&E: Phil Robertson Should Debate Dan Savage," *The Atlantic*, December 27, 2013, http://www.theatlantic.com/politics/archive/2013/12/a-em-duck-dynasty-em-solution-for-a-e-phil-robertson-should-debate-dan-savage/282668/

[4] Matt Wilstein, "Megyn Kelly and Guests Go After Alex Wagner's 'Blatantly Sexist' Tweet," *Mediaite*, January 29, 2014, http://www.mediaite.com/tv/megyn-kelly-and-guests-go-after-alex-wagners-blatantly-sexist-tweet/

[5] Ashley Lee, "Natasha Leggero 'Not Sorry' for Joke About Pearl Harbor Veterans," *The Hollywood Reporter*, January 3, 2014, http://www.hollywoodreporter.com/live-feed/natasha-leggero-not-sorry-joke-668443

[6] Jonathan Merritt, "The Real *Duck Dynasty* Scandal: Phil Robertson's Comments on Race," *The* Atlantic, December 19, 2014, http://www.theatlantic.com/politics/archive/2013/12/the-real-em-duck-dynasty-em-scandal-phil-robertsons-comments-on-race/282538/

[7] Wanda Carruthers, "Scarborough: Military Retirement Cuts are 'Sick' and 'Obscene'," *Newsmax*, December 18, 2013, http://www.newsmax.com/Newsfront/obscene-scarborough-budget-military/2013/12/18/id/542534/

[8] Patricia Kime, "Pensions Slashed Under Budget Bill Provision," *Army Times*, December 23, 2013, http://www.armytimes.com/article/20131223/BENEFITS/312300001/Pensions-slashed-under-budget-bill-provision

[9] David Brooks, "The Follower Problem," *The New York Times*, June 11, 2012, http://www.nytimes.com/2012/06/12/opinion/brooks-the-follower-problem.html?_r=0

[10] Maureen Dowd, "Still Mad as Hell," *The New York Times*, February 8, 2014, http://www.nytimes.com/2014/02/09/opinion/sunday/dowd-still-mad-as-hell.html

Credit

Lovett, Jon. "The Culture of Shut Up." *The Atlantic* Atlantic Media, 7 Apr. 2014. Web. © 2014 The Atlantic Media Co., as first published in *The Atlantic* Magazine. All rights reserved. Distributed by Tribune Content Agency, LLC.

Re-Thinking Objectivity: Columbia Journalism Review

Brent Cunningham

Brent Cunningham is managing editor of the Food & Environment Reporting Network *and has published a number of op-ed pieces in various periodicals, including* The Washington Post *and* The Nation. *His essays "Pastoral Romance" and "Last Meals" appeared in the 2012 and 2014 editions of* Best Food Writing, *respectively. In "Re-thinking Objectivity," originally published in the Columbia Journalism Review in July 2013, Cunningham examines how the quest for "fairness" in reporting leads instead to decontextualized information lacking in critical analysis, or to "lazy" objectivity that relies on biased information fed to journalists by those attempting to shape the story. Therefore, he argues, objectivity must be redefined to acknowledge journalistic subjectivity and to encourage reporters to critically examine the factual basis of their information.*

ে৪০ে৪০ে৪০

In a world of spin, our awkward embrace of an ideal can make us passive recipients of the news.

In his March 6 press conference[1], in which he laid out his reasons for the coming war, President Bush mentioned al Qaeda or the attacks of September 11 fourteen times in fifty-two minutes. No one challenged him on it, despite the fact that the CIA had questioned the Iraq-al Qaeda connection, and that there has never been solid evidence marshaled to support the idea that Iraq was involved in the attacks of 9/11.

When Bush proposed his $726 billion tax cut in January, his sales pitch on the plan's centerpiece—undoing the "double-taxation" on dividend earnings—was that "It's unfair to tax money twice." In the next two months, the tax plan was picked over in hundreds of articles and broadcasts, yet a Nexis database search turned up few news stories—notably, one by Donald Barlett and James Steele in *Time* on January 27, and another by Daniel Altman in the business section of *The New York Times* on January 21—that explained in detail what was misleading about the president's pitch: that in fact there is plenty of income that is doubly, triply, or even quadruply taxed, and that those other taxes affect many more people than the sliver who would benefit from the dividend tax cut.

Before the fighting started in Iraq, in the dozens of articles and broadcasts that addressed the potential aftermath of a war, much was written and said about the maneuverings of the Iraqi exile community and the shape of a postwar government, about cost and duration and troop numbers. Important subjects all. But few of those stories, dating from late last summer, delved deeply into the numerous and plausible complications of the aftermath. That all changed on February 26, when President Bush spoke grandly of making Iraq a model for retooling the entire Middle East. After Bush's speech, "aftermath" articles began to flow like the waters of the Tigris—including cover stories in *Time* and *The New York Times* Magazine—culminating in *The Wall Street Journal's* page-one story on March 17, just days before the first cruise missiles rained down on Baghdad, that revealed how the administration planned to hand the multibillion-dollar job of rebuilding Iraq to U.S. corporations. It was as if the subject of the war's aftermath was more or less off the table until the president put it there himself.

There is no single explanation for these holes in the coverage, but I would argue that our devotion to what we call "objectivity" played a role. It's true that the Bush administration is like a clenched fist with information, one that won't hesitate to hit back when pressed. And that reporting on the possible aftermath of a war before the war occurs, in particular, was a difficult and speculative story.

Yet these three examples—which happen to involve the current White House, although every White House spins stories—provide a window into a particular failure of the press: allowing the principle of objectivity to make us passive recipients of news, rather than aggressive analyzers and explainers of it. We all learned about objectivity in school or at our first job. Along with its twin sentries "fairness" and "balance," it defined journalistic standards.

Or did it? Ask ten journalists what objectivity means and you'll get ten different answers. Some, like *The Washington Post's* editor, Leonard Downie, define it so strictly that they refuse to vote lest they be forced to take sides. My favorite definition was from Michael Bugeja, who teaches journalism at Iowa State: "Objectivity is seeing the world as it is, not how you wish it were." In 1996 the Society of Professional Journalists acknowledged this dilemma and dropped "objectivity" from its ethics code. It also changed "the truth" to simply "truth."

Tripping Toward the Truth

As E.J. Dionne wrote in his 1996 book, *They Only Look Dead*, the press operates under a number of conflicting diktats: be neutral yet investigative; be disengaged but have an impact; be fair-minded but have an edge. Therein lies the nut of our tortured relationship with objectivity. Few would argue that complete objectivity is possible, yet we bristle when someone suggests we aren't being objective—or fair, or balanced—as if everyone agrees on what they all mean.

Over the last dozen years, a cottage industry of bias police has sprung up to exploit this fissure in the journalistic psyche, with talk radio leading the way followed by Shout TV and books like Ann Coulter's *Slander* and Bernard Goldberg's *Bias*. Now the left has begun firing back, with Eric Alterman's book *What Liberal Media?* (*CJR*, March/April) and a group of wealthy Democrats' plans for a liberal radio network. James Carey, a journalism scholar at Columbia, points out that we are entering a new age of partisanship. One result is a hypersensitivity among the press to charges of bias, and it shows up everywhere: In October 2001, with the war in Afghanistan under way, then—CNN chairman Walter Isaacson sent a memo to his foreign correspondents telling them to "balance" reports of Afghan "casualties or hardship" with reminders to viewers that this was, after all, in response to the terrorist attacks of September 11. More recently, a *CJR* intern, calling newspaper letters-page editors to learn whether reader letters were running for or against the looming war in Iraq, was told by the letters editor at *The Tennessean* that letters were running 70 percent against the war, but that the editors were trying to run as many pro-war letters as possible lest they be accused of bias.

Objectivity has persisted for some valid reasons, the most important being that nothing better has replaced it. And plenty of good journalists believe in it, at least as a necessary goal. Objectivity, or the pursuit of it, separates us from the unbridled partisanship found in much of the European press. It helps us make decisions quickly—we are disinterested observers after all—and it protects us from the consequences of what we write. We'd like to think it buoys our embattled credibility, though the deafening silence of many victims of Jayson Blair's fabrications would argue otherwise. And as we descend into this new age of partisanship, our readers need, more than ever, reliable reporting that tells them what is true when that is knowable, and pushes as close to truth as possible when it is not.

But our pursuit of objectivity can trip us up on the way to "truth." Objectivity excuses lazy reporting. If you're on a deadline and all you have is "both sides of the story," that's often good enough. It's not that such stories laying out the parameters of a debate have no value for readers, but too often, in our obsession with, as *The Washington Post's* Bob Woodward puts it, "the latest," we fail to push the story, incrementally, toward a deeper understanding of what is true and what is false. Steven R. Weisman, the chief diplomatic correspondent for *The New York Times* and a believer in the goal of objectivity ("even though we fall short of the ideal every day"), concedes that he felt obliged to dig more when he was an editorial writer, and did not have to be objective.

"If you have to decide who is right, then you must do more reporting," he says. "I pressed the reporting further because I didn't have the luxury of saying *X says* this and *Y says this* and you, dear reader, can decide who is right."

It exacerbates our tendency to rely on official sources, which is the easiest, quickest way to get both the "he said" and the "she said," and, thus, "balance." According to numbers from the media analyst Andrew Tyndall, of the 414 stories on Iraq broadcast on NBC, ABC, and CBS from last September to February, all but thirty-four originated at the White House, Pentagon, and State Department. So we end up with too much of the "official" truth.

More important, objectivity makes us wary of seeming to argue with the president— or the governor, or the CEO—and risk losing our access. Jonathan Weisman, an economics reporter for *The Washington Post*, says this about the fear of losing access: "If you are perceived as having a political bias, or a slant, you're screwed."

Finally, objectivity makes reporters hesitant to inject issues into the news that aren't already out there. "News is driven by the zeitgeist," says Jonathan Weisman, "and if an issue isn't part of the current zeitgeist then it will be a tough sell to editors." But who drives the zeitgeist, in Washington at least? The administration. In short, the press's awkward embrace of an impossible ideal limits its ability to help set the agenda.

This is not a call to scrap objectivity, but rather a search for a better way of thinking about it, a way that is less restrictive and more grounded in reality. As Eric Black, a reporter at the *Minneapolis Star Tribune*, says, "We need a way to both do our job and defend it."

An Ideals' Troubled Past

American journalism's honeymoon with objectivity has been brief. The press began to embrace objectivity in the middle of the nineteenth century, as society turned away from religion and toward science and empiricism to explain the world. But in his 1998 book, *Just the Facts*, a history of the origins of objectivity in U.S. journalism, David Mindich argues that by the turn of the twentieth century, the flaws of objective journalism were beginning to show. Mindich shows how "objective" coverage of lynching in the 1890s by *The New York Times* and other papers created a false balance on the issue and failed "to recognize a truth, that African-Americans were being terrorized across the nation."

After World War I, the rise of public relations and the legacy of wartime propaganda—in which journalists such as Walter Lippman had played key roles—began to undermine reporters' faith in facts. The war, the Depression, and Roosevelt's New Deal raised complex issues that defied journalism's attempt to distill them into simple truths. As a result, the use of bylines increased (an early nod to the fact that news is touched by human frailty), the political columnist crawled from the primordial soup, and the idea of "interpretive reporting" emerged. Still, as Michael Schudson argued in his 1978 book *Discovering the News*, journalism clung to objectivity as the faithful cling to religion, for guidance in an uncertain world. He wrote: "From the beginning, then, criticism of the 'myth' of objectivity has accompanied its enunciation. … Journalists came to believe in objectivity, to the extent that they did, because they wanted to, needed to, were forced by ordinary human aspiration to seek escape from their own deep convictions of doubt and drift."

By the 1960s, objectivity was again under fire, this time to more fundamental and lasting effect. Straight, "objective" coverage of McCarthyism a decade earlier had failed the public, leading Alan Barth, an editorial writer at *The Washington Post*, to tell a 1952 gathering of the Association for Education in Journalism: "There can be little doubt that the way [Senator Joseph McCarthy's charges] have been reported in most papers serves Senator McCarthy's partisan political purposes much more than it serves the purposes of the press, the interest of truth." Government lies about the U2 spy flights, the Cuban missile crisis, and the Vietnam War all cast doubt on the ability of "objective" journalism to get at anything close to the truth. The New Journalism of Tom Wolfe and Norman Mailer was in part a reaction to what many saw as the failings of mainstream reporting. In Vietnam, many of the beat reporters who arrived believing in objectivity eventually realized, if they stayed long enough, that such an approach wasn't sufficient. Says John Laurence, a former CBS News correspondent, about his years covering Vietnam: "Because the war went on for so long and so much evidence accumulated to suggest it was a losing cause, and that in the process we were destroying the Vietnamese and ourselves, I felt I had a moral obligation to report my views as much as the facts."

As a result of all these things, American journalism changed. "Vietnam and Watergate destroyed what I think was a genuine sense that our officials knew more than we did and acted in good faith," says Anthony Lewis, the former *New York Times* reporter and columnist. We became more sophisticated in our understanding of the limits of objectivity. And indeed, the parameters of modern journalistic objectivity allow reporters quite a bit of leeway to analyze, explain, and put news in context, thereby helping guide readers and viewers through the flood of information.

Still, nothing replaced objectivity as journalism's dominant professional norm. Some 75 percent of journalists and news executives in a 1999 Pew Research Center survey said it was possible to obtain a true, accurate, and widely agreed-upon account of an event. More than two-thirds thought it feasible to develop "a systematic method to cover events in a disinterested and fair way." The survey also offered another glimpse of the objectivity fissure: more than two-thirds of the print press in the Pew survey also said that "providing an interpretation of the news is a core principle," while less than half of those in television news agreed with that.

The More Things Change

If objectivity's philosophical hold on journalism has eased a bit since the 1960s, a number of other developments have bound us more tightly to the objective ideal and simultaneously exacerbated its shortcomings. Not only are journalists operating under conflicting orders, as E.J. Dionne argued, but their corporate owners don't exactly trumpet the need to rankle the status quo. It is perhaps important to note that one of the original forces behind the shift to objectivity in the nineteenth century was economic. To appeal to as broad an audience as possible, first the penny press and later the new wire services gradually stripped news of "partisan" context. Today's owners have squeezed the newshole, leaving less space for context and analysis.

If space is a problem, time is an even greater one. The nonstop news cycle leaves reporters less time to dig, and encourages reliance on official sources who can provide the information quickly and succinctly. "We are slaves to the incremental daily development," says one White House correspondent, "but you are perceived as having a bias if you don't cover it." This lack of time makes a simpleminded and lazy version of objectivity all the more tempting. In *The American Prospect* of November 6, 2000, Chris Mooney wrote about how "e-spin," a relentless diet of canned attacks and counterattacks e-mailed from the Bush and Gore campaigns to reporters, was winding up, virtually unedited, in news stories. "Lazy reporters may be seduced by the ease of readily provided research," Mooney wrote. "That's not a new problem, except that the prevalence of electronic communication has made it easier to be lazy."

Meanwhile, the Internet and cable news' Shout TV, which drive the nonstop news cycle, have also elevated the appeal of "attitude" in the news, making the balanced, measured report seem anachronistic. In the January/February issue of *CJR*, young journalists asked to create their dream newspaper wanted more point-of-view writing in news columns. They got a heavy dose of it during the second gulf war, with news "anchors" like Fox's Neil Cavuto saying of those who opposed the war, "You were sickening then; you are sickening now."

Perhaps most ominous of all, public relations, whose birth early in the twentieth century rattled the world of objective journalism, has matured into a spin monster so ubiquitous that nearly every word a reporter hears from an official source has been shaped and polished to proper effect. Consider the memo from the Republican strategist Frank Luntz, as described in a March 2 *New York Times* story, that urged the party—and President Bush—to soften their language on the environment to appeal to suburban voters. "Climate change" instead of "global warming," "conservationist" rather than "environmentalist." To the extent that the threat of being accused of bias inhibits reporters from cutting through this kind of manipulation, challenging it, and telling readers about it, then journalism's dominant professional norm needs a new set of instructions.

Joan Didion got at this problem while taking Bob Woodward to task in a 1996 piece in *The New York Review of Books* for writing books that she argued were too credulous, that failed to counter the possibility that his sources were spinning him. She wrote:

> The genuflection toward "fairness" is a familiar newsroom piety, in practice the excuse for a good deal of autopilot reporting and lazy thinking but in theory a benign ideal. In Washington, however, a community in which the management of news has become the single overriding preoccupation of the core industry, what "fairness" has often come to mean is a scrupulous passivity, an agreement to cover the story not as it is occurring but as it is presented, which is to say as it is manufactured.

Asked about such criticism, Woodward says that for his books he has the time and the space and the sources to actually uncover what really happened, not some manufactured version of it. "The best testimony to that," he says, "is that the critics never suggest how any of it is manufactured, that any of it is wrong." Then, objectivity rears its head. "What they seem to be saying," Woodward says of his critics, "is that I refuse to use the information I have to make a political argument, and they are right, I won't." Yet some of Woodward's critics do suggest how his material is manufactured. Christopher Hitchens, reviewing Woodward's latest book, *Bush at War*, in the June issue of The *Atlantic Monthly*, argues that, while reporting on a significant foreign-policy debate, Woodward fully presents the point of view of his cooperative sources, but fails to report deeply on the other sides of the argument. Thus he presents an incomplete picture. "Pseudo-objectivity in the nation's capital," Hitchens writes, "is now overripe for regime change."

To Fill the Void

Jason Riley is a young reporter at the *Louisville Courier-Journal*. Along with a fellow reporter, R.G. Dunlop, he won a Polk award this year for a series on dysfunction in the county courts, in which hundreds of felony cases dating back to 1983 were lost and never resolved. Riley and Dunlop's series was a classic example of enterprise reporting: poking around the courthouse, Riley came across one felony case that had been open for several years. That led to more cases, then to a drawer full of open cases. No one was complaining, at least publicly, about this problem. In a first draft, Riley wrote that the system was flawed because it let cases fall off the docket and just disappear for years. "I didn't think it needed attribution because it was the conclusion I had drawn after six months of investigation," he writes in an e-mail. But his editor sent it back with a note: "Says who?"

In a follow-up profile of the county's lead prosecutor, a man Riley has covered for three years, many sources would not criticize the prosecutor on the record. He "knew what people thought of him, knew what his strengths and weaknesses were," Riley says. "Since no one was openly discussing issues surrounding him, I raised many in my profile without attribution." Again his editors hesitated. There were discussions about the need to remain objective. "Some of my conclusions and questions were left out because no one else brought them up on the record," he says.

Riley discovered a problem on his own, reported the hell out of it, developed an understanding of the situation, and reached some conclusions based on that. No official sources were speaking out about it, so he felt obliged to fill that void. Is that bias? Good reporters do it, or attempt to do it, all the time. The strictures of objectivity can make it difficult. "I think most journalists will admit to feeding sources the information we want to hear, for quotes or attribution, just so we can make the crucial point we are not allowed to make ourselves," Riley says. "But why not? As society's watchdogs, I think we should be asking questions, we should be bringing up problems, possible solutions … writing what we know to be true."

Last fall, when America and the world were debating whether to go to war in Iraq, no one in the Washington establishment wanted to talk much about the aftermath of such a war. For the Bush administration, attempting to rally support for a preemptive war, messy discussions about all that could go wrong in the aftermath were unhelpful. Anything is better than Saddam, the argument went. The Democrats, already wary of being labeled unpatriotic, spoke their piece in October when they voted to authorize the use of force in Iraq, essentially putting the country on a war footing. Without the force of a "she said" on the aftermath story, it was largely driven by the administration, which is to say stories were typically framed by what the administration said it planned to do: work with other nations to build democracy. Strike a blow to terrorists. Stay as long as we need to and not a minute longer. Pay for it all with Iraqi oil revenue. There were some notable exceptions—a piece by Anthony Shadid in the October 20 *Boston Globe*, for instance, and another on September 22 by James Dao in *The New York Times*, pushed beyond the administration's broad assumptions about what would happen when

Saddam was gone—but most of the coverage included only boilerplate reminders that Iraq is a fractious country and bloody reprisals are likely, that tension between the Kurds and Turks might be a problem, and that Iran has designs on the Shiite region of southern Iraq. David House, the reader advocate for the *Fort Worth Star-Telegram*, wrote a piece on March 23 that got at the press's limitations in setting the agenda. "Curiously, for all the technology the news media have, for all the gifted minds that make it all work … it's a simple thing to stop the media cold. Say nothing, hide documents."

In November, James Fallows wrote a cover story for *The Atlantic Monthly* entitled "The Fifty-First State? The Inevitable Aftermath of Victory in Iraq." In it, with the help of regional experts, historians, and retired military officers, he gamed out just how difficult the aftermath could be. Among the scenarios he explored: the financial and logistical complications caused by the destruction of Baghdad's infrastructure; the possibility that Saddam Hussein would escape and join Osama bin Laden on the Most Wanted list; how the dearth of Arabic speakers in the U.S. government would hinder peacekeeping and other aftermath operations; how the need for the U.S., as the occupying power, to secure Iraq's borders would bring it face to face with Iran, another spoke in the "axis of evil"; the complications of working with the United Nations after it refused to support the war; what to do about the Iraqi debt from, among other things, UN-imposed reparations after the first Gulf War, which some estimates put as high as $400 billion.

Much of this speculation has since come to pass and is bedeviling the U.S.'s attempt to stabilize—let alone democratize—Iraq. So are some other post-war realities that were either too speculative or too hypothetical to be given much air in the pre-war debate. Looting, for instance, and general lawlessness. The fruitless (thus far) search for weapons of mass destruction. The inability to quickly restore power and clean water. A decimated health-care system. The difficulty of establishing an interim Iraqi government, and the confusion over who exactly should run things in the meantime. The understandably shallow reservoir of patience among the long-suffering Iraqis. The hidden clause in Halliburton's contract to repair Iraq's oil wells that also, by the way, granted it control of production and distribution, despite the administration's assurances that the Iraqis would run their own oil industry.

In the rush to war, how many Americans even heard about some of these possibilities? Of the 574 stories about Iraq that aired on NBC, ABC, and CBS evening news broadcasts between September 12 (when Bush addressed the UN) and March 7 (a week and a half before the war began), only twelve dealt primarily with the potential aftermath, according to Andrew Tyndall's numbers.

The Republicans were saying only what was convenient, thus the "he said." The Democratic leadership was saying little, so there was no "she said." "Journalists are never going to fill the vacuum left by a weak political opposition," says *The New York Times*'s Steven R. Weisman. But why not? If something important is being ignored, doesn't the press have an obligation to force our elected officials to address it? We have the ability, even on considerably less important matters than war and nation-building. Think of the dozens of articles *The New York Times* published between July 10, 2002 and March 31 about the Augusta National Country Club's exclusion of women members, including the one from November 25 that carried the headline "CBS Staying Silent in Debate on Women Joining Augusta." Why couldn't there have been headlines last fall that read: "Bush Still Mum on Aftermath," or "Beyond Saddam: What Could Go Right, and What Could Go Wrong?" And while you're at it, consider the criticism the *Times*'s mini-crusade on Augusta engendered in the media world, as though an editor's passion for an issue never drives coverage.

This is not inconsequential nitpicking. *The New Yorker*'s editor, David Remnick, who has written in support of going to war with Iraq, wrote of the aftermath in the March 31 issue: "An American presence in Baghdad will carry with it risks and responsibilities that will shape the future of the United States in the world." The press not only could have prepared the nation and its leadership for the aftermath we are now witnessing, but should have.

The Real Bias

In the early 1990s, I was a statehouse reporter for the *Charleston Daily Mail* in West Virginia. Every time a bill was introduced in the House to restrict access to abortion, the speaker, who was solidly pro-choice, sent the bill to the health committee, which was chaired by a woman who was also pro-choice. Of course, the bills never emerged from that committee. I was green and, yes, pro-choice, so it took a couple of years of witnessing this before it sunk in that—as the anti-abortion activists had been telling me from day one—the committee was stacked with pro-choice votes and that this was how "liberal" leadership killed the abortion bills every year while appearing to let the legislative process run its course. Once I understood, I eagerly wrote that story, not only because I knew it would get me on page one, but also because such political maneuverings offended my reporter's sense of fairness. The bias, ultimately, was toward the story.

Reporters are biased, but not in the oversimplified, left-right way that Ann Coulter and the rest of the bias cops would have everyone believe. As Nicholas Confessore argued in *The American Prospect*, most of the loudest bias-spotters were not reared in a newsroom. They come from politics, where everything is driven by ideology. Voting Democratic and not going to church—two bits of demography often trotted out to show how liberal the press is—certainly have some bearing on one's interpretation of events. But to leap to the conclusion that reporters use their precious column inches to push a left-wing agenda is specious reasoning at its worst. We all have our biases, and they can be particularly pernicious when they are unconscious. Arguably the most damaging bias is rarely discussed—the bias born of class. A number of people interviewed for this story said that the lack of socioeconomic diversity in the newsroom is one of American journalism's biggest blind spots. Most newsroom diversity efforts, though, focus on ethnic, racial, and gender minorities, which can often mean people with different skin color but largely the same middle-class background and aspirations. At a March 13 panel on media bias at Columbia's journalism school, John Leo, a columnist for *U.S. News & World Report*, said, "It used to be that anybody could be a reporter by walking in the door. It's a little harder to do that now, and you don't get the working-class Irish poor like Hamill or Breslin or me. What you get is people from Ivy League colleges with upper-class credentials, what you get is people who more and more tend to be and act alike." That, he says, makes it hard for a newsroom to spot its own biases.

Still, most reporters' real biases are not what political ideologues tend to think. "Politically I'm a reporter," says Eric Nalder, an investigative reporter at the *San Jose Mercury News*. Reporters are biased toward conflict because it is more interesting than stories without conflict; we are biased toward sticking with the pack because it is safe; we are biased toward event-driven coverage because it is easier; we are biased toward existing narratives because they are safe and easy. Consider the story—written by reporters around the country—of how Kenneth L. Lay, the former CEO of Enron, encouraged employees to buy company stock as he was secretly dumping his. It was a conveniently damning narrative, and easy to believe. Only it turned out, some two years later, to be untrue, leading *The New York Times's* Kurt Eichenwald to write a story correcting the record on February 9.

Mostly, though, we are biased in favor of getting the story, regardless of whose ox is being gored. Listen to Daniel Bice, an investigative columnist at the *Milwaukee Journal-Sentinel,* summarize his reporting philosophy: "Try not to be boring, be a reliable source of information, cut through the political, corporate, and bureaucratic bullshit, avoid partisanship, and hold politicians' feet to the fire." It would be tough to find a reporter who disagrees with any of that.

In his 1979 book *Deciding What's News,* the Columbia sociologist Herbert Gans defined what he called the journalist's "paraideology," which, he says, unconsciously forms and strengthens much of what we think of as news judgment. This consists largely of a number of "enduring values"—such as "altruistic democracy" and "responsible capitalism"—that are reformist, not partisan. "In reality," Gans writes, "the news is not so much conservative or liberal as it is reformist; indeed, the enduring values are very much like the values of the Progressive movement of the early twentieth century." My abortion story, then, came from my sense that what was happening violated my understanding of "altruistic democracy." John Laurence distills Gans' paraideology into simpler terms: "We are for honesty, fairness, courage, humility. We are against corruption, exploitation, cruelty, criminal behavior, violence, discrimination, torture, abuse of power, and many other things." Clifford Levy, a reporter for *The New York Times* whose series on abuse in New York's homes for the mentally ill won a Pulitzer this year, says, "Of all the praise I got for the series, the most meaningful was from other reporters at the paper who said it made them proud to work there because it was a classic case of looking out for those who can't look out for themselves."

This "paraideology," James Carey explains, can lead to charges of liberal bias. "There is a bit of the reformer in anyone who enters journalism," he says. "And reformers are always going to make conservatives uncomfortable to an extent because conservatives, by and large, want to preserve the status quo."

Gans, though, notes a key flaw in the journalist's paraideology. "Journalists cannot exercise news judgment," he writes, "without a composite of nation, society, and national and social institutions in their collective heads, and this picture is an aggregate of reality judgments … In doing so, they cannot leave room for the reality judgments that, for example, poor people have about America; nor do they ask, or even think of asking, the kinds of questions about the country that radicals, ultraconservatives, the religiously orthodox, or social scientists ask as a result of their reality judgments."

This understanding of "the other" has always been—and will always be—a central challenge of journalism. No individual embodies all the perspectives of a society. But we are not served in this effort by a paralyzing fear of being accused of bias. In their recent book *The Press Effect*, Kathleen Hall Jamieson and Paul Waldman make a strong case that this fear was a major factor in the coverage of the Florida recount of the 2000 presidential election, and its influence on journalists was borne out in my reporting for this piece. "Our paper is under constant criticism by people alleging various forms of bias," says the *Star-Tribune's* Eric Black. "And there is a daily effort to perform in ways that will make it harder to criticize. Some are reasonable, but there is a line you can cross after which you are avoiding your duties to truth-telling." In a March 10 piece critical of the press's performance at Bush's pre-war press conference, *USA Today's* Peter Johnson quoted Sam Donaldson as saying that it is difficult for the media—especially during war—"to press very hard when they know that a large segment of the population doesn't want to see a president whom they have anointed having to squirm." If we're about to go to war—especially one that is controversial—shouldn't the president squirm?

It is important, always, for reporters to understand their biases, to understand what the accepted narratives are, and to work against them as much as possible. This might be less of a problem if our newsrooms were more diverse—intellectually and socioeconomically as well as in gender, race, and ethnicity—but it would still be a struggle. There is too much easy opinion passing for journalism these days, and this is in no way an attempt to justify that. Quite the opposite. We need deep reporting and real understanding, but we also need reporters to acknowledge all that they don't know, and not try to mask that shortcoming behind a gloss of attitude, or drown it in a roar of oversimplified assertions.

Toward a Better Definition of Objectivity

In the last two years, Archbishop Desmond Tutu has been mentioned in more than 3,000 articles on the Nexis database, and at least 388 (11 percent) included in the same breath the fact that he was a Nobel Peace Prize winner. The same search criteria found that Yasser Arafat turned up in almost 96,000 articles, but only 177 (less than .2 percent) mentioned that he won the Nobel prize. When we move beyond stenography, reporters make a million choices, each one subjective. When, for example, is it relevant to point out, in a story about Iraq's weapons of mass destruction, that the U.S. may have helped Saddam Hussein build those weapons in the 1980s? Every time? Never?

The rules of objectivity don't help us answer such questions. But there are some steps we can take to clarify what we do and help us move forward with confidence. A couple of modest proposals:

Journalists (and journalism) must acknowledge, humbly and publicly, that what we do is far more subjective and far less detached than the aura of objectivity implies—and the public wants to believe. If we stop claiming to be mere objective observers, it will not end the charges of bias but will allow us to defend what we do from a more realistic, less hypocritical position.

Secondly, we need to free (and encourage) reporters to develop expertise and to use it to sort through competing claims, identify and explain the underlying assumptions of those claims, and make judgments about what readers and viewers need to know to understand what is happening. In short, we need them to be more willing to "adjudicate factual disputes," as Kathleen Hall Jamieson and Paul Waldman argue in *The Press Effect*. Bill Marimow, the editor of the *Baltimore Sun,* talks of reporters "mastering" their beats. "We want our reporters to be analysts," he told a class at Columbia in March. "Becoming an expert, and mastering the whole range of truth about issues will give you the ability to make independent judgments."

Timothy Noah, writing in *The Washington Monthly* for a 1999 symposium on objectivity, put it this way: "A good reporter who is well-steeped in his subject matter and who isn't out to prove his cleverness, but rather is sweating out a detailed understanding of a topic worth exploring, will probably develop intelligent opinions that will inform and perhaps be expressed in his journalism." This happens every day in ways large and small, but it still happens too rarely. In a March 18 piece headlined "Bush Clings to Dubious Allegations About Iraq," *The Washington Post*'s Walter Pincus and Dana Milbank laid out all of Bush's "allegations" about Saddam Hussein "that have been challenged—and in some cases disproved—by the United Nations, European governments, and even U.S. intelligence." It was noteworthy for its bluntness, and for its lack of an "analysis" tag. In commenting on that story, Steven Weisman of *The New York Times* illustrates how conflicted journalism is over whether such a piece belongs in the news columns: "It's a very good piece, but it is very tendentious," he says. "It's interesting that the editors didn't put it on page one, because it would look like they are calling Bush a liar. Maybe we should do more pieces like it, but you must be careful not to be argumentative."

Some reporters work hard to get these same "argumentative" ideas into their stories in more subtle ways. Think of Jason Riley's comment about "feeding information" to sources. Steven Weisman calls it making it part of the "tissue" of the story. For example, in a March 17 report on the diplomatic failures of the Bush administration, Weisman worked in the idea that the CIA was questioning the Iraq-al Qaeda connection by attributing it to European officials as one explanation for why the U.S. *casus belli* never took hold in the UN.

The test, though, should not be whether it is tendentious, but whether it is true.

There are those who will argue that if you start fooling around with the standard of objectivity you open the door to partisanship. But mainstream reporters by and large are not ideological warriors. They are imperfect people performing a difficult job that is crucial to society. Letting them write what they know and encouraging them to dig toward some deeper understanding of things is not biased, it is essential. Reporters should feel free, as Daniel Bice says, to "call it as we see it, but not be committed to one side or the other." Their professional values make them, Herbert Gans argues, akin to reformers, and they should embrace that aspect of what they do, not hide it for fear of being slapped with a bias charge. And when actual bias seeps in—as it surely will—the self-policing in the newsroom must be vigorous. Witness the memo John Carroll, editor of the *Los Angeles Times,* wrote last month to his staff after a front-page piece on a new Texas abortion law veered left of center: "I want everyone to understand how serious I am about purging all political bias from our coverage."

Journalists have more tools today than ever to help them "adjudicate factual disputes." In 1993, before the computer-age version of "precision journalism" had taken root in the newsroom, Steve Doig helped *The Miami Herald* win a Pulitzer with his computer-assisted stories that traced damage done by Hurricane Andrew to shoddy home construction and failed governmental oversight of builders. "Precision journalism is arguably activist, but it helps us approach the unobtainable goal of objectivity more than traditional reporting strategies," says Doig, who now teaches computer-assisted reporting at Arizona State University. "It allows you to measure a problem, gives you facts that are less controvertible. Without the computer power, our Hurricane Andrew stories would have essentially been finger-pointing stories, balanced with builders saying there is no way any structure could have withstood such winds."

On April 1, Ron Martz, a reporter from the *Atlanta Journal-Constitution* embedded with the Army in Iraq, delivered a "war diary" entry on National Public Radio in which he defended his battlefield decision to drop his reporter's detachment and take a soldier's place holding an intravenous drip bag and comforting a wounded Iraqi civilian. The "ethicists," Martz said on NPR, tell us this is murky territory. That Martz, an accomplished reporter, should worry at all that his reputation could suffer from something like this says much about journalism's relationship with objectivity. Martz concluded that he is a human being first and a reporter second, and was comfortable with that. Despite all our important and necessary attempts to minimize our humanity, it can't be any other way.

Note

1   Press conference was held on March 6, 2003.

Credit _____

Cunningham, Brent. "Re-thinking Objectivity." *Columbia Journalism Review* 11 July 2003. Web.

Good News for the Future? Young People, Internet Use, and Political Participation

Tom P. Bakker and Claes H. de Vreese

Tom P. Bakker holds a Ph.D. from The Amsterdam School of Communication Research. He worked on the project Citizen Journalism, Media and Politics from 2008 to 2011, as well as at various news outlets. Claes H. de Vreese is a Professor of Political Communication at The Amsterdam School of Communication Research, University of Amsterdam. He has published extensively on politics and the media. In "Good News for the Future? Young People, Internet Use, and Political Participation," first published in Communication Research *in 2011, the authors examine the effect the Internet has on the civic and political engagement of young people. Their research suggests that, contrary to widespread assumptions, Internet use among young people, and specifically social networking, appears to encourage greater civic and political engagement both online and offline.*

CEDORNOCEO

Introduction

Much research on youth and politics from the last decade shows increasing detachment of younger people from politics. Most discussions revolve around declining political interest, dropping participation, and low turnout at elections (e.g., Delli Carpini, 2000; Phelps, 2004; Pirie & Worcester, 2000). Although the assumption that political participation among the young has been low for a long time is generally accepted, the role of the media in affecting (non)participatory behavior has become particularly interesting with the ever-growing popularity of the Internet among younger people and the possible effects of the new medium. The use of new media for political ends in the United States was visible during the 2008 U.S. presidential elections. President Obama actively and successfully employed social media like Facebook, Twitter, and YouTube as communication tools, capitalizing on the heavy use of the Internet for political activities by younger people (Smith & Rainie, 2008). Also, in most Western European countries there seems high potential for the Internet, considering the high usage levels over the last few years (Eurostat, 2009) and the continuing debates on decreasing participation levels among youth.

A considerable amount of research is already available on the ways the Internet affects civic or political involvement. Although findings have sometimes been inconclusive, recent studies acknowledge that Internet use is not a unidimensional concept and thus does not—if at all—affect all groups in society similarly; rather, its effects depend on a complex combination of personal and social characteristics, usage patterns, and the specific content and context of the medium. More specifically, Shah, Kwak, and Holbert (2001) have shown that modeling specified Internet use (as opposed to "overall Internet use") as a predictor of social capital worked best for younger generations (people under 35 in this case). Similar arguments about differential effects have earlier been made concerning the effects of watching television (McLeod & McDonald, 1985; Norris, 1996).

A plethora of both specific and generic terms have been used to cover diverging forms of civic and political involvement, ranging from *social capital* (e.g., Putnam, 2000), *civic literacy* (Milner, 2002), and *political* and *civic engagement* to more concrete terms like *membership, political knowledge,* and *turnout.* In this article, we focus on *political participation.* In a comprehensive overview, Delli Carpini (2004, p. 396) defines political participation as part of a wider notion of "democratic engagement" which includes most of the terms mentioned above. While confining ourselves to politics, we claim that the understanding of political participation should not be limited to institutional and traditional ways. The definitions and boundaries of political participation have been subjects of discussion for decades (for an early overview and discussion, see Conge, 1988), but contemporary research simply cannot ignore online ways of participation. This article focuses on offline and online political participation in the Netherlands. Just like in the United States and many other Western European countries, Internet usage among Dutch youth is very high, while at the same time there are debates about declines in participation. Our study finally aims to generate general insights into the role of specific uses of the Internet in affecting participatory behavior among the so-called Internet generation.

A Closer Look at Decline in Participation

Historically, the participation of citizens in the political process has been considered a crucial element for a functioning and healthy democracy. Irrespective of the various changes in the social and political landscape on both international and national levels during the last decades, the significance of participatory behavior of citizens is at the core in several key works on democracy (e.g., Held, 2006). In the light of this alleged importance, serious concerns have been raised over the rate of political participation among young and future generations. Recent reports from western countries show low or decreasing levels of participation. However, questions arise if *all* forms of political participation are declining or if the existing literature is biased by a disproportional focus on institutional and limited measures of participatory behavior. As—among others—Verba, Schlozman, and Brady (1995) have made clear, political participation has several dimensions, is changing over time, and requires different levels of input of time, money, and skills. It may well be that participatory acts that require a substantial amount of input in offline settings are more accessible and attractive for some people when they can be carried out in an online context (e.g., sending an e-mail to a politician is faster, cheaper, and easier than sending a letter).

Some suggest that it is not so much the levels of interest or participation that are being challenged but rather the attitudes toward politics that are changing. For example, younger people are thought to be more skeptical and to show more political apathy (e.g., Henn, Weinstein, & Wring, 2002), something that should not be equated with nonparticipation or disengagement. Younger people may form a new generation that is less attracted by traditional forms of political engagement (Phelps, 2004; Zukin, Keeter, Andolina, Jenkins, & Delli Carpini, 2006). Such assertions have led to a call for a broader and more contemporary notion of political or civic participation (Dahlgren, 2000; de Vreese, 2006; Dunleavy, 1996; Livingstone, Bober, & Helsper, 2005; O'Toole, Lister, Marsh, Jones, & McDonagh, 2003; Phelps, 2005; Russell, 2004; Verba et al., 1995) and to look beyond established and institutional measures of participation like party membership, attendance at political meetings, or voter turnout. Taking a broader approach, Zukin et al. (2006) concluded that "simple claims that today's youth (…) are apathetic and disengaged from *civic* life are simply wrong" (pp. 188–189).

The Internet is a natural medium for alternative and digital ways of political participation. It offers—potentially—new modes of easily accessible, low-cost forms of participation. The web and all other online applications are heavily used by younger people. For example, in 2007, the average level of Internet use[1] in the 27 European Union member states was 60%, whereas this was 88% for the age group of 16 to 24, peaking at 99% in the Netherlands and 100% in Denmark, Finland, and Iceland (Eurostat, 2007). In the United States, younger people also belong to the group of heaviest Internet users. While in May 2008 the overall percentage of Internet users[2] among the adult American population was 73%, this percentage was 90% for the age group 18 to 29 (Pew Internet & American Life Project, 2008). The Internet offers a wide scope of possibilities to engage in political activities like visiting political blogs, researching political information, following online news, participating in forums, discussing politics by e-mail, or organizing electronic petitions.

There have been divergent expectations about the development of the Internet and how it may affect certain aspects of civic and political life. Supporters of a so-called utopian view not only praise the wide-ranging technical possibilities but also commend the social potential of the Internet to increase political engagement and participation. Followers of a more dystopian view consider the Internet more as a social threat, disconnecting people from "real" life (Kraut et al., 1998; Nie & Erbring, 2002) or even endangering key elements of a healthy democracy (Sunstein, 2001). Many empirical studies from recent years, however, have not found evidence for either strong positive or negative effects of Internet use on (offline forms of) political engagement (see Boulianne, 2009). Nevertheless, as we shall see, studies that have included more specified forms of Internet use in their model were able to shed more light under what circumstances, or for which audience, effects actually *do* appear.

Media and Politics: An Unclear Relationship

The notion that media, including the Internet, serve multiple functions and lead to different effects is commonly adopted in the field of political communication. A range of studies—usually employing multivariate analyses—have addressed the relationships between particular uses of the Internet and forms of political and civic engagement (e.g., Quintelier & Vissers, 2008; Scheufele & Nisbet, 2002; Shah, McLeod, & Yoon, 2001). Tolbert and McNeal (2003), for example, found that being exposed to election news on the Internet increased the probability that people would vote during the 1996 and 2000 U.S. presidential elections, leading to the idea that the Internet has a mobilizing potential. Focusing on civic engagement, Shah et al. (2001) showed that "information exchange" on the Internet was a better predictor than "overall Internet use." Xenos and Moy (2007), however, show that positive effects of online news on engagement are higher for people with more political interest, and, also, Bimber (2003) argues that mainly already politically engaged citizens benefit from the Internet's potential.

The rapid growth of Internet use and the alleged declining levels of political involvement of younger people have made the relationship between these two a popular and much debated issue. New media may well challenge the role or fill some of the gap left by traditionally strong socializers such as family, church, and school. Especially, the role played by parents for their children as key socializers with regard to politics is changing. In the past decades, trends of increasing individualization and volatile electoral behavior are observed (Dalton, 2002). Although traditionally parents were stable voters and played an important role, they are now increasingly becoming floating voters and losing ground as political socializers. Taking this development into account, media in general, and the Internet in particular, are becoming more central in the process of affecting participatory behavior. As Delli Carpini (2004) notes, "As one of several socializing agents, the media provide much of the 'raw material' that make up social and political beliefs, attitudes, and schema" (p. 408).

Looking first at the role of "traditional" news media, newspaper use repeatedly proved to be positively related to various forms of civic and political engagement. Eveland and Scheufele (2000) showed that reading newspapers positively impacted political participation and voting, and Weaver and Drew (2001) found positive relationships between paying attention to campaign news in newspapers and voting (see also McLeod, Scheufele, & Moy, 1999; Scheufele, 2002). Jeffres, Lee, Neuendorf, and Atkin (2007) showed that readership of newspapers was positively related with different forms of community activities and social capital. Also, television news use, although less consistently, has been found to—directly (Norris, 1996) or indirectly (Shah, Cho, Eveland, & Kwak, 2005)—impact political participation in a positive direction.

The impact of news consumption has also been tested in online contexts and showed similar positive relationships. Tolbert and McNeal (2003) showed that using online news increased voting probability, and Quintelier and Vissers (2008) found that consuming online news positively related to political participation among teenagers, while both studies included a large set of control variables (see also Esser & de Vreese, 2007; Kenski & Stroud, 2006; Shah et al., 2005) We therefore hypothesize, *ceteris paribus,* the following:

> *Hypothesis 1 (H1):* News consumption via newspapers, television, and the Internet is positively related to political participation.

Besides news use, discussing politics with family or friends is considered an important factor as regard to political participation. Various studies have convincingly linked political discussion with participatory behavior (Kim, Wyatt, & Katz, 1999; McLeod et al., 1999; Wyatt, Katz, & Kim, 2000) and knowledge (Eveland, 2004; Eveland & Thomson, 2006). Parallel to the relationships between *offline* discussion and participation, positive associations have been suggested between *online* discussion and political knowledge and participation (Hardy & Scheufele, 2005; Price & Cappella, 2002). This leads us to our second hypothesis:

> *Hypothesis 2 (H2):* Interactive online communication is positively related to political participation.

Although there seems to be wide agreement on the potential benefits of Internet use, some have argued that time spent on the Internet (or watching television) reduces the available time to engage in meaningful civic and political activities (Nie & Erbring, 2002; Putnam, 1995, 2000), a process that is generally referred to as *time displacement.* These assertions, however, have been countered in other research (e.g., Shah, Schmierbach, Hawkins, Espino, & Donavan, 2002).

Because of the high development pace of the Internet and the phenomenon's relative newness in social science, research approaches and findings vary widely and theories on the potential effects of the new medium are neither too stable nor convincing. Although scholars agree on the assumption that the Internet leads to differential effects for different types of users, recent research on the relationship between media use and politics is still very limited in the examination of the multidimensional relationship between Internet use and political participation. Previous research (Pasek, Kenski, Romer, & Jamieson, 2006) acknowledges the varied functions media can serve, but the multidimensional character of the Internet in analyses is often overlooked. Although most researchers aim at determining the role that media play in younger people's lives with regard to political participation, for the most part solely informational uses or general indicators (e.g., web use, e-mail) are taken into consideration with regard to the Internet. Limited specification of Internet use in survey research may lead scholars to underestimate the actual magnitude of Internet effects (see also Boulianne, 2009). We argue that given the high level of Internet use among younger people along with their diverging usage patterns, the multidimensional character of the new medium deserves greater attention. Following this need to specify the type of use and online activity, we hypothesize the following:

> *Hypothesis 3 (H3):* Specified media usage is a stronger predictor of political participation than time spent with a medium.

Another often overlooked but important aspect when tapping political or civic participation is the various digital possibilities the Internet offers to engage in political activities, which then leads to the expectation that intensive use of the Internet does not *necessarily* lead to decreased participation. As noted earlier, the Internet can be used to be politically active in various ways (visiting political websites, discussing politics in discussion forums, signing online petitions) and requires different levels of skills or energy. Moreover, many online activities, like signing petitions or sending political messages, have also been measured in an offline form (e.g., McLeod et al., 1999; Putnam, 2000; Verba et al., 1995). Given the popularity and relative ease of online political participation, such activities should not be neglected when measuring participatory behavior. However, taking into account the theory of time displacement, increased online participatory behavior may lead to lower levels of offline participation. Given the centrality of the Internet among younger people, we therefore hypothesize the following:

> *Hypothesis 4 (H4):* Internet use is a stronger predictor for newer forms of political participation than traditional forms.

Our last expectation relates to intrinsic preferences toward specific media content. Prior (2005) proposes a measure of relative entertainment preference (REP), which is aimed at understanding the political implications of people's preference for news or entertainment content. Prior's results point at a negative relationship between REP and political knowledge and voter turnout. For this research, we will focus on the potential link between REP and political participation, to see if this proposition can be extended. We do so—in analogy to our Internet use measures—also to acknowledge that it is the type of use of a medium that matters and not the duration of the use. Our last hypothesis therefore reads as follows:

> *Hypothesis 5 (H5):* There is a negative relationship between REP and political participation.

Method

We designed an online survey in the Netherlands to explore the possible relationships between different media uses and political participation. Ten thousand people in the age group of 16 to 24 were sampled by the marketing company TAPPS. These people were invited by e-mail to fill in the questionnaire. The sampling frame consists of a selection of databases that are composed of different modes of recruitment including both offline and online modes. The survey was administered by the Amsterdam School of Communication Research (ASCoR) in the spring of 2006. To maximize the response rate, the survey was kept relatively short (average response time was less than 10 minutes) and incentives were raffled off among the participants.

An online survey design was chosen, given our key interest in the relationship between different forms of political participation and Internet use patterns. Although online surveys are critiqued for their skewed distributions (i.e., only Internet users), in the Netherlands, Internet access among 16 to 24 years is almost 100%, and our interest is not a comparison between online and offline users. The questionnaire was successfully completed by 2,409 respondents ($M = 19.2$ years, $SD = 2.29$), resulting in a response rate of 24% (AAPOR RR1).[3]

Dependent Variables

Given the high Internet usage among younger people, we tapped two discrete forms of participatory behavior, labeled *traditional participation* and *digital participation*. A factor analysis (principal component analysis with Varimax rotation) yielded two factors for both forms of participation, which we tagged *passive* and *active participation*.

Digital participation was measured by asking people about the frequency they participated in online political activities, ranging on a 5-point scale from *never* to *very often.* Following the factor analysis, the variables *digital passive participation* and *digital active participation* were created, respectively explaining 42% (eigenvalue 3.82) and 12% (eigenvalue 1.07) of the variance.[4] Digital passive participation (M = 1.70, SD = 0.69) was measured by asking respondents to indicate how often they, in relation to politics, (1) visited websites of the municipality, (2) visited websites of the government and public administration, and (3) visited websites with political content. The three items showed to be internally consistent (α = .77). Digital active participation (M = 2.05, SD = 0.69) involved more active forms of participation and was gauged by asking how often the respondent in relation to politics (1) reacted online to a message or article on the Internet, (2) signed online petitions, and (3) participated in online polls. The items formed an acceptable internally consistent scale (α = .59).

A similar approach was used to tap traditional participation. For this measure, people again were asked with what frequency (5-point scale, *never* to *very often*) they participated in political activities, but this time in an offline setting. Factor analysis led to the creation of traditional passive participation (explained variance 15%, eigenvalue 1.02) and traditional active participation (explained variance 45%, eigenvalue 3.16). Respondents' traditional passive participation (M = 1.80, SD = 0.73) was made up of three items (α = .63), asking people how often they (1) retrieved books or information about political or social issues, (2) signed petitions, and (3) followed newspapers and television in election times to learn about politics and political parties. Traditional active participation (M = 1.21, SD = 0.41) consisted of four items (α = .75), asking how often the respondents (1) sent letters to newspapers or magazines to comment on articles, (2) protested or complained by mail or telephone about decisions taken by the government or public administration, (3) participated in demonstrations, and (4) actively engaged in discussions during debates or lectures.

Independent Variables

Media variables. To assess the types of media and media content that respondents usually consume, a set of detailed questions was asked, following Slater's argument (2004, p. 169) that a lack of specified measures of media use could, among others, lead to underestimates of its possible effects. In this article, specificity of media exposure measures is taken into account by assessing uses of newspaper, television, and Internet.

Newspapers. Respondents were asked to indicate how much time they spent reading paid and free newspapers on an average day (in 10-minute intervals), leading to *reading time paid dailies* (M = 2.66, SD = 1.03) and *reading time free dailies* (M = 2.67, SD = 0.84). Participants were also asked how often (in days) during an average week they read the following newspapers: *AD/Algemeen Dagblad, Metro, NRC Handelsblad,*

NRC.next, Het Parool, Spits, De Telegraaf, Trouw, de Volkskrant, and a regional daily. Additive index scores were created for quality newspapers *(NRC Handelsblad, NRC. next, Het Parool, Trouw,* and *de Volkskrant; M* = 1.10, *SD* = 0.24), popular newspapers *(AD/Algemeen Dagblad* and *De Telegraaf; M* = 1.40, *SD* = 0.57), and free newspapers *(Metro and Spits; M* = 2.05, *SD* = 0.90).

Television. The setup for the television questions corresponded with the design of the newspaper section. First the respondents were asked how long (in 0.5-hour intervals) they watched television on an average day, leading to creation of the variable *viewing time television* (*M* = 6.97, *SD* = 2.30). The respondents then were asked how often (in days) they tuned into different national, regional, international, and thematic channels. A factor analysis revealed two forms of viewing behavior: *public television viewing* (eigenvalue 1.85, explained variance 14.3%) and *commercial television viewing* (eigenvalue 3.98, explained variance 30.6%). Public television viewing (*M* = 1.83, *SD* = 0.73) consisted of the channels Nederland 1, Nederland 2, and Nederland 3, and commercial television viewing (*M* = 2.41, *SD* = 0.66) was formed by RTL4, RTL5, RTL7, SBS6, Net5, and Veronica/JETIX. Both the public and the commercials channels formed reliable scales (Cronbach's α = .78).

An additional measure was used to tap the respondents' relative preference for entertainment- or news-related content on television. The REP is based on Prior's REP (Prior, 2005) and was measured by letting the respondents choose, in five rounds, between their preference for an entertainment program or a news/current affairs program. Consequently, the total amount of choices (five) was divided by the amount of choices for entertainment programs (ranging between 0 and 5) and a REP ratio was computed between 0 and 1 (*M* = 0.73, *SD* = 0.24).

Internet. First, respondents were asked how much time they spent online on an average day (15 minutes or less, 30 minutes, 45 minutes, 1 hour, 1.5 hours, 2 hours, 2.5 hours, 3 hours, 3.5 hours, 4 hours, or 4.5 hours or more), resulting in the variable *time spent online* (*M* = 6.88, *SD* = 2.64).

As noted earlier, it is considered relevant to examine not only informational or overall use of media types but rather include detailed measures of media use (Slater, 2004). For example, taking into account the large battery of possible Internet activities, Norris and Jones (1998) distinguish between four different types of Internet users, labeled *researchers, home consumers, political expressives,* and *party animals.* Shah et al. (2001) discriminated between using the Internet for social recreation, product consumption, financial management, or information exchange (see also Quintelier & Vissers, 2008). In our survey, we presented our respondents with a list of 16 surfing activities and 4 communication activities and asked to indicate how often (5-point scale, ranging between *never* and *very often*) they took part in those activities. After factor analysis, four categories were determined: Internet news use (eigenvalue 1.37, explained variance 8.65%), services (eigenvalue 2.91, explained variance 18.2%), music (eigenvalue 1.99, explained variance 12.4%), and club/organization (eigenvalue 1.10, explained variance 6.9%). Internet news use ($M = 2.05$, $SD = 0.83$) is the combined measure of visiting newspaper websites, visiting news sites and news blogs, and visiting showbizz news sites ($\alpha = .59$). Services ($M = 2.39$, $SD = 0.68$) is formed by online banking, job searching, housing sites, looking for product information, holiday bookings, and online shopping ($\alpha = .65$). Music ($M = 3.59$, $SD = 1.11$) is a two-item measure of downloading music and software and listening to music on your PC ($\alpha = .69$). Club/organization ($M = 2.46$, $SD = 1.31$) is created by asking people how often they visited the website of an organization or club they were a member of. Respondents were also asked how often (5-point scale, between *never* and *very often*) they participated in online communication activities. The three variables were e-mail ($M = 4.25$, $SD = 0.77$), social networking (chat and online communities; eigenvalue = 1.54, explained variance = 38.5%; $M = 3.33$, $SD = 0.98$), and forum ($M = 2.29$, $SD = 1.24$).

Control variables. Respondents were asked to indicate their gender (1 = *male*, 2 = *female*) and level of education. A dummy variable was used to check for differences between respondents below and above legal voting age, which is 18 in the Netherlands ($1 \geq 18$). Political talk ($M = 2.28$, $SD = 1.11$) was measured by asking on a 5-point scale, ranging between *never* and *very often*, how often the respondent talked with friends about local or national political issues. Political interest ($M = 2.85$, $SD = 1.12$) was tapped by asking to what extent people agreed with the statement "Politics is interesting" (5-point scale, ranging between *totally disagree* and *totally agree*). Although both political talk and political interest are generally used as dependent variables, here they were purposefully implemented as control variables in order to provide a conservative test of the four main dependent political participation variables. Political talk and political interest can be expected to account for a considerable amount of the variance in the dependent variables, but inserting both variables in the early stage as control variables can assist in clarifying whether particular media use explains forms of political participation, while both political talk and interest are controlled for.

Analysis

To test our hypotheses, hierarchical multiple regressions analyses were run for the four forms of participation. The independent variables were grouped into four blocks that were consecutively taken into the regression. The variables in the first block were used as control variables, consisting of gender, legal voting age, education, political interest, and political talk. The second block was formed by measures of *duration* of newspaper, television, and Internet use. The third and fourth blocks were formed by respectively traditional media variables (newspapers and television) and Internet variables.

As already indicated earlier, by using political interest and political talk as control variables, a conservative test could be conducted of the participation measures. Also, entering media duration variables at an early stage allowed us to both test for main effects of media duration use and differential effects based on specified use of newspapers, television, and Internet, helping us to address the expectation (H3) that specified media usage (block 3 and 4) would be a stronger predictor of political participation than time spent with a medium (block 2), with possible effects weakening or diminishing when participation forms are regressed on all variable blocks in the final model.

Results

When looking at the results of all four regression analyses (Tables 1 to 4), we find support for our hypothesis that specified media usage is a stronger predictor of political participation than time spent with a medium (H3). Almost all initial significant beta coefficients in block 2 (time spent with a medium) vanish when the remaining blocks (block 3 and 4, specified media use) are entered in the third and fourth step of the analysis. Only in the regression model for traditional passive participation, a significant positive association remains for *reading time paid dailies* (Table 1). No significant effects are found for gender and education, except for modest negative significant associations in the model for traditional active participation (Table 2). In the models for active participation (both online and offline), a negative effect was found for legal voting age.[5]

Examining both the traditional media block and the Internet block, we find that using the Internet for news is a positive predictor for all four forms of participation. However, quality newspaper reading only shows significant positive associations with traditional forms of participation (Tables 1 and 2). No negative effects are found for reading popular or free newspapers (with one exception). Public television viewing (often seen as strongly correlated with news viewing) only proves to be a positive predictor of passive forms of participation, while commercial viewing is not a significant predictor for any type of participatory behavior. Given the systematic positive associations of news use on the Internet and the mixed results of newspaper reading and watching (public) television, we can partially confirm H1 that news consumption via newspapers, television, and the Internet is positively related to political participation. As expected, respondents' entertainment preference was negatively related to political participation, so H5 can be confirmed.

Table 1. Predicting Traditional Passive Participation

	M1	M2	M3	M4	M5
Control Variables					
Gender	.00	.00	.02	.02	.03
Education	.01	.01	.00	.00	.00
Legal voting age	.04**	.04*	.03	.01	.03
Political talk	.55***	.55***	.51***	.48***	.01
Political interest	.24***	.23***	.19***	.18***	.01
Duration					
Reading time paid dailies		.07***	.06***	.04**	.01
Reading time free dailies		−.01	−.01	−.02	.01
Viewing time television		−.01	−.01	.00	.01
Time spent online		.01	.01	−.03	.00
Traditional media					
Quality newspaper reading			.04*	.03*	.05
Popular newspaper reading			−.02	−.03*	.02
Free daily reading			.00	−.02	.01
Public television viewing			.08***	.06***	.02
Commercial television viewing			.00	−.02	.02
Relative entertainment preference			−.09***	−.10***	.05
Internet					
Internet new use				.10***	.01
Services				.06***	.02
Music				.00	.01
Club/organization				.02	.01
E-mail				.05***	.01
Social networking				.01	.01
Forum				.04*	.01
N				2,409	
R^2 change		.004	.017	.021	
Total R^2 (adjusted)	.502	.506	.523	.544	

Note: Entries are standardized beta coefficients and standard errors.

*p ≤ .05. **p ≤ .01. *** p ≤ .001.

Table 2. Predicting Traditional Active Participation

	M1	M2	M3	M4	SE
Control Variables					
Gender	−.09***	−.08***	−.06**	−.06**	.02
Education	−.04*	−.04	−.03	−.04*	.00
Legal voting age	−.01	−.02	−.04	−.05*	.02
Political talk	.26***	.26***	.23***	.19***	.01
Political interest	.13***	.12***	.08***	.07***	.01
Duration					
Reading time paid dailies		.06**	.03	.01	.01
Reading time free dailies		.03	.00	−.01	.01
Viewing time television		−.01	−.04*	−.03	.00
Time spent online		.06**	.06**	.01	.00
Traditional media					
Quality newspaper reading			.11***	.12***	.03
Popular newspaper reading			.01	−.01	.01
Free daily reading			.08***	.07***	.01
Public telvision viewing			.06*	.03	.01
Commercial television viewing			.06**	.04	.01
Relative entertainment preference			−.03	−.04	.04
Internet					
Internet new use				.09***	.01
Services				.09***	.01
Music				−.04*	.01
Club/organization				.03	.01
E-mail				−.03	.01
Social networking				.06**	.01
Forum				.10***	.01
N				2,409	
R^2 change		.007	.026	.034	
Total R^2 (adjusted)	.130	.137	.163	.197	

Note: Entries are standardized beta coefficients and standard errors.

*p ≤ .05. **p ≤ .01. *** p ≤ .001.

Table 3. Predicting Digital Passive Participation

	M1	M2	M3	M4	SE
Control Variables					
Gender	−.06***	−.05**	−.02	−.03	.03
Education	.02	.02	.01	.01	.01
Legal voting age	.09***	.09***	.08***	.00	.03
Political talk	.31***	.31***	.27***	.20***	.01
Political interest	.27***	.26***	.21***	.19***	.01
Duration					
Reading time paid dailies		.05**	.02	−.01	.01
Reading time free dailies		.02	.02	.00	.02
Viewing time television		.01	−.01	.02	.01
Time spent online		.07***	.07***	.01	.00
Traditional media					
Quality newspaper reading			.02	.02	.05
Popular newspaper reading			.00	−.02	.02
Free daily reading			.01	−.02	.01
Public telvision viewing			.13***	.09***	.02
Commercial television viewing			.02	−.01	.02
Relative entertainment preference			−.10***	−.10***	.06
Internet					
Internet new use				.18***	.02
Services				.18***	.02
Music				−.04*	.01
Club/organization				.05**	.01
E-mail				.07***	.02
Social networking				−.01	.01
Forum				.06***	.01
N				2,409	
R^2 change		.007	.029	.086	
Total R^2 (adjusted)	.282	.289	.318	.404	

Note: Entries are standardized beta coefficients and standard errors.

*$p \leq .05$. **$p \leq .01$. *** $p \leq .001$.

Table 4. Predicting Digital Active Participation

	M1	M2	M3	M4	SE
Control Variables					
Gender	−.07***	−.05**	−.04	−.01	.03
Education	−.02	.00	−.01	−.01	.01
Legal voting age	−.12***	−.14***	.15***	−.13***	.03
Political talk	.31***	.32***	.29***	.22***	.01
Political interest	.03	.03	.01	.01	.01
Duration					
Reading time paid dailies		.03	.02	−.02	.01
Reading time free dailies		.06	.05*	.03	.02
Viewing time television		.03	−.01	.03	.01
Time spent online		.13***	.13***	−.01	.00
Traditional media					
Quality newspaper reading			.02	.01	.05
Popular newspaper reading			.00	−.03	.02
Free daily reading			.04	.00	.01
Public telvision viewing			.07**	.02	.02
Commercial television viewing			.07**	.03	.02
Relative entertainment preference			−.05*	−.05**	.06
Internet					
Internet new use				.18***	.02
Services				.07***	.02
Music				.05*	.01
Club/organization				.04*	.01
E–mail				.05**	.02
Social networking				.03	.01
Forum				.36***	.01
N				2,409	
R^2 change		.023	.012	.202	
Total R^2 (adjusted)	.123	.146	.158	.360	

Note: Entries are standardized beta coefficients and standard errors.

*$p \leq .05$. **$p \leq .01$. ***$p \leq .001$.

Looking at the Internet block, a considerable amount of variables are (modest) positive predictors of participation. Concerning surfing activities, particularly news, service, and club/organization are significantly and positively related to most forms of participation. The same tendency is found for online forms of communication. Predominantly significant positive relationships were found between online forms of communication (mainly e-mail and forum use) and participation, supporting our expectation that interactive online communication is positively related to participation (H2).

Comparing the predictive power of the Internet block on the four dependent variables, higher amounts of explained variance were found for digital forms of participation (passive 8.6%, active 20.2%) than for traditional participation, supporting H4 (Internet use is a stronger predictor for newer forms of political participation than for traditional forms). However, several Internet variables are also significant positive predictors for traditional ways of participation.[6]

Discussion

The shortcomings in the communication environment are often highlighted when the shortcomings of today's democratic practices are discussed. The empirical evidence for the negative effects of suboptimal communications is at best mixed and more complex than most assumed relationships (see also Shah, McLeod, & Yoon, 2001; Tolbert & McNeal, 2003). This study particularly tackled the relationships between various types of media use and various forms of political participation for the citizens of tomorrow, young people aged 16 to 24. We found that various types of media use are positively linked to measures of political participation. In addition to all kinds of informational uses, noninformational uses of the web (e.g., online communication and visiting nonnews websites) also had positive relationships with diverse forms of participation. With conventional wisdom and much extant research focusing on the *negative* role played by the media in understanding younger people's political participation, this article has shown otherwise. Although high usage of particular (entertainment) media or a total detachment from any news media may indeed be disadvantageous for participatory behavior, a broader look at the use of media is unarguably relevant.

The findings of this study support our expectation that tapping specific uses of newspapers, television, and Internet improves our understanding of the relationships between media use and participatory behavior. Reversely, overall *duration* of specific media use proves to have weak predictive power. This finding is supported in related studies (e.g., Shah et al., 2001). While established positive effects of news use are indeed found in this article, the inclusion of other online activities, like using digital services and engaging in online communication and discussion, also shows positive relationships with most forms of political participation. This augments our argument that most effects of media use on political participation are *positive* in nature.

Moreover, this study extends Putnam's view (2000) that social networks are beneficial to participatory behavior. However, while Putnam, in his work on the building of social capital, stresses the importance of physical presence and reality, we extend this argument to also show that "being connected" online is positively related to both on and offline forms of participation. Although results for the four different forms of participation pointed in the same direction, the strength of associations differed. Forum use, for example, proved to be a much stronger predictor of digital active participation than of other forms, while traditional media use proved to be a (slightly) better predictor of traditional forms of participation than digital forms. Overall, however, several positive associations have been found between use of the Internet and both (digital and traditional) forms of participation, corroborating our expectation that online activities may be equally important measures in research on younger people's participatory behavior.

Although we have found associations between media use and participatory behavior of youth, the cross-sectional setup of the analysis does not permit us to make firm assertions about the causal direction of the relationship. It may very well be that specific media use drives on the intrinsic motivation of people to be politically active. This potentially reverse, reciprocal, or maybe even reinforcing process of media selection deserves special attention in current and future media effects research, using more complex combinations of both cross-sectional and overtime analysis of panel data (Slater, 2007). Longitudinal analysis could also be very useful in revealing cohort effects for different (media) generations. Although an online survey is a very useful instrument regarding our sample (young people) and the subject of this study (Internet use), the online invitations and surveys may have led to a somewhat skewed distribution of our sample. Hence, we are unable to make comparisons with youth that are not online or hardly use the Internet and might be active newspaper readers.

While the current study has limitations that should be considered and explored in future research, we have tried to improve the understanding of the varied functions of Internet use and to determine certain online usage patterns of younger people (e.g., consumer-related use, communication, online networking) as potential predictors of political participation (see also Quintelier & Vissers, 2008; Shah et al., 2001). The article demonstrates the limitations of research designs that are heavily focused on overall measures of (news) media use, passing over the wide-ranging and diverging uses and usage patterns of active online citizens. In a research field where Internet and younger generations are of key interest, scholars should not limit their approach to only the established offline and institutional ways of participation and media use. When research takes into account both offline and online political participation, including institutional and alternative ways of participatory behavior, a better understanding can be developed of the challenges and changes political participation is really facing in the current millennium.

Notes

[1]   Internet use is defined as the percentage of individuals who used the Internet in the last year.

[2]   An Internet user is defined as someone who at least occasionally uses the Internet or sends and receives e-mail.

[3]   While this response rate may seem low, it should be noted that random digit dialing (RDD) samples in the Netherlands typically yield response rates around 30%. Moreover, Krosnick (1999) shows that low a response rate is not per se an issue if the sample is not too far off the targeted population.

[4]   Our original factor analysis included three additional items, but these were removed because they suffered from extreme positive skewness or did not load clearly on one of the two extracted components.

[5]   Additional analyses suggest that the negative coefficients appear because of the negative associations with participation for respondents between 22 and 24 years old. Although we are not sure about the cause of this finding, it may be that the participatory acts that were measured become less relevant, interesting or accessible for this group, for example because of life changes such as working and thus having less free time to engage in participatory acts.

[6]   We emphasize that our test is rather conservative, given the controls for not only demographics but also for political talk and political interest which account for a large share of the explained variance. The robustness of our findings is augmented by this conservative estimate.

Works Cited

Bimber, B. (2003). *Information and American Democracy: Technology in the Evolution of Political Power.* Cambridge, UK: Cambridge University Press.

Boulianne, S. (2009). "Does Internet Use Affect Engagement? A Meta-Analysis of Research." *Political Communication, 26,* 193–211.

Conge, P. J. (1988). "The Concept of Political Participation: Toward a Definition." *Comparative Politics, 20,* 241–249.

Dahlgren, P. (2000). "The Internet and the Democratization of Civic Culture." *Political Communication, 17,* 335–340.

Dalton, R. J. (2002). *Citizen Politics: Public Opinion and Political Parties in Advanced Industrial Democracies* (3rd ed.). New York: Chatham House.

de Vreese, C. H. (2006). "10 Observations About the Past, Present, and Future of Political Communication. Inaugural Lecture Delivered at the University of Amsterdam, Chair in Political Communication." Amsterdam: Amsterdam University Press.

Delli Carpini, M. X. (2000). "Gen.com: Youth, Civic Engagement, and the New Information Environment." *Political Communication, 17,* 341–349.

Delli Carpini, M. X. (2004). "Mediating Democratic Engagement: The Impact of Communications on Citizens' Involvement in Political and Civic Life." In L. L. Kaid (Ed.), *Handbook of Political Communication* (395–434). Mahwah, NJ: Lawrence Erlbaum.

Dunleavy, P. (1996). "Political Behavior: Institutional and Experiential Approaches." In R. Goodin & H.-D. Klingemann (Eds.), *A New Handbook of Political Science* (276–294). Oxford, UK: Oxford University Press.

Esser, F., & de Vreese, C. H. (2007). "Comparing Young Voters' Political Engagement in the United States and Europe." *American Behavioral Scientist, 50,* 1195–1213.

Eurostat. (2007). *Individuals—Internet use 2007.* Retrieved April 3, 2008, from http://epp.eurostat. ec.europa.eu/.

Eurostat. (2009). *Data in Focus 46/2009, Internet Usage in 2009, Households and Individuals.* Retrieved December 22, 2009, from http://epp.eurostat.ec.europa.eu/cache/ITY_PUBLIC/4-08122009-BP/EN/4-08122009-BP-EN.PDF.

Eveland, W. P., Jr. (2004). "The Effect of Political Discussion in Producing Informed Citizens: The Roles of Information, Motivation, and Elaboration." *Political Communication, 21,* 177–193.

Eveland, W. P., Jr., & Scheufele, D. A. (2000). "Connecting News Media Use With Gaps in Knowledge and Participation." *Political Communication, 17,* 215–237.

Eveland, W. P., Jr., & Thomson, T. (2006). "Is It Talking, Thinking, or Both? A Lagged Dependent Variable Model of Discussion Effects on Political Knowledge." *Journal of Communication, 56,* 523–542.

Hardy, B. W., & Scheufele, D. A. (2005). "Examining Differential Gains From Internet Use: Comparing the Moderating Role of Talk and Online Interactions." *Journal of Communication, 55*(1), 71–84.

Held, D. (2006). *Models of democracy.* Cambridge, UK: Polity.

Henn, M., Weinstein, M., & Wring, D. (2002). "A Generation Apart? Youth and Political Participation in Britain." *British Journal of Politics and International Relations, 4,* 167–192.

Jeffres, L. W., Lee, J.-W., Neuendorf, K., & Atkin, D. (2007). "Newspaper Reading Supports Community Involvement." *Newspaper Research Journal,* 28(1), 6–23.

Kenski, K., & Stroud, N. J. (2006). Connections Between Internet Use and Political Efficacy, Knowledge, and Participation." *Journal of Broadcasting & Electronic Media, 50,* 173–192.

Kim, J., Wyatt, R. O., & Katz, E. (1999). "News, Talk, Opinion, Participation: The Part Played by Conversation in Deliberative Democracy." *Political Communication, 16,* 361–385.

Kraut, R., Patterson, M., Lundmark, V., Kiesler, S., Mukopadhyay, T., & Scherlis, W. (1998). "Internet Paradox: A Social Technology that Reduces Social Involvement and Psychological Well-Being?" *American Psychologist, 53,* 1017–1031.

Krosnick, J. A. (1999). "Survey Research." *Annual Review of Psychology, 50,* 537–567.

Livingstone, S., Bober, M., & Helsper, E. J. (2005). "Active Participation or Just More Information? Young People's Take-Up of Opportunities to Act and Interact on the Internet." *Information, Communication & Society, 8,* 287–314.

McLeod, J. M., & McDonald, D. G. (1985). "Beyond Simple Exposure: Media Orientations and Their Impact on Political Processes." *Communication Research, 12*(1), 3–33.

McLeod, J. M., Scheufele, D. A., & Moy, P. (1999). "Community, Communication, and Participation: The Role of Mass Media and Interpersonal Discussion in Local Political Participation." *Political Communication, 16,* 315–336.

Milner, H. (2002). *Civic Literacy: How Informed Citizens Make Democracy Work.* Hanover, NH: University Press of New England.

Nie, N. H., & Erbring, L. (2002). "Internet and Mass Media: A Preliminary Report." *IT & Society, 1*(2), 134–141.

Norris, P. (1996). "Does Television Erode Social Capital? A Reply to Putnam." *PS: Political Science and Politics, 29,* 474–480.

Norris, P., & Jones, D. (1998). "Editorial: Virtual Democracy." *International Journal of Press/Politics, 3*(2), 1–4.

O'Toole, T., Lister, M., Marsh, D., Jones, S., & McDonagh, A. (2003). "Tuning Out or Left Out? Participation and Nonparticipation Among Young People." *Contemporary Politics, 9*(1), 45–61.

Pasek, J., Kenski, K., Romer, D., & Jamieson, K. H. (2006). "America's Youth and Community Engagement: How Use of Mass Media is Related to Civic Activity and Political Awareness in 14- to 22-Year-Olds." *Communication Research, 33*(3), 115–135.

Pew Internet & American Life Project. (2008). *Pew Internet & American Life Survey, May 2008.* Retrieved December 22, 2009, from http://www.pewinternet.org/Static-Pages/Trend-Data/Usage-Over-Time.aspx/.

Phelps, E. (2004). "Young Citizens and Changing Electoral Turnout, 1964–2001." *Political Quarterly, 75,* 238–248.

Phelps, E. (2005). "Young Voters at the 2005 Britain General Election." *Political Quarterly, 76,* 482–487.

Pirie, M., & Worcester, R. (2000). *The Big Turn-Off: Attitudes of Young People to Government, Citizenship and Community.* London: Adam Smith Institute.

Price, V., & Cappella, J. N. (2002). "Online Deliberation and its Influence: The Electronic Dialogue Project in Campaign 2000." *IT & Society, 1*, 303–329.

Prior, M. (2005). "News vs. Entertainment: How Increasing Media Choice Widens Gaps in Political Knowledge and Turnout." *American Journal of Political Science, 49*, 577–592.

Putnam, R. D. (1995). "Tuning In, Tuning Out: The Strange Disappearance pf Social Capital in America." *PS: Political Science and Politics, 28*, 664–683.

Putnam, R. D. (2000). *Bowling Alone: The Collapse and Revival of American Community*. New York: Simon & Schuster.

Quintelier, F., & Vissers, S. (2008). "The Effect of Internet Use on Political Participation: An Analysis of Survey Results for 16-Year-Olds in Belgium." *Social Science Computer Review, 26*, 411–427.

Russell, A. (2004). "The Truth About Youth? Media Portrayals of Young People and Politics in Britain." *Journal of Public Affairs, 4*, 347–354.

Scheufele, D. A. (2002). "Examining Differential Gains From Mass Media and Their Implications for Participatory Behavior." *Communication Research, 29*(1), 46–65.

Scheufele, D. A., & Nisbet, M. C. (2002). "Being a Citizen Online: New Opportunities and Dead Ends." *Harvard International Journal of Press/Politics, 7*(3), 55–75.

Shah, D. V., Cho, J., Eveland, W. P., Jr., & Kwak, N. (2005). "Information and Expression in a Digital Age: Modeling Internet Effects on Civic Participation." *Communication Research, 32*, 531–565.

Shah, D. V., Kwak, N., & Holbert, R. L. (2001). "'Connecting' and 'Disconnecting' With Civic Life: Patterns of Internet Use and the Production of Social Capital." *Political Communication, 18*, 141–162.

Shah, D. V., McLeod, J. M., & Yoon, S. (2001). "Communication, Context, and Community: An Exploration of Print, Broadcast and Internet Influences." *Communication Research, 28*, 464–506.

Shah, D. V., Schmierbach, M., Hawkins, J., Espino, R., & Donavan, J. (2002). "Nonrecursive Models of Internet Use and Community Engagement: Questioning Whether Time Spent Online Erodes Social Capital." *Journalism & Mass Communication Quarterly, 79*, 964–987.

Slater, M. D. (2004). "Operational and Analyzing Exposure: The Foundation of Media Effects Research." *Journalism & Mass Communication Quarterly, 81*, 168–183.

Slater, M. D. (2007). "Reinforcing Spirals: The Mutual Influence of Media Selectivity and Media Effects and Their Impact on Individual Behavior and Social Identity." *Communication Theory, 17*, 281–303.

Smith, A., & Rainie, L. (2008). *The Internet and the 2008 election*. Washington, DC: Pew Internet & American Life Project.

Sunstein, C. (2001). *Republic.com*. Princeton, NJ: Princeton University Press.

Tolbert, C. J., & McNeal, R. S. (2003). "Unraveling the Effects of the Internet on Political Participation?" *Political Research Quarterly, 56*, 175–185.

Verba, S., Schlozman, K. L., & Brady, H. E. (1995). *Voice and Equality: Civic Voluntarism in American Politics*. Cambridge, MA: Harvard University Press.

Weaver, D., & Drew, D. (2001). "Voter Learning and Interest in the 2000 Presidential Election: Did the Media Matter?" *Journalism & Mass Communication Quarterly, 78*, 787–798.

Wyatt, R. O., Katz, E., & Kim, J. (2000). "Bridging the Spheres: Political and Personal Conversation in Public and Private Spaces." *Journal of Communication, 50*(1), 71–92.

Xenos, M., & Moy, P. (2007). "Direct and Differential Effects of the Internet on Political and Civic Engagement." *Journal of Communication, 57*, 704–718.

Zukin, C., Keeter, S., Andolina, M., Jenkins, K., & Delli Carpini, M. X. (2006). *A New Engagement? Political Participation, Civic Life, and the Changing American Citizen*. New York: Oxford University Press.

Credit

Bakker, T. P., and C. H. de Vreese. "Good News for the Future? Young People, Internet Use, and Political Participation." *Communication Research* 38.4: 451–70. Print. Copyright © 2011 by *Communication Research*. Reprinted by Permission of SAGE Publications.

Unit 2

Ethics and Education

Based on current trends, the average bachelor's student entering college this year will graduate with over $30,000 worth of debt. Sixty percent of all undergraduates will graduate with unpaid loans, which is only shocking until one considers that the cost of their college experience, including tuition, fees, books, and housing, will be well over $100,000 by the end of four years of degree courses at most public universities. At the same time, the advent of distance learning technologies, Massive Open Online Courses (MOOCs), diversity and disability initiatives, and open admissions over recent decades has made the university experience more accessible than ever. The great paradox of the modern academy is that it must be both celebrated for its progress and condemned for failing to meet the financial and professional needs of its students.

At the same time, the role of students themselves is changing. Involved, engaged scholarship demands more of students than ever before in terms of personal, moral, and scholastic development. Students of the 21st century are expected to involve themselves in the contemporary issues of their time, hold themselves to a higher standard of academic honesty and excellence, respect and endeavor to integrate experiences and views opposite their own, to be—at the most fundamental level—members not only of an institution, but of a supportive and productive community of scholars who aim to shape and change the world around them.

Education in America is at a crossroads. Changes in focus, funding, and mission have redefined the university and its relationships within the community in ways that will have uncertain and long-lasting consequences. It is not, however, the responsibility of the institution alone to address these issues—active and mindful students must also recognize their role in defining their educations and the spaces in which they find meaning and engage with the ideas, technologies, and demographics that will shape the next century.

Who Are You and What Are You Doing Here?

Mark Edmundson

Mark Edmundson is a professor of English at the University of Virginia. Throughout his career, he has published books and essays on such topics as the importance of studying the humanities, the cultural significance of sports, and what it means to be a teacher. Edmundson originally published "Who Are You and What Are You Doing Here?" in Oxford American, *a magazine that features writers from and essays about the American South. In "Who Are You and What Are You Doing Here?," Edmundson addresses a problem-solution essay to college students. His tone is urgent; he wants college students to think deeply about what they want out of their college experience because, he argues, college students face many challenges to achieving a "real" education. Edmundson, therefore, offers a vision of what the ideal college learning experience can and should be.*

ርጽ⊙ርჰ⊙ርጽ⊙

A message in a bottle to the incoming class.

ርጽ⊙ርჰ⊙ርጽ⊙

Welcome and congratulations: Getting to the first day of college is a major achievement. You're to be commended, and not just you, but the parents, grandparents, uncles, and aunts who helped get you here.

It's been said that raising a child effectively takes a village: Well, as you may have noticed, our American village is not in very good shape. We've got guns, drugs, two wars, fanatical religions, a slime-based popular culture, and some politicians who—a little restraint here—aren't what they might be. To merely survive in this American village and to win a place in the entering class has taken a lot of grit on your part. So, yes, congratulations to all.

You now may think that you've about got it made. Amidst the impressive college buildings, in company with a high-powered faculty, surrounded by the best of your generation, all you need is to keep doing what you've done before: Work hard, get good grades, listen to your teachers, get along with the people around you, and you'll emerge in four years as an educated young man or woman. Ready for life.

Do not believe it. It is not true. If you want to get a real education in America you're going to have to fight—and I don't mean just fight against the drugs and the violence and against the slime-based culture that is still going to surround you. I mean something a little more disturbing. To get an education, you're probably going to have to fight against the institution that you find yourself in—no matter how prestigious it may be. (In fact, the more prestigious the school, the more you'll probably have to push.) You can get a terrific education in America now—there are astonishing opportunities at almost every college—but the education will not be presented to you wrapped and bowed. To get it, you'll need to struggle and strive, to be strong, and occasionally even to piss off some admirable people.

I came to college with few resources, but one of them was an understanding, however crude, of how I might use my opportunities there. This I began to develop because of my father, who had never been to college—in fact, he'd barely gotten out of high school. One night after dinner, he and I were sitting in our kitchen at 58 Clewley Road in Medford, Massachusetts, hatching plans about the rest of my life. I was about to go off to college, a feat no one in my family had accomplished in living memory. "I think I might want to be pre-law," I told my father. I had no idea what being pre-law was. My father compressed his brow and blew twin streams of smoke, dragon-like, from his magnificent nose. "Do you want to be a lawyer?" he asked. My father had some experience with lawyers, and with policemen, too; he was not well-disposed toward either. "I'm not really sure," I told him, "but lawyers make pretty good money, right?"

My father detonated. (That was not uncommon. My father detonated a lot.) He told me that I was going to go to college only once, and that while I was there I had better study what I wanted. He said that when rich kids went to school, they majored in the subjects that interested them, and that my younger brother Philip and I were as good as any rich kids. (We were rich kids minus the money.) Wasn't I interested in literature? I confessed that I was. Then I had better study literature, unless I had inside information to the effect that reincarnation wasn't just hype, and I'd be able to attend college thirty or forty times. If I had such info, pre-law would be fine, and maybe even a tour through invertebrate biology could also be tossed in. But until I had the reincarnation stuff from a solid source, I better get to work and pick out some English classes from the course catalog. "How about the science requirements?"

"Take 'em later," he said, "you never know."

My father, Wright Aukenhead Edmundson, Malden High School Class of 1948 (by a hair), knew the score. What he told me that evening at the Clewley Road kitchen table was true in itself, and it also contains the germ of an idea about what a university education should be. But apparently almost everyone else—students, teachers, and trustees and parents—sees the matter much differently. They have it wrong.

Education has one salient enemy in present-day America, and that enemy is education—university education in particular. To almost everyone, university education is a means to an end. For students, that end is a good job. Students want the credentials that will help them get ahead. They want the certificate that will give them access to Wall Street, or entrance into law or medical or business school. And how can we blame them? America values power and money, big players with big bucks. When we raise our children, we tell them in multiple ways that what we want most for them is success—material success. To be poor in America is to be a failure—it's to be without decent health care, without basic necessities, often without dignity. Then there are those back-breaking student loans—people leave school as servants, indentured to pay massive bills, so that first job better be a good one. Students come to college with the goal of a diploma in mind—what happens in between, especially in classrooms, is often of no deep and determining interest to them.

In college, life is elsewhere. Life is at parties, at clubs, in music, with friends, in sports. Life is what celebrities have. The idea that the courses you take should be the primary objective of going to college is tacitly considered absurd. In terms of their work, students live in the future and not the present; they live with their prospects for success. If universities stopped issuing credentials, half of the clients would be gone by tomorrow morning, with the remainder following fast behind.

The faculty, too, is often absent: Their real lives are also elsewhere. Like most of their students, they aim to get on. The work they are compelled to do to advance—get tenure, promotion, raises, outside offers—is, broadly speaking, scholarly work. No matter what anyone says, this work has precious little to do with the fundamentals of teaching. The proof is that virtually no undergraduate students can read and understand their professors' scholarly publications. The public senses this disparity and so thinks of the professors' work as being silly or beside the point. Some of it is. But the public also senses that because professors don't pay full-bore attention to teaching they don't have to work very hard—they've created a massive feather bed for themselves and called it a university.

This is radically false. Ambitious professors, the ones who, like their students, want to get ahead in America, work furiously. Scholarship, even if pretentious and almost unreadable, is nonetheless labor-intensive. One can slave for a year or two on a single article for publication in this or that refereed journal. These essays are honest: Their footnotes reflect real reading, real assimilation, and real dedication. Shoddy work—in which the author cheats, cuts corners, copies from others—is quickly detected. The people who do this work have highly developed intellectual powers, and they push themselves hard to reach a certain standard: That the results have almost no practical relevance to the students, the public, or even, frequently, to other scholars is a central element in the tragicomedy that is often academia.

The students and the professors have made a deal: Neither of them has to throw himself heart and soul into what happens in the classroom. The students write their abstract, over-intellectualized essays; the professors grade the students for their capacity to be abstract and over-intellectual—and often genuinely smart. For their essays can be brilliant, in a chilly way; they can also be clipped off the Internet, and often are. Whatever the case, no one wants to invest too much in them—for life is elsewhere. The professor saves his energies for the profession, while the student saves his for friends, social life, volunteer work, making connections, and getting in position to clasp hands on the true grail, the first job.

No one in this picture is evil; no one is criminally irresponsible. It's just that smart people are prone to look into matters to see how they might go about buttering their toast. Then they butter their toast.

As for the administrators, their relation to the students often seems based not on love but fear. Administrators fear bad publicity, scandal, and dissatisfaction on the part of their customers. More than anything else, though, they fear lawsuits. Throwing a student out of college, for this or that piece of bad behavior, is very difficult, almost impossible. The student will sue your eyes out. One kid I knew (and rather liked) threatened on his blog to mince his dear and esteemed professor (me) with a samurai sword for the crime of having taught a boring class. (The class was a *little* boring—I had a damned cold—but the punishment seemed a bit severe.) The dean of students laughed lightly when I suggested that this behavior might be grounds for sending the student on a brief vacation. I was, you might say, discomfited, and showed up to class for a while with my cellphone jiggered to dial 911 with one touch.

Still, this was small potatoes. Colleges are even leery of disciplining guys who have committed sexual assault, or assault plain and simple. Instead of being punished, these guys frequently stay around, strolling the quad and swilling the libations, an affront (and sometimes a terror) to their victims.

You'll find that cheating is common as well. As far as I can discern, the student ethos goes like this: If the professor is so lazy that he gives the same test every year, it's okay to go ahead and take advantage—you've both got better things to do. The Internet is amok with services selling term papers and those services exist, capitalism being what it is, because people purchase the papers—lots of them. Fraternity files bulge with old tests from a variety of courses.

Periodically the public gets exercised about this situation, and there are articles in the national news. But then interest dwindles and matters go back to normal.

One of the reasons professors sometimes look the other way when they sense cheating is that it sends them into a world of sorrow. A friend of mine had the temerity to detect cheating on the part of a kid who was the nephew of a well-placed official in an Arab government complexly aligned with the U.S. Black limousines pulled up in front of his office and disgorged decorously suited negotiators. Did my pal fold? Nope, he's not the type. But he did not enjoy the process.

What colleges generally want are well-rounded students, civic leaders, people who know what the system demands, how to keep matters light, not push too hard for an education or anything else; people who get their credentials and leave the professors alone to do their brilliant work, so they may rise and enhance the rankings of the university. Such students leave and become donors and so, in their own turn, contribute immeasurably to the university's standing. They've done a fine job skating on surfaces in high school—the best way to get an across-the-board outstanding record—and now they're on campus to cut a few more figure eights.

In a culture where the major and determining values are monetary, what else could you do? How else would you live if not by getting all you can, succeeding all you can, making all you can?

The idea that a university education really should have no substantial content, should not be about what John Keats was disposed to call Soul-making, is one that you might think professors and university presidents would be discreet about. Not so. This view informed an address that Richard Brodhead gave to the senior class at Yale before he departed to become president of Duke. Brodhead, an impressive, articulate man, seems to take as his educational touchstone the Duke of Wellington's precept that the Battle of Waterloo was won on the playing fields of Eton. Brodhead suggests that the content of the courses isn't really what matters. In five years (or five months, or minutes), the student is likely to have forgotten how to do the problem sets and will only hazily recollect what happens in the ninth book of *Paradise Lost*. The legacy of their college years will be a legacy of difficulties overcome. When they face equally arduous tasks later in life, students will tap their old resources of determination, and they'll win.

All right, there's nothing wrong with this as far as it goes—after all, the student who writes a brilliant forty-page thesis in a hard week has learned more than a little about her inner resources. Maybe it will give her needed confidence in the future. But doesn't the content of the courses matter at all?

On the evidence of this talk, no. Trying to figure out whether the stuff you're reading is true or false and being open to having your life changed is a fraught, controversial activity. Doing so requires energy from the professor—which is better spent on other matters. This kind of perspective-altering teaching and learning can cause the things which administrators fear above all else: trouble, arguments, bad press, etc.

After the kid-samurai episode, the chair of my department not unsympathetically suggested that this was the sort of incident that could happen when you brought a certain intensity to teaching. At the time I found his remark a tad detached, but maybe he was right.

So, if you want an education, the odds aren't with you: The professors are off doing what they call their own work; the other students, who've doped out the way the place runs, are busy leaving the professors alone and getting themselves in position for bright and shining futures; the student-services people are trying to keep everyone content, offering plenty of entertainment and building another state-of-the-art workout facility every few months. The development office is already scanning you for future donations. The primary function of Yale University, it's recently been said, is to create prosperous alumni so as to enrich Yale University.

So why make trouble? Why not just go along? Let the profs roam free in the realms of pure thought, let yourselves party in the realms of impure pleasure, and let the student-services gang assert fewer prohibitions and newer delights for you. You'll get a good job, you'll have plenty of friends, you'll have a driveway of your own.

You'll also, if my father and I are right, be truly and righteously screwed. The reason for this is simple. The quest at the center of a liberal-arts education is not a luxury quest; it's a necessity quest. If you do not undertake it, you risk leading a life of desperation—maybe quiet, maybe, in time, very loud—and I am not exaggerating. For you risk trying to be someone other than who you are, which, in the long run, is killing.

By the time you come to college, you will have been told who you are numberless times. Your parents and friends, your teachers, your counselors, your priests and rabbis and ministers and imams have all had their say. They've let you know how they size you up, and they've let you know what they think you should value. They've given you a sharp and protracted taste of what they feel is good and bad, right and wrong. Much is on their side. They have confronted you with scriptures—holy books that, whatever their actual provenance, have given people what they feel to be wisdom for thousands of years. They've given you family traditions—you've learned the ways of your tribe and your community. And, too, you've been tested, probed, looked at up and down and through. The coach knows what your athletic prospects are, the guidance office has a sheaf of test scores that relegate you to this or that ability quadrant, and your teachers have got you pegged. You are, as Foucault might say, the intersection of many evaluative and potentially determining discourses: you boy, you girl, have been made.

And—contra Foucault—that's not so bad. Embedded in all of the major religions are profound truths. Schopenhauer, who despised belief in transcendent things, nonetheless thought Christianity to be of inexpressible worth. He couldn't believe in the divinity of Jesus, or in the afterlife, but to Schopenhauer, a deep pessimist, a religion that had as its central emblem the figure of a man being tortured on a cross couldn't be entirely misleading. To the Christian, Schopenhauer said, pain was at the center of the understanding of life, and that was just as it should be.

One does not need to be as harsh as Schopenhauer to understand the use of religion, even if one does not believe in an otherworldly god. And all of those teachers and counselors and friends—and the prognosticating uncles, the dithering aunts, the fathers and mothers with their hopes for your fulfillment—or their fulfillment in you— should not necessarily be cast aside or ignored. Families have their wisdom. The question "Who do they think you are at home?" is never an idle one.

The major conservative thinkers have always been very serious about what goes by the name of common sense. Edmund Burke saw common sense as a loosely made, but often profound, collective work, in which humanity has deposited its hard-earned wisdom—the precipitate of joy and tears—over time. You have been raised in proximity to common sense, if you've been raised at all, and common sense is something to respect, though not quite—peace unto the formidable Burke—to revere.

You may be all that the good people who raised you say you are; you may want all they have shown you is worth wanting; you may be someone who is truly your father's son or your mother's daughter. But then again, you may not be.

For the power that is in you, as Emerson suggested, may be new in nature. You may not be the person that your parents take you to be. And—this thought is both more exciting and more dangerous—you may not be the person that you take yourself to be, either. You may not have read yourself aright, and college is the place where you can find out whether you have or not. The reason to read Blake and Dickinson and Freud and Dickens is not to become more cultivated, or more articulate, or to be someone who, at a cocktail party, is never embarrassed (or who can embarrass others). The best reason to read them is to see if they may know you better than you know yourself. You may find your own suppressed and rejected thoughts flowing back to you with an "alienated majesty." Reading the great writers, you may have the experience that Longinus associated with the sublime: You feel that you have actually created the text yourself. For somehow your predecessors are more yourself than you are.

This was my own experience reading the two writers who have influenced me the most, Sigmund Freud and Ralph Waldo Emerson. They gave words to thoughts and feelings that I had never been able to render myself. They shone a light onto the world and what they saw, suddenly I saw, too. From Emerson I learned to trust my own thoughts, to trust them even when every voice seems to be on the other side. I need the wherewithal, as Emerson did, to say what's on my mind and to take the inevitable hits. Much more I learned from the sage—about character, about loss, about joy, about writing and its secret sources, but Emerson most centrally preaches the gospel of self-reliance and that is what I have tried most to take from him. I continue to hold in mind one of Emerson's most memorable passages: "Society is a joint-stock company, in which the members agree, for the better securing of his bread to each shareholder, to surrender the liberty and culture of the eater. The virtue in most request is conformity. Self-reliance is its aversion. It loves not realities and creators, but names and customs."

Emerson's greatness lies not only in showing you how powerful names and customs can be, but also in demonstrating how exhilarating it is to buck them. When he came to Harvard to talk about religion, he shocked the professors and students by challenging the divinity of Jesus and the truth of his miracles. He wasn't invited back for decades.

From Freud I found a great deal to ponder as well. I don't mean Freud the aspiring scientist, but the Freud who was a speculative essayist and interpreter of the human condition like Emerson. Freud challenges nearly every significant human ideal. He goes after religion. He says that it comes down to the longing for the father. He goes after love. He calls it "the overestimation of the erotic object." He attacks our desire for charismatic popular leaders. We're drawn to them because we hunger for absolute authority. He declares that dreams don't predict the future and that there's nothing benevolent about them. They're disguised fulfillments of repressed wishes.

Freud has something challenging and provoking to say about virtually every human aspiration. I learned that if I wanted to affirm any consequential ideal, I had to talk my way past Freud. He was—and is—a perpetual challenge and goad.

Never has there been a more shrewd and imaginative cartographer of the psyche. His separation of the self into three parts, and his sense of the fraught, anxious, but often negotiable relations among them (negotiable when you come to the game with a Freudian knowledge), does a great deal to help one navigate experience. (Though sometimes—and this I owe to Emerson—it seems right to let the psyche fall into civil war, accepting barrages of anxiety and grief for this or that good reason.)

The battle is to make such writers one's own, to winnow them out and to find their essential truths. We need to see where they fall short and where they exceed the mark, and then to develop them a little, as the ideas themselves, one comes to see, actually developed others. (Both Emerson and Freud live out of Shakespeare—but only a giant can be truly influenced by Shakespeare.) In reading, I continue to look for one thing—to be influenced, to learn something new, to be thrown off my course and onto another, better way.

My father knew that he was dissatisfied with life. He knew that none of the descriptions people had for him quite fit. He understood that he was always out-of-joint with life as it was. He had talent: My brother and I each got about half the raw ability he possessed and that's taken us through life well enough. But what to do with that talent—there was the rub for my father. He used to stroll through the house intoning his favorite line from Groucho Marx's ditty "Whatever it is, I'm against it." (I recently asked my son, now twenty-one, if he thought I was mistaken in teaching him this particular song when he was six years old. "No!" he said, filling the air with an invisible forest of exclamation points.) But what my father never managed to get was a sense of who he might become. He never had a world of possibilities spread before him, never made sustained contact with the best that had been thought and said. He didn't get to revise his understanding of himself, figure out what he'd do best that might give the world some profit.

My father was a gruff man, but also a generous one, so that night at the kitchen table at 58 Clewley Road he made an effort to let me have the chance that had been denied to him by both fate and character. He gave me the chance to see what I was all about, and if it proved to be different from him, proved even to be something he didn't like or entirely comprehend, then he'd deal with it.

Right now, if you're going to get a real education, you may have to be aggressive and assertive.

Your professors will give you some fine books to read, and they'll probably help you understand them. What they won't do, for reasons that perplex me, is to ask you if the books contain truths you could live your lives by. When you read Plato, you'll probably learn about his metaphysics and his politics and his way of conceiving the soul. But no one will ask you if his ideas are good enough to believe in. No one will ask you, in the words of Emerson's disciple William James, what their "cash value" might be. No one will suggest that you might use Plato as your bible for a week or a year or longer. No one, in short, will ask you to use Plato to help you change your life.

That will be up to you. You must put the question of Plato to yourself. You must ask whether reason should always rule the passions, philosophers should always rule the state, and poets should inevitably be banished from a just commonwealth. You have to ask yourself if wildly expressive music (rock and rap and the rest) deranges the soul in ways that are destructive to its health. You must inquire of yourself if balanced calm is the most desirable human state.

Occasionally—for you will need some help in fleshing-out the answers—you may have to prod your professors to see if they take the text at hand—in this case the divine and disturbing Plato—to be true. And you will have to be tough if the professor mocks you for uttering a sincere question instead of keeping matters easy for all concerned by staying detached and analytical. (Detached analysis has a place—but, in the end, you've got to speak from the heart and pose the question of truth.) You'll be the one who pesters his teachers. You'll ask your history teacher about whether there is a design to our history, whether we're progressing or declining, or whether, in the words of a fine recent play, *The History Boys*, history's "just one fuckin' thing after another." You'll be the one who challenges your biology teacher about the intellectual conflict between evolution and creationist thinking. You'll not only question the statistics teacher about what *numbers* can explain but what they can't.

Because every subject you study is a language and since you may adopt one of these languages as your own, you'll want to know how to speak it expertly and also how it fails to deal with those concerns for which it has no adequate words. You'll be looking into the reach of every metaphor that every discipline offers, and you'll be trying to see around their corners.

The whole business is scary, of course. What if you arrive at college devoted to pre-med, sure that nothing will make you and your family happier than a life as a physician, only to discover that elementary-school teaching is where your heart is?

You might learn that you're not meant to be a doctor at all. Of course, given your intellect and discipline, you can still probably be one. You can pound your round peg through the very square hole of medical school, then go off into the profession. And society will help you. Society has a cornucopia of resources to encourage you in doing what society needs done but that you don't much like doing and are not cut out to do. To ease your grief, society offers alcohol, television, drugs, divorce, and buying, buying, buying what you don't need. But all those too have their costs.

Education is about finding out what form of work for you is close to being play—work you do so easily that it restores you as you go. Randall Jarrell once said that if he were a rich man, he would pay money to teach poetry to students. (I would, too, for what it's worth.) In saying that, he (like my father) hinted in the direction of a profound and true theory of learning.

Having found what's best for you to do, you may be surprised how far you rise, how prosperous, even against your own projections, you become. The student who eschews medical school to follow his gift for teaching small children spends his twenties in low-paying but pleasurable and soul-rewarding toil. He's always behind on his student-loan payments; he still lives in a house with four other guys (not all of whom got proper instructions on how to clean a bathroom). He buys shirts from the Salvation Army, has intermittent Internet, and vacations where he can. But lo—he has a gift for teaching. He writes an essay about how to teach, then a book—which no one buys. But he writes another—in part out of a feeling of injured merit, maybe— and that one they do buy.

Money is still a problem, but in a new sense. The world wants him to write more, lecture, travel more, and will pay him for his efforts, and he likes this a good deal. But he also likes staying around and showing up at school and figuring out how to get this or that little runny-nosed specimen to begin learning how to read. These are the kinds of problems that are worth having and if you advance, as Thoreau said, in the general direction of your dreams, you may have them. If you advance in the direction of someone else's dreams—if you want to live someone else's life rather than yours— then get a TV for every room, buy yourself a lifetime supply of your favorite quaff, crank up the porn channel, and groove away. But when we expend our energies in rightful ways, Robert Frost observed, we stay whole and vigorous and we don't weary. "Strongly spent," the poet says, "is synonymous with kept."

Credit _____

Edmundson, Mark. "Who Are You and What Are You Doing Here?" *Oxford American* 74. 22 Aug. 2011. Print.

Marketization of Education: An Ethical Dilemma

Samuel M. Natale and Caroline Doran

Samuel Natale is a professor of Strategic Management at Adelphi University in New York. He has a Ph.D. in Education and Psychology. Natale's co-author, Caroline Doran, has a Ph.D. in Organizational Management. In "Marketization of Education: An Ethical Dilemma," Natale and Doran describe a problematic trend in higher education, namely that many universities are too focused on the business of training students, who have come to be seen as education consumers. This training mentality is in contrast to the traditional idea of college as a space for intellectual growth, rich faculty scholarship, and citizenship development, all ideas that Edmundson mentions in "Who Are You and What Are You Doing Here?" After describing several ways that the "corporatized" university affects faculty, enrolled students, and prospective students, Natale and Doran offer some solutions that could help to fight against this trend toward marketization.

⳹⳼⳹⳼⳹⳼

> It is still a rather common misconception that marketing should be primarily focused on admissions. Such a mindset fails to consider that students will often have much greater value to the institution as alumni. Thus, it is important to establish strong relationships with students before they even arrive at the college, continue to build upon those relationships while they are attending college, and ideally extend the value of those relationships across a lifetime. If IHEs do not consider the entire lifetime value chain of a student and connect the links in the chain with concepts such as IMC, they will undoubtedly lose considerable opportunities to advance their institutions. (Edmiston 2009, p. 173)

Education considered in such a context reduces students to a revenue stream and colleges to businesses; this is the contemporary face of education.

As educational leaders seek solutions to the complex problems facing their institutions, including rapidly shifting mission and changes which perhaps capture fewer and fewer qualified students, many perceive the marketization of education as a viable answer. Although the adoption of business practices may initially benefit universities, it remains questionable whether these new approaches benefit students and faculty. Focusing resources to elevate university rankings and to drive student enrollment may improve the institution's revenues; however, is it wise to redirect the efforts of faculty from their core responsibility as educators?

Shifting Priorities and How They Affect Universities and Faculty

The University Within the Context of the State's and Society's Goals

In recent years, the dwindling supply of federal funds coupled with the growth of consumer culture and growing fervor for corporate capitalism have done much to transform higher education (Molesworth et al. 2009). In such a society, students seek to secure a degree, rather than experience an education, with their goals limited to the acquisition of skills needed for employment and maximizing income. Within this context, universities are being pushed to produce knowledgeable students that society and employers deem valuable—not knowledge for its own sake or classical approaches that focus more on the process and ability to think. Additionally, higher learning institutions are being asked to graduate more students while maintaining the same standards of quality, closing achievement gaps, and becoming more efficient and productive organizations (Lingenfelter 2006).

The issue of accountability and the measurement of outcomes are now commonplace in education (Sigler 2007). Such accountability is usually couched in the language of accounting. The kinds of questions advanced by such a discourse include: Does the academy provide good value for money? Is money being spent wisely and well? Is there an appropriate social return on the billions of dollars that are invested in higher education, both directly and indirectly, by students and their parents, the state and corporations? In such a discourse, "wisely and well" are redefined by an increasing concern with the economic and vocational relevance of what is taught rather than by an older set of more liberal concerns. Do students have the requisite knowledge and skills to make them employable in a modern economy? Students may well be versed in the details of medieval history or the poetry of William Blake, but what can they *do*? Are they able to communicate and work in teams? Do they understand business? Do they have the key or core skills necessary for work?

Furthermore, newer economic and cultural imperatives mean that the state's interest in the university is considerably more intrusive and less benign. Concerns with economic competitiveness, for example, mean that the state's interests in the university are vested along new lines and dimensions. Because the state encourages or coerces universities to produce graduates who have more useful knowledge and who have developed the right kind of core generic skills, the modern university is at increasing risk of losing its distinctive and balanced character by emphasizing, for example, newer business values rather than the older academic ones.

Society's relationship with knowledge is also changing: it is shifting to one where society is increasingly concerned with the utility of knowledge. A new model of higher education appears to be developing in which the pursuit of knowledge related to the "practical" rather than the pursuit of knowledge related to what is "true" or "good" has become the dominant goal. The knowledge society is interested only in *certain kinds* of knowledge and values only *certain kinds* of learning. Therefore, students are torn between self-development and the need to have marketable skills. More so than in the past, students are focused on preparation for the workplace and are overly concentrated on content related only to the job (Molesworth et al. 2009). Such a new discourse potentially rips the roots of the university from its time-honored position.

Universities were once thought of as institutions for the public good, serving the interests of the community and the citizens of the world. A question central to the education debate, with the growing proportion of education being provided by non-traditional sources, is whether education is still a public good or whether it contributes to the development of society as opposed to the development of individuals (Knight 2006). Today education is largely viewed as a marketable commodity. Education, once seen as a process, has been reduced to job preparation, making higher education a product in which one invests for the purpose of one's future employment opportunities in business and technology. Of the more than 1.5 million degrees that were granted in 2007–2008, the most common degrees were: 21% in business, 10.5% in the social sciences and history, 7% in health science, and 6.5% in education (IES 2009). Furthermore, rather than guiding and supporting the student in becoming more intellectually complex, universities and colleges that are highly commercialized serve to prepare the student to become a participant in the consumer culture and no longer strive to encourage the student's reflection and critical thinking.

The University Within the Context of Financial Goals

The concern of any institution with a strong corporate orientation is to meet the demands of the student (consumer) in the most efficient (cost-effective) manner. Adoption of business practices by educational institutions is transforming the educational landscape. As business practices are accepted in education, students have been transformed into consumers, and, in some institutions, programs are deemed successful only when they drive revenue production or support the acquisition of corporate funding. Many institutions are headed by presidents who are paid like corporate executives, and recruitment of university leaders often focuses on the business acumen of candidates, rather than their expertise as educators or their commitment to learning (Marris 2005).

The changes in higher education reach far beyond vocabulary and run deeply into the heart of institutions. In an environment of academic production, courses that do not garner interest from large numbers of students may be eliminated. To improve the efficiency of faculty, universities may seek to reduce the hours that academics spend in discussions with students, creating an atmosphere of passive, reproductive learning that does not encourage critical thinking and reflection by the student (Molesworth et al. 2009).

The University Within the Context of Other Organizations' Goals

Corporations that desire greater tailoring of information fund universities to serve their own needs. But corporate sponsorship of research may be placing faculty members in a position where they face conflicts of interest and commitment. Faculty may be diverted from teaching to financially productive research and become preoccupied with producing research for corporations, securing grants from businesses, and engaging in consultant assignments with corporate clients (Kaplan 1996).

In the past, research largely consisted of individual scholars engaged in a quest for new knowledge in their fields of study. Today there are research programs, collective projects with multiple researchers, consisting of individuals who are expendable and interchangeable. Some of today's research programs may no longer represent a search for knowledge; instead, they have become structured programs controlled by management with clearly defined business goals heavily influenced by corporations. Research is expensive and only certain disciplines generate funding. As corporate dollars pour in to support pharmaceutical, technology, and biomedical research, research in other disciplines is no longer attractive because it cannot secure funding.

The ethical concern with this research focus, as posed by Yassi et al. (2010), is that the more universities come to depend on research funding from businesses, the more researchers are compelled not to deviate in their findings from the interests of those who fund them. Should their findings be incongruent with their funders, they risk their careers, which raises the question, or at least *should* raise the question, regarding the integrity of contemporary university research.

Training and the Contemporary Model of Education

Historically, the university was seen as a community that nurtured ideas and innovations, built the morals of its students, and contributed to democracy through producing political and social leaders (Tilak 2009). This is no longer the case. Concerns with accountability, knowledge, and student abilities pave the way for new forms of assessment, monitoring, and surveillance, where supposedly liberal processes are valued less than the measurable outcomes of higher education. Given the new grounding in absolute pragmatism, the university is pressured to produce graduates who are ready to blend into the workforce or into those agencies of society responsible for social change. Curriculum that has been distorted to focus heavily on technology and business has undermined the core values of higher education. The earlier commitment of higher education institutions to a core curriculum is being eroded as they become training centers for industry (Miscamble 2006). The former distinction between education and training has collapsed here into a new hybrid. The study of the humanities may no longer be valued in this new environment. One wonders why though, when the actual outcomes of an effective liberal education involve, "the ability to listen carefully, to read critically, to write accurately and persuasively, and to analyze exactly" (Ryan 1999, p. 17). There is now so much focus on workplace skills, that there is little value to knowing anything that cannot help students become more "marketable" in the workforce, garner a raise, or advance a career. Having read the *Iliad* is not likely to help in any of these respects.

Faculty and the Contemporary Model of Education: The Teacherpreneur

While universities become increasingly focused on the application of business practices, one might question whether this new paradigm of higher education dismisses what was once thought to be the role of faculty members. In the new corporate model of higher education, faculty members are seen as providers of customer service and transmitters of industry-relevant skills. Professors are often no longer seen as scholars; rather they are viewed as employees with publications (Molesworth et al. 2009).

The new vision of higher education as an economic institution and knowledge as a product is likely to not be aligned with the fundamental values of many faculty members. Some claim higher education has been transformed, while many other and more seasoned academics see it as the death of the university as they have known it. As leaders of higher education institutions grow obsessed with the corporate vision of profit, faculty members are relegated to positions where they are less involved in the mission of their institutions (Thacker 2005). The role of faculty is changing dramatically.

Schools are commonly recruiting faculty from industry and now focus on their industry skills as opposed to their critical thinking skills (Molesworth et al. 2009). In fact, scholarship may no longer be a requisite skill for teaching in higher education. Even though business is the most commonly pursued undergraduate degree, the most common degree at the master's level is education, followed by business. The greatest number of degrees granted in 2009 at the doctorate level were related to health and clinical sciences, followed by education, engineering, biological and biomedical sciences, psychology, and physical sciences (IES 2009). Therefore, what is emerging is a trend whereby pursuing a terminal degree in business is less common than in other fields, perhaps because so much focus is now placed on field experience among new business faculty. In an effort to satisfy the consumers' demand for preparation for the workplace, colleges and universities seek to maximize their connection with corporations, which may mean recruiting faculty from industry, drawing into question the qualifications of such individuals to be mentors in a deep and meaningful learning process. Moreover, the new financial demands lead to hiring more adjuncts (Meyerson 2005).

In earlier times, faculty members enjoyed significant autonomy over their teaching and research, but with the new emphasis on corporate management, this too has changed. Furthermore, the move to external accountability driven by financial rather than intellectual goals transforms faculty into employees through competence-based audits and assessments, and changes a community of scholars into a training ground for corporate workers with too much emphasis on finances and too little focus on the education of students (Gibbs 2006). More important, professors often feel compelled to focus on what will allow students to pass as opposed to focusing on critical thinking and reflection. Furthermore, because students are so focused on the post-graduation job hunt, they are overly focused on the outcomes of assessments (Molesworth et al. 2009). Combined, these relegate professors' role to one concentrated on grade-related outcomes, rather than on the process of learning.

Moreover, in an environment where higher education institutions have become research centers for corporations, the qualifications for faculty members, which were once thought to be scholarship and the ability to mentor students, are being replaced by the candidate's skill as an entrepreneur. Corporate influence is particularly widespread in the fields of medicine, biotechnology, and pharmacology. The media has exposed numerous tales of corporate funding by the tobacco, energy, and pharmaceutical industries where university-based researchers received millions of dollars to produce research in support of their corporate benefactors (Bridenthal 2005). Humanities, however, are less able to create marketable products for industry and attract less corporate funding, which has resulted in a trend toward higher salaries for top researchers who garner major corporate funding while adjuncts are teaching at barely livable salaries. Moral and civic-focused courses are often offered only at the introductory level, and some senior faculty members are unwilling to teach these lower level courses because they value their research activities over teaching.

Faculty members are often faced with balancing professionalism and commercialism in today's higher education environment. While institutions may no longer hire faculty to be active members of a rigorous intellectual community, faculty members may now see their positions in the university as mere platforms for moving forward entrepreneurial agendas. And, every faculty member must have such an agenda or feel at risk. As objectivity of university-based research is questioned, the integrity of higher education is also questioned. This issue of teacher as entrepreneur (teacherpreneur) is exacerbated by disparity in pay. While salaries for university and college presidents may approach the levels of corporate executives, compensation for professors has barely increased (Marris 2005). The average salary for male professors in 2009 was $79,706 and $65,638 for females (IES 2009).

Statistics indicate a steady increase in part-time faculty positions and a reduction in tenure-track positions (Altbach 2009). Only 49% of full-time professors had tenure in 2008 compared to 56% in 1994 (IES 2009). There were 0.7 million full-time and 0.7 million part-time faculty in 2007, and the rate of part-time to full-time staff in education has also been growing. Between 1997 and 2007, part-time staff increased by 39%, whereas full-time staff rose by only 25%. Much of the growth in part-time staff can be attributed to the hiring of part-time faculty (IES 2009). For those teachers who are not fully employed outside of the school, they are likely teaching at multiple institutions to make a living. This should pose an ethical quandary for institutions and students: in many cases, these teachers are not making an acceptable living as they do not have a permanent full-time job. This impacts commitment to an institution and its students; professors who teach at multiple institutions at one time teach well beyond what is considered a full-time load for full-time professors.

Furthermore, in recent years, many not-for-profit universities have launched for-profit online and other degree-granting programs in which faculty members are expected to teach. With this additional workload, professors may find it difficult to be committed to the responsibilities once thought to be the essence of academic life: teaching, research, participation in the academic community, and governance of their institutions. Again, the ethical dilemma is whether the issue of fairness or reasonableness has been taken off the table for a cadre of employees that is seeing the core of their work changing like a daily menu. This surely impacts morale, which has a negative effect on schools and students.

Shifting Priorities and How They Affect Learning, Students, and Society

Between 1988 and 1998, enrollment in colleges grew by 11% but, between 1998 and 2008, enrollment grew by 32% (IES 2009). In sync with the public's growing interest in acquiring a college education, this era has seen great changes in the *modus operandi* on the supply side. What has emerged in the last 20 years, therefore, is an increasing focus on the marketization of education (Newman and Jahdi 2009).

The economic strife and reduced availability of federal funds for higher education in the 1990s created an atmosphere ripe for the leaders of America's colleges and universities to find the marketing strategies of the business community appealing, as they pursued their quest for new sources of funds with the added rivalry of the "for profit" sector. History indicates that securing funding has long been a challenge for American colleges and universities. Many of the private higher education institutions were funded through donations from nineteenth-century industrialists, who later turned their attention to philanthropic activities. Following World War II, the GI Bill provided funding for the expansion of many colleges and universities, but a decline in the population in the 1970s and 1980s drove institutions to seek new methods of financial support (Hossler 2004). In these years, new trends such as federal funding for science and engineering research, as well as a growing application of aggressive marketing practices, including the use of financial aid for student recruitment, began to emerge (Miscamble 2006).

One of the problems imposed by the state on higher education is that state leaders view schools as having an independent income stream in the form of tuition and consequently, expect students to pay an increasingly larger proportion for the cost of their education (Sigler 2007). Tuition as a percentage of college's revenue has increased 10 points over the last 25 years. Tuition now comprises 36.3% of school revenues (SHEEO 2009). Student-derived revenue is now more important than ever, making student satisfaction more important than ever. Consequently, parents have become customers, students are now consumers, and education and research, once believed to be processes, are now seen as products (Miscamble 2006). Terms of the managerial vocabulary, such as performance assessment, quality control, and competitive edge, are also now commonplace in discussions of higher education. It is not difficult to understand how this new vocabulary has been so readily adopted, when one considers that corporate lawyers and business leaders hold the majority of positions on the governing boards of most universities and colleges in America (Miscamble 2006).

Colleges now operate as bottom line-oriented organizations and the marketization of higher education has been accompanied by the adoption of a managerialist ideology and a new drive for quality and efficiency, which has resulted in increased bureaucracy in many institutions (Lock and Lorenz 2007). Consequently, the composition of the varying employment classifications in educational institutions has also changed considerably, directly reflecting a shift in the importance of the administrative function of education. For example, the percentage of non-teaching professionals has risen from 10 to 20% between 1979 and 2007 (IES 2009). From the perspective of an institution with a strong corporate focus, these changes may appear to be process improvements in that universities may be more cost-efficient and able to produce more graduates at a lower per capita cost, but this type of administrative approach to education is unrealistic (Goldspink 2007).

Enrollment Management and Student Aid

There are now more students (consumers) than ever interested in pursuing a college degree, and these consumers are paying a higher percentage of their education—schools are relying more heavily than ever on tuition dollars. Therefore, the contemporary face of education is extremely competitive. Schools have developed enrollment management strategies to allow them to be competitive and to influence whom and how many students they matriculate. Some of the practices employed in enrollment management are not without controversy, however, and they largely center on institutions' use of campus-based financial aid to attract preferential students. The use of need-based financial assistance has long been seen as an appropriate method of promoting diversity and inclusion of less affluent students in the college community, but merit awards, which have become increasingly popular both in private and public institutions, serve a different end.

Colleges offer merit-based aid to high scoring students to improve their rankings, elevate their prestige, and support their brand image. As the focus has shifted away from promoting the promise of social justice, access to quality education for low income students is being pushed aside in the pursuit of a corporate vision. One reason is that merit-based aid is instrumental in increasing the cost of getting an education (Lingenfelter 2006). Students from middle or higher income families are more likely than students from lower income families to receive merit-based aid (IES 2009). Also, with limited financial aid resources available, merit-based awards have resulted in fewer students receiving need-based aid (Ehrenberg 2005). Merit-based aid increased 212%, while need-based aid increased only 47% between 1996 and 2004 (Marklein 2007). Moreover, while colleges are using merit-based aid to woo students they deem as most desirable, they are also spending more money on recruiting, leaving fewer resources available for faculty salaries and the education of students.

Enrollment Management and Rankings

Furthermore, rankings have taken on greater meaning in an environment where colleges are actively competing for students' tuition dollars. Students frequently turn to the rankings of universities when formulating their application decisions (Thacker 2005). Playing the rankings game has undoubtedly contributed to the marketization of higher education. Because students and their families are paying a larger proportion of students' education, they are demanding information on retention rate, graduation rates, and job prospects—information that will indicate their return on investment (Sigler 2007). The down side to this is that, over the past decade, rankings have become increasingly important, causing educational institutions to redirect funds to improving their rankings in such publications as *U.S. News and World Report* (Lingenfelter 2006).

The rankings game is not always played fairly either. It is possible to improve a college's rankings in terms of 6-year graduation rates by relaxing standards, admitting highly qualified students, or throwing a lot of money at support services. Colleges can also improve their rankings by improving their spend-per-student, which discourages schools from being financially prudent. This increases the need for tuition or forces faculty to look for research funds (Ehrenberg 2005). Furthermore, schools are pressuring faculty into helping improve rankings (Hossler 2000). Diver (2005) highlights other practices, such as:

> failing to report low SAT scores from foreign students, "legacies," recruited athletes, or members of other 'special admission' categories; exaggerating per capita instructional expenditures by misclassifying expenses for athletics, faculty research, and auxiliary enterprises; artificially driving up the number of applicants by counting as a completed application the first step of a 'two-part' application process; and inflating the yield rate by rejecting or wait-listing the highest achievers in the applicant pool (who are least likely to come if admitted). (p. 137)

There is an ethical issue with chasing ranking status. Playing the rankings game has refocused colleges on recruiting high potential students and persuading students who will likely have better grades from leaving for out-of-state schools through discounting tuition (Lingenfelter 2006). Also, the number of students receiving Pell grants in the top ranks seems to decrease as ranks improve, pointing to the use of the adjustment of tuition to influence rankings (Meredith 2004). An incidental outcome of this is that access to college for the financially disadvantaged would intuitively have to be more difficult. The ethical concern with rankings should be the emphasis it puts on seeking highly qualified students, deflecting attention from the tradition of wanting to make access to higher education equitable (Ehrenberg 2005).

Enrollment management has become a critical tool in playing the rankings game, and enrollment management in most public and private higher education institutions has gained increased importance. Enrollment management offices are concerned with the positioning of the university's brand in the marketplace and are often leaders in designing marketing, pricing, and financial aid strategies employed to attract the institution's target consumer. A commonly used tool used to deploy information regarding a school's message is the college view book (Klassen 2000). In a study examining the content of view books, Klassen (2000) found universities communicate what they are about to prospective students through their view books. As an example of how view books are used as marketing tools, schools ranked in the top 15 of the *U.S. News and World Report* ranking of U.S. colleges and universities primarily employ imagery in their view books of engagement between students and professors, cultural events, and artistic activities. On the other hand, imagery used by tier four schools focuses on graduation, alumni events, and posteducational endeavors. According to Klassen (2000), the message sent by each type of university is that graduation can be achieved with little disruption in terms of jobs, relationship, children, etc. Schools are creating a vision of Utopia … degrees without any hassles.

> By excising the disagreeable but common routines of ordinary life, all of the view books examined here have unwittingly sidestepped the very longings that have compelled young people for centuries to seek a higher education: service to humanity and their fellow citizens, commitment to family and work, and the search for higher meaning. (p. 21)

Ethically, these types of enrollment management/marketing practices are questionable. From the student's perspective, it is difficult to evaluate higher education as a consumer product and, for many students, the brand image of the institution as presented in such materials as the view books becomes the deciding factor. Studies indicate that students are influenced by effective advertising campaigns that begin to blur the lines between marketing a school and selling it (Nicholls et al. 1995).

Issues of Rigor and Utility of Learning

Colleges and universities are in threat of becoming institutions whose primary service is to prepare the student for lifelong consumerism rather than a "better life." People must remain more important than the acquisition of things. Student consumerism is pervasive in the U.S., where they believe that, regardless of effort, students deserve the degree they pay for and, should they not feel satisfied with the services rendered, they are justified in challenging the provider of that service—the teacher—about the perceived weakness of the teacher's performance. In addition, students are lazier, harder to motivate, and bored; they do not want to be there; they want to get to work

(Ng and Forbes 2009). There is no room for rigor or meaningful journeys in such an environment, and the marketization of education is largely to blame. When students are not happy, they can threaten to take their needed tuition dollars elsewhere, just as they would change car insurance to obtain a policy with better value. The problem is that these students are not forced to see that they are an integral part of the process and not just an addendum by administrators vying for rankings and tuition dollars.

Furthermore, obtaining a degree solely focused on employment denies students the opportunity to transform themselves on a personal level. The problem with this focus on content at the expense of critical thinking is that society no longer has the large number of creative critical thinkers required in a capitalist society (Raduntz 2007, p. 242). Moreover, the ethical issue posed by this orientation to please and not engage the student is that, for all the heartache evoked, the new model of business is not serving the universities any more adequately, as we hear from Arum and Roska in *Academically Adrift: Limited Learning on College Campuses*—at least 45% of undergraduates demonstrated "no improvement in critical thinking, complex reasoning, and writing skills in the first two years of college, and 36 percent showed no progress in four years" (Benton 2011). According to Benton, this is "just the beginning of the bad news" (para 1). Professors often feel compelled to focus on what will allow students to pass as opposed to focusing on critical thinking and reflection (Molesworth et al. 2009). In the long term, this can only spell demise on a personal and societal level, and teachers and schools, rather than improving society, are adding to its burden. Again, the marketization of education plays no small part in schools' failure to improve the future of society.

Problems and Solutions

What to Do about Rankings?

The marketing of colleges in the U.S. is now more prevalent than at any other time in history (Klassen 2000), and this calls for an urgent conversation on the commercialization of education. First and foremost, the issue of rankings needs to be addressed. According to Lingenfelter (2006, p. 6):

> In the past dozen years both state governments and institutions have spent increasing amounts of money for what amounts to expensive efforts to improve their rankings in *U.S. News and World Report*. Institutions are discounting tuition to attract more students with better grades and test scores, and some of our states have been discounting tuition to keep better students at home.

Recommendations have been made that institutions should no longer cooperate with organizations that issue rankings. In fact, this is just what some schools have chosen to do. Colin Diver, president of Reed College, describes the school's lack of cooperation with *U.S. News & World Report* ranking system as follows:

> By far the most important consequence of sitting out the rankings game, however, is the freedom to pursue our own educational philosophy, not that of some news magazine. ... We are free to admit the students we think will thrive at Reed and contribute to its intellectual atmosphere, rather than those we think will elevate our standing on *U.S. News's* list. ... Pleasing students *can* mean superb educational programs precisely tailored to their needs; but it can also mean dumbing down graduation requirements, lessening educational rigor, inflating grades, and emphasizing nonacademic amenities. At Reed we have felt free to pursue an educational philosophy that maintains rigor and structure—including a strong core curriculum in the humanities, extensive distribution requirements, a junior qualifying examination in one's major, a required senior thesis, uninflated grades (not reported to students unless they request them), heavy workloads, and graduate-level standards in many courses. We have also felt free to resist pressure to provide an expensive and highly selective program of varsity athletics and other nonacademic enticements simply for their marketing advantages. ... Unlike many of our rankings-sensitive peers, we feel no pressure to use part-time adjunct faculty or teaching assistants as an inexpensive but educationally dubious technique for even further increasing the percentage of small classes. (pp. 137–139)

What to Do about Branding?

The financial feasibility of many colleges is now dependent on marketing and maintaining market share (Edirisooriya 2009). Because the competitive landscape in education is now so competitive, schools feel they have no alternative but to differentiate themselves through branding. No person could argue for complete removal of a business model as it seems critical in these difficult economic times and, while one may question the appropriateness of marketing an institution, marketing in higher education is now a global phenomenon. Many in higher education are not pleased with their new roles as marketing representatives, and many members of the higher education community do not have the experience to be skillful marketers. Furthermore, there is a degree of whitewashing enveloping the educational landscape as a result of this branding effort that might be considered misleading and unethical that needs to be addressed. Obtaining a degree should be hard work, it should require personal sacrifice, it should require personal accountability, and students who are not capable should be allowed to fail. Society should not be burdened with graduates who are not up to par and schools need to accept their responsibility in this regard by not attempting to sell utopia. Then, when students enroll, they are prepared to work hard for their degrees and will not expect to sail through the process simply because they are paying. Perhaps, institutions might then consider transforming their marketing-focused enrollment management offices into counseling services that encourage students to become participants in learning rather than consumers of education.

What to Do about Faculty Morale?

Faculty spend 58% of their time teaching, 20% of the balance in research and scholarship, and 22% on issues, such as administration and professional development (IES 2009). With so many part-time and adjunct faculty, there is considerable pressure on full-time faculty to publish to meet standards for accreditations, such as AACSB, to serve on committees, and to engage in administrative effort. This is deeply problematic in an entrepreneurial environment. According to Goldspink (2007), faculty morale is low because so much focus is being placed on additional administrative responsibilities in an effort to achieve operational efficiencies. This also detracts from learning outcomes. Furthermore, Benton (2011, para 17) writes:

> Students may be enjoying high self-esteem, but college teachers seem to be suffering from a lack of self-confidence. It starts in graduate school, when we begin to fear we are destined for unemployment, when we compare our pay with that of comparably educated professionals, and when we realize that—for all the sacrifices that we've made, often with idealistic motives—we are held in slight regard. Many people even think of us as subversives who 'hate America.' During the latest economic crisis—perhaps the endpoint of a 40-year slide—many of us have felt as if we've become expendable, if we are employed at all. That makes it hard for us to make strong demands on our students, or, perhaps more important, to stand up for any kind of change in our institutions.

A holistic approach is necessary to address the problem of low faculty morale, which has become epidemic. This issue is a broad social one. Educators are no longer valued as they once were. A good place to start addressing this issue is to support a return of academic power to the faculty in the teacher-student dyad. Administrators need to examine the efficacy of anonymous student evaluations in determining teaching quality as it gives no voice to faculty. Administrators need to reevaluate the level of administrative burden placed on faculty when the ranks of full-time faculty are falling. These are becoming embedded ethical issues.

What to Do about Critical Thinking and Dumbing Down?

The university was once seen as the center for investigation and critical thinking, and it would be a tremendous loss to society if higher education became an activity solely driven by the demands of a capitalist culture. Higher education has now come to be a means of securing material affluence, and education may no longer be viewed as a potentially transformative experience able to affect the student's intellectual perspective of the world.

The student as consumer perspective causes harm. It has the propensity to lower quality and promote a passive, disengaged student body. Because the consumer is always right, implicit in the student as consumer model is that students must be happy with the services rendered. When the consumer is an integral part of the delivery of education, one would have to question this consumer satisfaction orientation. Further, when the outcome of learning is reduced to a grade, with the student as a consumer and the teacher as the provider, the faculty is perceived as solely responsible for learning. This is problematic. According to Rojstaczer and Healy (2010), grade inflation has been on an upward trajectory since the 1980s, and it is very probable that this is as a result of student-based teacher evaluation. According to Benton (2011), it has become difficult to give students honest feedback as teachers must now envelop students with praise and encouragement to avoid student disappointment, thus retarding student growth. This new form of higher education is not likely to prepare students for corporate careers because it does not provide them with the opportunity to become critical thinkers, who are able to innovate and cope with change. Compounding this is the growing number of adjunct or part-time faculty whose performance is measured in large part by student evaluations and who are not always in sync with the institution's mission (Benton 2011).

Contemporary education is currently situated uneasily between "traditional" and "relevant." Teachers must once again emphasize supporting personal student transformation, even if they are under pressure from management and students to focus on the skills that support a job search (Molesworth et al. 2009). Faculty must concur on this.

What to Do about Ethical Issues in Research?

Externally funded research raises a host of ethical concerns. Yassi et al. (2010) call on universities to address the ethical issues posed by non-university funded research rather than jeopardize the integrity of research and scholarship. They also call for schools to deal swiftly with researchers who subordinate research integrity to their career goals and the demands of those funding their research.

What to Do about the Export Market?

Higher education, which was once viewed as contributing to the social and moral well-being of society, is now viewed through the lens of neoliberalism (Gibbs 2001), and we are also exporting this viewpoint. Education is now a highly exported product and its commodification in an international context raises the ethical urgency to act immediately to ensure that the standard of education that is being exported is up to par.

The commercialization of education in a cross-border context calls for vigilant oversight in the provision of education and the portability of qualifications (Matsuura 2006). By 2025, there will be 7.2 million students worldwide (Bohm et al. 2002). The international market in higher education is valued in excess of $30 billion with the U.S. ranking as the leading player. Exporting higher education programs to less developed countries has become big business. Non-traditional schools use virtual universities, branch campuses, and corporate universities and are creating a "new paradigm" of higher education (Matsuura 2006). This engages directly with the contemporary debate as to whether this increase in cross-border education undermines the traditional values of education in terms of the relevance of service, research, and learning/teaching (Knight 2006). Furthermore, according to Daniel (2006):

> Cross-border provision without concern for equity and social justice has generated a backlash that manifests itself as restrictive regulations and punitive measures. This clearly indicates that the providers from the developed world must instill confidence and trust within the developing world by forging partnerships, facilitating the development of quality assurance mechanisms, and building indigenous human resource capacity.

Final Thoughts

Issues such as academic freedom are becoming less important than accountability; truth is deemed less important than utility; performance is to be valued over thoughtfulness. The system of higher education that has worked for centuries was founded on the belief that education was a process. Today's system cannot work because it views higher education as a product from a perspective of economic value. If a university in a consumer-driven culture is to educate students to participate as informed purchasers in the market economy, then the institution must prepare students by doing more than developing their sense of economic self-interest; it requires a university that mentors students in developing a moral understanding of humanity (Gibbs 2001).

In this belief system, the values of free-market policies, entrepreneurship, deregulation, and reduced government funding have replaced the commitment to social outcomes. With this major revision of higher education, universities are no longer seen as centers for intellectual activity. If the marketization of higher education continues, there may come a time when academics will become skills trainers with the sole purpose of transmitting knowledge to prepare students for employment—already, educators have taken a back seat to trainers and business managers (Raduntz 2007, p. 242)—and they will bear little resemblance to the scholars who once filled the halls of the universities and filled the minds of their students with ideas, questions, and visions.

Works Cited

Altbach, P. G. (2009, April 30). "It's the Faculty, Stupid!" *The Times Higher Education Supplement, 1894*, 40.

Benton, T. H. (2011, February). "A Perfect Storm in Undergraduate Education, Part I." *The Chronicle of Higher Education*. Retrieved from http://chronicle.com/article/A-Perfect-Storm-in/126451/.

Bohm, A., Davis, D., Meares, D., & Pearce, D. (2002). *The Global Student Mobility 2025 Report: Forecasts of the Global Demand for International Education*. Canberra: IDP.

Bridenthal, R. (2005, August). Review of the book *University, Inc: The Corporate Corruption of Higher Education*, by J. Washburn. *Radical Teacher, 73*, 35–37.

Daniel, J. (2006). Preface. In J. Knight (Ed.), *Higher Education Crossing Borders: A Guide to the Implications of the General Agreement on Trade in Services (GATS) for Cross-Border Education*. Commonwealth of Learning and UNESCO.

Diver, C. (2005, November). "Is There Life After Rankings?" *The Atlantic*. Retrieved from http://www.reed.edu/president/speeches/atlantic_ monthly05Diver.pdf.

Edirisooriya, G. (2009). "A Market Analysis of the Latter Half of the Nineteenth-Century American Higher Education Sector." *History of Education, 38*(1), 115–132.

Edmiston, D. (2009). "An Examination of Integrated Marketing Communication in U.S. Public Institutions of Higher Education." *International Journal of Educational Advancement, 8*(3), 152–175.

Ehrenberg, R. C. (2005). "Method or Madness? Inside the *U.S. News & World Report* College Rankings." *Journal of College Admission, 189*, 29–35.

Gibbs, P. (2001). "Higher Education as a Market: A Problem or Solution?" *Studies in Higher Education, 26*(1), 85–94.

Goldspink, C. (2007). "Rethinking Educational Reform." *Educational Management Administration & Leadership, 35*(1), 27–50.

Hossler, D. (2000). "The Problem with College Rankings." *About Campus, 5*, 20–24.

Hossler, D. R. (2004). "How Enrollment Management has Transformed—or Ruined—Higher Education." *Chronicle of Higher Education, 34*, B3.

IES (2009). "*Digest of Education Statistics:* Chapter 3 Post Secondary Education." Retrieved from http://nces.ed.gov/programs/digest/ d09/ch_3.asp.

Kaplan, G. R. (1996). "Profits R Us: Notes on the Commercialization of America's Schools." *Phi Delta Kappan, 78*(3), 1–12. Retrieved March 17, 2011, from EBSCO*host*.

Klassen, M. L. (2000). "Lots of Fun, Not Much Work, and No Hassles: Marketing Images of Higher Education." *Journal of Marketing for Higher Education, 10*(2), 11–26.

Knight, J. (2006). *Higher Education Crossing Borders: A Guide to the Implications of the General Agreement on Trade in Services (GATS) for Cross-Border Education*. Commonwealth of Learning and UNESCO.

Lingenfelter, P. E. (2006). "The Unfunding of Public Education." Presented at the Public Affairs Week, Baruch College, City College of New York. Retrieved from http://www.sheeo.org/ about/paulpres/baruch%20college.pdf.

Lock, G., & Lorenz, C. (2007). "Revisiting the University Front." *Studies in Philosophy and Education, 26*, 405–418.

Marklein, M. B. (2007). "Colleges Taking Another Look at Value of Merit-Based Aid." *USA Today*. Retrieved from http://www.usa today.com/news/education/2007-03-14-merit-aid_N.htm.

Marris, E. (2005). "Corporate Culture Nets Big Bucks for University Heads." *Nature, 434*, 1059.

Matsuura, K. (2006). Foreword. In J. Knight (Ed.), *Higher Education Crossing Borders: A Guide to the Implications of the General Agreement on Trade in Services (GATS) for Cross-Border Education*. Commonwealth of Learning and UNESCO.

Meredith, M. (2004). "Why Do Universities Compete in the Ratings Game? An Empirical Analysis of the Effects of the *U.S. News and World Report* College Rankings." *Research in Higher Education, 45*(5), 443–461.

Meyerson, G. (2005, August). Review of the book *Universities in the Marketplace: The Commercialization of Higher Education*, by D. Bok. *Radical Teacher, 73*, 33–35.

Miscamble, W. D. (2006). "The Corporate University: A Catholic Response." *America*, 14–17.

Molesworth, M., Nixon, E., & Scullion, R. (2009). "Having, Being and Higher Education: The Marketisation of the University and the Transformation of the Student into Consumer." *Teaching in Higher Education, 14*(3), 277–287.

Newman, S., & Jahdi, K. (2009). "Marketisation of Education: Marketing, Rhetoric and Reality." *Journal of Further and Higher Education, 33*(1), 1–11.

Ng, I. C. L., & Forbes, J. (2009). Education as Service: The Understanding of University Experience Through the Service Logic. *Journal of Marketing for Higher Education, 19*(1), 38–64.

Nicholls, J., Harris, J., Morgan, E., Clarke, K., & Sims, D. (1995). "Marketing Higher Education: The MBA Experience." *International Journal of Educational Management, 9*(2), 31–38.

Raduntz, H. (2007). Chapter 13: "The Marketization of Education within the Global Capitalist Economy." In *Globalizing Education: Policies, Pedagogies, & Politics* (pp. 231–245). New York: Peter Lang Publishing, Inc.

Rojstaczer, S., & Healy, C. (2010). "Grading in American Colleges and Universities." Retrieved from http://gradeinflation.com/tcr2010 grading.pdf.

SHEEO. (2009). *State Higher Education Finance FY 2008*. Retrieved from www.sheeo.org/finance/shef_fy08.pdf.

Sigler, W. (2007). "The Age of Outcomes." *College and University, 83*(2), 53–56, 58–60.

Thacker, L. (2005). "Confronting the Commercialization of Admissions." *Chronicle of Higher Education, 51*(25), B26. Retrieved March 17, 2011, from EBSCO*host*.

Tilak, J. B. G. (2009). "Higher Education: A Public Good or a Commodity for Trade?" *Prospects, 38*, 449–466.

Yassi, A., Dharamsi, S., Speigel, J., Rojas, A., Dean, E., & Woolard, R. (2010). "The Good, the Bad, and the Ugly of Partnered Research: Revisiting the Sequestration Thesis and the Role of Universities in Promoting Social Justice." *International Journal of Health Services, 40*(3), 485–505.

Credit

Natale, Samuel M. and Doran, Caroline. "Marketization of Education: An Ethical Dilemma." *Journal of Business Ethics* 7 July 2011: 187–96. Web. *Journal of Business Ethics* is published by Springer-Verlag Dordrecht. Reproduced with permission of Springer-Verlag Dordrecht via Copyright Clearance Center.

A Question of Honor

Cheating on Campus Undermines the Reputation of Our Universities and the Value of Their Degrees. Now Is the Time for Students Themselves to Stop It.

William M. Chace

William M. Chace's academic career includes serving as president of Emory University, as president of Wesleyan University, and as Professor of English at Stanford University. "A Question of Honor" originally appeared in The American Scholar, *a publication of the esteemed academic honor society Phi Beta Kappa. Like Edmundson and Natale and Doran, Chace is concerned with problems in higher education. The particular problem that he focuses on is cheating. In the first part of the essay, Chace explores the complexities of what cheating is, and he offers several reasons for why students cheat and how they are able to get away with it. Chace concludes the essay with an idealistic vision of what can be done to address the problem.*

CR80CR80CR80

One of the gloomiest recent reports about the nation's colleges and universities reinforces the suspicion that students are studying less, reading less, and learning less all the time: "American higher education is characterized," sociologists Richard Arum and Josipa Roksa said last year, "by limited or no learning for a large proportion of students." Their book, *Academically Adrift*, joins a widening, and often negative, reassessment of what universities contribute to American life. Even President Obama has gotten into the act, turning one problem with higher education into an applause line in his latest State of the Union address. "So let me put colleges and universities on notice," he said: "If you can't stop tuition from going up, the funding you get from taxpayers will go down. Higher education can't be a luxury—it is an economic imperative that every family in America should be able to afford."

Where should we lay the blame for the worsening state of one of the foundations of American civilization, one that has long filled us with justifiable pride? The big public universities are already bogged down by diminishing financial support from the states; private education is imperiled by tuition costs that discourage hundreds of thousands of middle-class and poorer students from applying. Some schools have made heroic attempts to diversify their student bodies, but too little financial aid is available to make access possible for all the applicants with academic promise.

What is happening inside the classroom for those who do get in? Who is teaching the students? Less and less often it is a member of an institution's permanent faculty, and rarer still one of its distinguished professors. More and more of the teaching has been parceled out to part-time instructors who have no hope of landing a full-time position. Because of this, their loyalty to the school that hired them, and to the students they will probably meet in just one course and never again, has diminished.

Amid such melancholy reports from the front, campus amusements that have nothing to do with education—intercollegiate athletics leads the festivities—sop up money, keep coaches in the headlines, and divert public attention from the essential mission of education: to strengthen the minds of young people and to prepare them to cope with the demands of life.

Perhaps that is why, when the public is asked about colleges and universities, the response is increasingly negative with each passing year. According to the Pew Research Center, most American citizens (57 percent) say that higher education "fails to provide good value for the money students and their families spend." Within the innermost sanctum of the academy the view is almost the same: "About four-in-ten college presidents say the system is headed in the wrong direction," according to Pew. If university presidents, who by profession and temperament routinely find every glass more than half-full, are so disconsolate, the public can't be expected to be optimistic.

Were this situation to get any worse, it could legitimately be called a crisis. But American colleges and universities are not going under anytime soon. Despite their problems, they employ hundreds of thousands of people, keep towns and even cities financially afloat, and offer cultural resources and, yes, athletic and other entertainments. They adorn the nation with their well-kept campuses. The research done on those campuses makes us safer, improves our health, and inspires our nobler human impulses. Along the way, colleges and universities provide multiyear habitat for millions of postadolescents who, more often than not, are bewilderingly short of ideas about what to do after leaving secondary school. And they continue to offer a haven to those who finish their undergraduate years and do not or cannot enter the present bleak job market. Most of these students are happy to find themselves— for four, five, or even six years—with other people their age, with whom they can develop social skills while entertaining each other and themselves and exposing their minds to selected academic topics. For all these reasons, the college experience in this country long ago became one of its most acceptable rites of passage. The schools are there because they serve a variety of needs. The challenge is to make them better.

But now they are up against a spectrum of problems whose magnitude they have never faced before. What can they do—amid financial pressures, dwindling public esteem, pre-professional anxieties on the part of their students, and eroded faculty loyalty—to recover the prestige they once enjoyed?

One answer, I believe, rests in what they can do, and must do, about a large and ugly presence on almost every campus: academic dishonesty. Cheating now hurts American higher education; it might well be cheating that can begin to save it.

CREOCEEOCRE

In college and university classrooms across the country, every student sooner or later faces the apparently simple task of writing an essay. The essay might focus on a philosophical topic (the argumentative structure of John Stuart Mill's *On Liberty*, for example), or the student's interpretation of a play (Harold Pinter's *The Homecoming*, say), or a political issue (the likely shape of demographic changes in the United States in the next 20 years). The topics are endless, but the ground rules are not: be clear, employ the rules of logic, and most pointedly, be original.

The last requirement is where the system gets confused. No teacher really expects any student essay to revolutionize our understanding of the world, to be so original that the firmament begins to wobble. The opportunity to be truly original has gotten rarer through the eons. As Mark Twain put it, "What a good thing Adam had. When he said a good thing he knew nobody had said it before." No, originality means something more modest: that the student, after much reflection and weighing of the assembled evidence, has written in a way that reflects the particular contours of his or her thinking. The turns and twists of the prose, the things emphasized and the things neglected, the way the essay opens and closes, and how errors, some small and some large, inevitably infiltrate the prose—these features, constituting the essay's fingerprint, are evidence that the student has written something original. But truth to tell, it's not working that way. Today, lots of students cheat. They use the work of others. They buy essays. They plagiarize. Still, even though the Web makes cheating easier than ever before, and thus more prevalent, the phenomenon of cheating is nothing new. Students have been at it for a long time.

Eighty years ago, Dean Clarence W. Mendell of Yale University declared that the problem of cheating at his school was widespread enough to require instant reform: "It is altogether imperative that the growing disregard of this traditional standard on the part of many unthinking undergraduates should be wiped out." He sternly added, "the faculty has but one attitude toward cheating, an attitude shared, we believe, by the undergraduate body." But 45 years later, in 1976, another Yale dean, Eva Balogh, described cheating at the school as "rampant." New Haven hadn't changed much, and Yale was no isolated case. That same year, on the other side of the country, the student newspaper at the University of Southern California reported that as many as 40 percent of students there were plagiarizing their written work.

The first comprehensive study of cheating at colleges and universities (5,000 students at almost 100 institutions) was completed in 1964. It found that 75 percent of the students had engaged in one form or another of academic dishonesty. A generation later, in 2001, an authoritative survey conducted by Donald L. McCabe of Rutgers and his colleagues concluded that cheating was now "prevalent" across the country and that "some forms of cheating have increased dramatically in the last 30 years."

Indeed, every study over the decades has concluded that cheating at American colleges and universities is rampant. Despite Dean Mendell's desire long ago to wipe it out, grim admonitions from college presidents year after year, and any number of cheating eruptions around the nation, dishonesty, indigenous to almost every campus, flourishes. A recent survey by the online journal *Inside Higher Ed* of more than a thousand chief academic officers at schools nationwide revealed that more than two-thirds of them believe that cheating has become a much worse problem than it once was. But, interestingly enough, fewer than a quarter of them thought it was on the rise on their own campuses.

Students cheat for many reasons, some of them even doing so without malign intent, either because they don't understand the rules of academic honesty or are confused about the assignment. Some students cheat because of pressures to succeed in a competitive world. Some cheat because they are lazy, tired, or indifferent. Some, overwhelmed by the oceanic wash of information pouring in upon them as they open their computers to the Web, conclude that there is nothing new to say. And some cheat because they look at all academic tasks as exciting opportunities to fool the system as well as the teacher.

They learn early. The Josephson Institute of Ethics sampled more than 40,000 public and private high school students and found that three-fifths of them admitted to having cheated on a test. Nearly half of these were honors students; a third had cheated twice or more in the previous year. In high school, every applicant to college is given an open invitation to cheat—the personal essay that college admissions offices require. How many students write these essays without help? How many parents write them?

How many friends, counselors, and commercial agencies write them? No one knows, but the pressure to get such help must be precisely as strong as the pressure to write the kind of essay that will win respect from an admissions dean. The temptation to cross the line shows up early in a young person's life.

As with any transgressive cultural activity both scorned and widespread (running red lights, using recreational drugs, evading taxes), some cheaters are exposed while others go untouched. For every cheating student who is nabbed, another slips under the radar. Nor is the radar kept in good working order. Some teachers know when a student's work is fraudulent but elect to do nothing. It takes time, and time is expensive; bringing a student before a campus judicial council is also labor intensive, and the outcome is unpredictable; students or their parents can retain attorneys to fight the charges and endlessly complicate the procedure; administrators cannot be counted on to back up professors making accusations. Professors like the elevation of teaching but not the grubby business of prosecuting. For the increasing number of adjunct instructors, vigilance about cheating could put their professional futures at risk. They could earn an unappealing tag: "high maintenance." And some teachers have concluded that the only person hurt by cheating is the cheater, and so they wash their hands of the entire business.

On many campuses, dishonesty is simply accepted as an unwelcome but ubiquitous feature of teaching and learning, the equivalent of friction in the pedagogical machine. Reflect on what Dean Mendell said, but perhaps only dimly understood, all those decades ago. The "unthinking undergraduates" at Yale who were cheating made up part of the undergraduate body at Yale as a whole that presumably shared the faculty's revulsion toward cheating. Denouncing a wrong does not necessarily mean being innocent of committing it. Most students know that cheating surrounds them, but few see ways to do anything about it, even when they hold it in contempt. Some of those who cheat are morally offended by others who cheat, but they too are, for obvious reasons, disinclined to complain. In every cultural domain, we grow accustomed to breaches that, with time and repetition, we wind up believing are normal.

But how does cheating become tolerated, assimilated, and ultimately absorbed into our understanding of normality? The answer partly resides in the peculiar kind of wrong it is. Compared with the violation of copyright, a crime punishable in a court of law, cheating at school is "only" a moral and ethical wrong. Plagiarism, one of the most common forms of cheating, often leaves behind no apparent victim; the author from whose body of work the plagiarist extracts a useful portion might never know anything has happened; and the work, despite the theft, remains in the author's possession (lawyers call this "usufruct"). The downloading without attribution of finished essays from the Internet, another immensely popular way of completing classroom assignments, harms no honest author, as copying them for publication would. And if several students conspire to compose an essay in the name of one, who is the exploited party? Any outrage can seem tolerable if it looks victimless.

Consider, moreover, with what emollients any feeling of guilt about cheating can be soothed in a student's mind. To begin, the culture outside the campus gates seems long ago to have accepted dishonesty when it comes to the writings of certain important people. Just how much of *Profiles in Courage* did John F. Kennedy write and how much did Theodore Sorensen write? How strongly do we care? What should we say about the Rev. Martin Luther King Jr.'s doctoral dissertation at Boston University, once we know that it is filled with the writings of others, copied down paragraph after paragraph, in vast profusion? Think also of Roger Clemens, Barry Bonds, and almost everyone involved in international cycling—sports figures about whom allegations of cheating are now featured in every newspaper in the land. What of the plagiarism of prize-winning historians Doris Kearns Goodwin and Stephen E. Ambrose, not to mention the elaborate transfer, generations ago, of the ideas of German philosophers into the "philosophy" of Samuel Taylor Coleridge? Don't we just note such derelictions and then generously move on to matters more pressing?

The much-quoted aphorism by T. S. Eliot that "immature poets imitate; mature poets steal" can give license enough to a student faced with the chore of writing an original senior thesis on, say, Eliot himself. That immature student, emboldened by fantasies, can think himself into maturity by doing no more than what Eliot said the great customarily do: steal.

CRIACSRIACSRIA

Yet another social reality erodes the moral offensiveness of cheating, a reality that universities and colleges find themselves ill equipped to cope with. Given that so much professional life—the legal and medical systems, entrepreneurial capitalism, the operations of established companies and the public sector, the very working life that many college graduates will enter—is based on the pooling of ideas and the energy of teamwork, how is it that the academic world can demand wholly independent work and originality? Indeed, students can wonder why colleges observe the principles of solitary labor when they will soon work in offices where ideas are meant to be merged and where the inspiration of one person achieves value only when coupled with the inspiration of many others.

Nowhere is this tension between the ethical code of the campus and that of the working world more awkwardly felt than in the discipline of computer science. On campuses, students taking courses in this fertile area of study are urged to work independently to develop their skills, but if they are fortunate enough upon graduation to get a job with a firm making use of such skills, they will join highly ambitious teams of men and women who, to succeed, will merge their talent and their scientific knowledge to create something—a new piece of money-making software, for instance—that not one of them, working alone, could have come up with.

On campus, solitary independence; off campus, collective energy. The contradiction between these two methods partially explains why the greatest incidence of cheating at high-powered universities like Stanford and others occurs among students enrolled in computer science courses. Those students must hold in their minds that a wrong in one place is highly prized in another. Nor is it irrelevant, as one imagines the incentives to cheat, to consider the attractive beginning salaries offered to successful computer-science graduates of schools such as Stanford. The urge to succeed can yield to the temptation to cheat if a good job awaits just beyond the campus gates.

Few students are ignorant of the prevailing ethical standards of their home institutions. Should those standards be strong and consistently enforced, and should those institutions provide example after example of moral courage, students who cheat do so with the knowledge that they are violating a code of honor that has substance. But if the institutions themselves exhibit questionable ethical standards—leaving a trail of shoddy compromise, corner cutting, and breaches of trust—those students come to understand that honor is only a word and not a practice. Since nothing more quickly leaps into a young person's mind than the recognition of hypocrisy, cheating becomes easier once institutional duplicity is detected.

In colleges and universities, then, where primary teaching duties are given over to part-time instructors so that well-paid professors can devote themselves to research projects; where tuition is very high but certain classes are large and crowded; where extra tutorial help is lavishly provided to students on athletic scholarships (many of whom never would be admitted on academic grounds) and only rarely to students who play no intercollegiate sports; where the values seem to be corporate rather than academic; where, as at Claremont McKenna College, an administrator submits false SAT scores to publications like *U.S. News & World Report* in order to boost the school's "selective" reputation; and where, as a consequence, campus morale is low, some students can and will respond as one would to any organization proclaiming one set of values while practicing another. Students entering colleges and universities are told that these places are, and have been, "special." When they turn out to be commonplace, standards will triumph.

Students are under personal, parental, and pre-professional pressures that have never been more intense. Getting into the right school, and achieving in such a way that one can then proceed to the next right station in life, makes the college experience for many young people more a matter of getting ahead—acquiring the proper credential—than undergoing a unique ritual devoted to self-knowledge and meeting intellectual growth. If resources beyond oneself are needed to get ahead—even illicit resources such as the writings of others, all easily acquired by a few keyboard strokes in the privacy of one's room, and all gained with no apparent sense of injury to anyone else—so be it. Nothing seems lost; forward motion has been sustained.

The most appalling aspect of the rise of cheating on campus in recent times is that some professors themselves have offered sophisticated defenses of plagiarism. An ambitious student can now turn to the writings of teachers who have made ingenious theoretical defenses for the very cheating practices proscribed by the universities at which they teach. If a student faces the accusation that his work is not original, that student can respond: Don't you know that the idea of "originality" has been hammered into nothingness by thinkers such as Michel Foucault? After all, he proclaimed four decades ago that the very idea of an author, any author, is dead, and hence there is no one around to claim originality. Instead, wrote Foucault, in *What Is an Author?*, we should welcome a new world in which the inhibiting codes of authorship have been cast to the winds:

> All discourses, whatever their status, form, value, and whatever the treatment to which they will be subjected, would then develop in the anonymity of a murmur. We would no longer hear the questions that have been rehashed for so long: Who really spoke? Is it really he and not someone else? With what authenticity or originality? ... And behind all these questions, we would hear hardly anything but the stirring of an indifference: What difference does it make who is speaking?

Once a student adopts, under so impressive an aegis as Foucault, an indifference about authorship, the coast is clear and all noisome ethical restrictions can be jettisoned. *Perspectives on Plagiarism* (1999), edited by Lise Buranen and Alice Myers Roy, brings together essays demonstrating the problem. Gilbert Larochelle, who teaches political philosophy at the University of Quebec and who is a professorial devotee of the celebrated philosopher, puts it this way: "Can plagiarism still exist in an intellectual universe where it has become impossible to differentiate the representation from the referent, the copy from the original, and the copyist from the author?" Another teacher, Debora Halbert of Otterbein College, inspired by both Foucault and feminism, ups the ante and provides students who might be thinking of plagiarizing with dreams of anti-establishment revolution: "Appropriation or plagiarism are acts of sedition against an already established mode of knowing, a way of knowing indebted to male creation and property rights. … No concept of intellectual property should exist in a feminist future." Yet another professor, Marilyn Randall of the University of Western Ontario, writes that "later critical discourse whole-heartedly adopts the notion of plagiarism as an intentional political act" and, perhaps sensitive to the unattractive connotations of the word itself, repackages plagiarism as "discursive repetition." Buoyed up by such sophisticated arguments, and keen to be part of a bright new future, students might well be ashamed if they did *not* cheat.

A less theoretical defense of cheating comes by way of something called "patchwriting." It combines low-level Foucauldian thinking ("no such thing as originality") with American confessionalism ("folks, let's be honest, everybody cheats all the time"). It argues that whatever we write is no more than proof that we are forever standing on the shoulders of giants. We're fooling ourselves if we believe that we are writing something that has not, in so many words, been written before. Human beings can't be original. As a species, we endlessly use and reuse what has been used and reused before, forever recycling the logic, the words, the turns of phrase, and all the rest. So why not, says a chief apologist for patchwriting, go easy on the students? Teach them, says Rebecca Moore Howard of Syracuse University, that it's okay to download essays from the Internet, to pluck useful phrases or even paragraphs from Wikipedia, and to cobble whatever seems to fit together into the semblance of an essay ready for grading. "[Patchwriting] is a form of verbal sculpture, molding new shapes from preexisting materials, Howard writes. "It is something that all academic writers do. Patchwriting belongs not in a category with cheating on exams and purchasing term papers but in a category with the ancient tradition of learning through apprenticeship and mimicry." It's really how we all write anyway, if only we had the courage as patchwriters to say so.

What explains this peculiar defense of plagiarism? Pedagogical and professional anxiety may be one cause: if we go after cheaters, pursuing them all the way to the judicial councils, we will have done nothing, say the defenders, but reinforce the barriers between teachers and students, the invidious social hierarchies separating those possessing the standards (even if they are ill-paid teachers of composition) and those supplying the tuition (even if they are freshmen and sophomores). In the interests of both candor and classroom egalitarianism, why not let everyone in on the secret about writing: plagiarism is at the heart of prose; it's how it gets done. Once that forbidden truth is out in the open, genuine teaching can begin. Neither students nor teacher will feel inferior any longer. They will hold in common the abiding truth of writing: it's all patched together.

And yet. As I have written these words, one by one, knowing all the while that none of them is original with me, all of them (except "usufruct") drawn from the common well of English diction, and recognizing that neither my sentence construction nor my way of organizing paragraphs is unique to me, and while I have gone to many sources to find the information I've needed to write, I believe this essay is mine, mine alone, and would not exist had I not written it. I don't believe I have patched, or that I've plagiarized. As it is with me, so it has always been with writers, and so it will always be. The arguments protecting or even championing plagiarism fall before the palpable evidence of originality, modest and grand, ephemeral and enduring, as it has existed in writing everywhere.

CR

Almost every reader of this essay began, I assume, with the presumption that plagiarism is a serious wrong. Most readers will find its assorted defenders more ridiculous than credible, whether they are disciples of postmodern theory or teachers warning students away from the allegedly phony attractions of originality. Such readers can find kinship, then, with the students who do not cheat. To them we must turn our attention. Both groups have a stake in a clean system. For the students, it means grades honestly earned; for the readers, it means the hope that this country's educational enterprise is ethically sound. Together the two groups can find much to respect in what another kind of composition teacher, Augustus M. Kolich, expressed a generation ago:

> [P]lagiarism cuts deeply into the integrity and morality of what I teach my students, and it sullies my notions about the sanctity of my relationship to students. It is a lie, and although lies are often private matters between two people, plagiarism is never merely private because it breaches a code of behavior that encompasses my classroom, my teaching, my university, and my society.

Here, then, is the situation: abundant evidence that something is wrong, coupled with an abiding sense that the wrong is pernicious and widespread, and highly resistant to remedies. So, to quote Vladimir Lenin's famous pamphlet (whose title was plagiarized from a novel by Nikolai Chernyshevsky): *What Is to Be Done?*

Assuming that something should be done, one response could be to stiffen the apparatus of policing. Internet sites such as "Turnitin," to which students and teachers can submit student work to see if it contains material from essays already on electronic file, could be employed by more and more teachers to track down those who misuse the material. Penalties could be increased; the pursuers could try to become more clever than the pursued; teaching could take on an even more suspicious and hostile attitude. But this plan of attack might well underestimate the resourceful talents of young people—versed as they are in every aspect of the digital world—to outwit even vigilant professorial hawks.

But another strategy already exists. Some institutions, rare but sturdily resolute in spirit, have fought the infection of cheating for decades. Many of them, but hardly all, are small liberal arts colleges. They have had history and tradition at their back. All of them have expended both time and social capital in encouraging honesty and trust. Instead of a campus culture in which adversarial tensions between administrators and students are a given and where cheating is presumed, these institutions convey to the students themselves the authority to monitor the ethical behavior of their classmates. Every student on these campuses is informed, directly and formally, what honor means and why it is important. Every student is presumed to want every classmate to observe the principles of honor. This puts everyone at the same moral starting line. Then students are expected to act as if the work of one is in fact the responsibility of all. Nothing about this is perfunctory. Indeed, at these schools, academic honor is a dominating concern.

Which are these colleges and universities, few in number and proud of their traditions? Washington and Lee, Haverford, Rice, Cal Tech, and the University of Virginia are among them. At some of them, the students themselves hear cases of alleged honor violations and render the judgments with no members of the faculty joining them. Professors note the violation; students then take charge. At such schools, when students cheat, students mete out the justice, which can be swift and uncompromising. At a few of these schools, there exists what is called the "single sanction": any violation of the honor code means permanent expulsion. At all these places, honor has been enshrined as fundamental to the history and the life of the institution. Known to every student who enrolls, the code of honor is already in practice while they matriculate; it is remembered with respect after they graduate. By maintaining such systems, these campuses are less likely to be collections of individuals than, at their best, small societies of truthful men and women. They see the dangers of cheating for what they are: practices in which many students can be hurt by the dishonesty of a few. And not just students but, in the words of Professor Kolich, the university as a whole, and the larger society beyond the gates.

Can the number of such campuses increase? More than 100 American campuses have some form of honor code already, even if many of them give only lip service to the concept. What would it take to transform classrooms throughout the United States into arenas of moral practice? How would American higher education look then? Might it have in hand one small but powerful argument to turn aside the criticisms hurled against it by those who think that it has lost its ethical bearings and who see it as given over to misplaced values such as pre-professional practicalities or simple-minded political correctness? Such critics—noisy and passionate—might be brought to attention with the news that moral instruction, at the foundation of some of the nation's best schools, had been given a central position at other schools across the country.

If such a reconsideration of one of the essential purposes of higher education were to take place, things on American campuses could begin to seem quite different. Instead of training a suspicious eye on students, professors could turn to them with an understanding of how much they have at stake, and how much they fear they can lose, as long as cheating thrives. In those students who do not cheat resides a core of strength, a habit of mind and morality, thus far employed at too few schools. Those schools should remind themselves of one central fact: at their best, students are dedicated to learning. Students who cheat undermine who they are. At its core, cheating is self-destructive.

The lesson is about students and what they alone can do, not about schools and what they have failed to do. The institutions, after all, can always find ways to walk away from the problem. Although no school welcomes negative publicity about academic dishonesty, administrators can always point the finger downward at those who break the rules. And professors can always distance themselves in the same way. So it is the students who stand at the center of this drama.

Doubters might say that what works at small schools couldn't work at larger ones. Big universities, sprawling with students, promote anonymity, and with anonymity comes blamelessness. At such places, no one is responsible for anything and honor codes are bound to fail. But even big places are composed of individual classes, each taught by one teacher, often in small rooms where, once again, principles of individual honor and personal responsibility can be secured and, once again, those with the most to lose can act to bring honesty to bear. Keep in mind that though universities might be large or small, the average student-teacher ratio today is excellent, according to a 2010 survey by *U.S. News & World Report*: slightly less than 15-to-one, with liberal arts colleges averaging 12.2 students per faculty member, and national universities averaging 15.5 students per faculty member. The numbers are small enough to permit, if not to encourage, local and intimate moral responsibility.

To do nothing is not an answer. Once the emptiness of such a response to so serious a problem is recognized, a form of education beneficial to all can come. To encourage moral awareness is to appreciate what rests at the heart of what it means to teach. In the end, it also rests at the heart of what it means to learn.

Should such a pattern of student responsibility spread more widely across the nation, classroom after classroom will benefit. Students will more fully understand how legitimate societies are established and how they survive—by a consensual agreement that they will govern themselves by rule, by mutual respect, and by vigilance. At that point, universities and colleges will be able to recover some of the trust and respect they have lost. They will be able to say, with authority, that the essential virtue of honorable behavior is both promoted and protected on campus.

Credit
Chace, William M. "A Question of Honor: Cheating on Campus Undermines the Reputation of Our Universities and Their Degrees. Now Is the Time for Students Themselves to Stop It." Copyright of *American Scholar* is the property of Phi Beta Kappa Society, Spring 2012: 20–32. Print.

The Shame of College Sports

Taylor Branch

Taylor Branch is a Pulitzer Prize winning author and civil rights historian. His most notable work is America in the King Years, *a narrative of Dr. Martin Luther King, Jr. and the civil rights era. The October 2011 cover story of* The Atlantic, *an esteemed publication known for its long form essays that cover politics, culture, business and more, was "The Shame of College Sports." This controversial essay ignited a national conversation about the NCAA and how—or whether—it serves student-athletes' best interests. Similar to Natale and Doran's criticism of the revenue-focused mentality in higher education administration, Branch denounces the revenue-focused mentality in the NCAA, which, according to Branch, results in the exploitation of athletes and showcases the NCAA's hypocrisy.*

CREOCREOCREO

"I'm not hiding," Sonny Vaccaro told a closed hearing at the Willard Hotel in Washington, D.C., in 2001. "We want to put our materials on the bodies of your athletes, and the best way to do that is buy your school. Or buy your coach."

Vaccaro's audience, the members of the Knight Commission on Intercollegiate Athletics, bristled. These were eminent reformers—among them the president of the National Collegiate Athletic Association, two former heads of the U.S. Olympic Committee, and several university presidents and chancellors. The Knight Foundation, a nonprofit that takes an interest in college athletics as part of its concern with civic life, had tasked them with saving college sports from runaway commercialism as embodied by the likes of Vaccaro, who, since signing his pioneering shoe contract with Michael Jordan in 1984, had built sponsorship empires successively at Nike, Adidas, and Reebok. Not all the members could hide their scorn for the "sneaker pimp" of schoolyard hustle, who boasted of writing checks for millions to everybody in higher education.

"Why," asked Bryce Jordan, the president emeritus of Penn State, "should a university be an advertising medium for your industry?"

Vaccaro did not blink. "They shouldn't, sir," he replied. "You sold your souls, and you're going to continue selling them. You can be very moral and righteous in asking

103

me that question, sir," Vaccaro added with irrepressible good cheer, "but there's not one of you in this room that's going to turn down any of our money. You're going to take it. I can only offer it."

William Friday, a former president of North Carolina's university system, still winces at the memory. "Boy, the silence that fell in that room," he recalled recently. "I never will forget it." Friday, who founded and co-chaired two of the three Knight Foundation sports initiatives over the past 20 years, called Vaccaro "the worst of all" the witnesses ever to come before the panel.

But what Vaccaro said in 2001 was true then, and it's true now: corporations offer money so they can profit from the glory of college athletes, and the universities grab it. In 2010, despite the faltering economy, a single college athletic league, the football-crazed Southeastern Conference (SEC), became the first to crack the billion-dollar barrier in athletic receipts. The Big Ten pursued closely at $905 million. That money comes from a combination of ticket sales, concession sales, merchandise, licensing fees, and other sources—but the great bulk of it comes from television contracts.

Educators are in thrall to their athletic departments because of these television riches and because they respect the political furies that can burst from a locker room. "There's fear," Friday told me when I visited him on the University of North Carolina campus in Chapel Hill last fall. As we spoke, two giant construction cranes towered nearby over the university's Kenan Stadium, working on the latest $77 million renovation. (The University of Michigan spent almost four times that much to expand its Big House.) Friday insisted that for the networks, paying huge sums to universities was a bargain. "We do every little thing for them," he said. "We furnish the theater, the actors, the lights, the music, and the audience for a drama measured neatly in time slots. They bring the camera and turn it on." Friday, a weathered idealist at 91, laments the control universities have ceded in pursuit of this money. If television wants to broadcast football from here on a Thursday night, he said, "we shut down the university at 3 o'clock to accommodate the crowds." He longed for a campus identity more centered in an academic mission.

The United States is the only country in the world that hosts big-time sports at institutions of higher learning. This should not, in and of itself, be controversial. College athletics are rooted in the classical ideal of *Mens sana in corpore sano*—a sound mind in a sound body—and who would argue with that? College sports are deeply inscribed in the culture of our nation. Half a million young men and women play competitive intercollegiate sports each year. Millions of spectators flock into football stadiums each Saturday in the fall, and tens of millions more watch on television. The March Madness basketball tournament each spring has become a major national event, with upwards of 80 million watching it on television and talking about the games around the office water cooler. ESPN has spawned ESPNU, a channel dedicated to college sports, and Fox Sports and other cable outlets are developing channels exclusively to cover sports from specific regions or divisions.

With so many people paying for tickets and watching on television, college sports has become Very Big Business. According to various reports, the football teams at Texas, Florida, Georgia, Michigan, and Penn State—to name just a few big-revenue football schools—each earn between $40 million and $80 million in profits a year, even after paying coaches multimillion-dollar salaries. When you combine so much money with such high, almost tribal, stakes—football boosters are famously rabid in their zeal to have their alma mater win—corruption is likely to follow.

Scandal after scandal has rocked college sports. In 2010, the NCAA sanctioned the University of Southern California after determining that star running back Reggie Bush and his family had received "improper benefits" while he played for the Trojans. (Among other charges, Bush and members of his family were alleged to have received free airfare and limousine rides, a car, and a rent-free home in San Diego, from sports agents who wanted Bush as a client.) The Bowl Championship Series stripped USC of its 2004 national title, and Bush returned the Heisman Trophy he had won in 2005. Last fall, as Auburn University football stormed its way to an undefeated season and a national championship, the team's star quarterback, Cam Newton, was dogged by allegations that his father had used a recruiter to solicit up to $180,000 from Mississippi State in exchange for his son's matriculation there after junior college in 2010. Jim Tressel, the highly successful head football coach of the Ohio State Buckeyes, resigned last spring after the NCAA alleged he had feigned ignorance of rules violations by players on his team. At least 28 players over the course of the previous nine seasons, according to Sports Illustrated, had traded autographs, jerseys, and other team memorabilia in exchange for tattoos or cash at a tattoo parlor in Columbus, in violation of NCAA rules. Late this summer, Yahoo Sports reported that the NCAA was investigating allegations that a University of Miami booster had given millions of dollars in illicit cash and services to more than 70 Hurricanes football players over eight years.

The list of scandals goes on. With each revelation, there is much wringing of hands. Critics scold schools for breaking faith with their educational mission, and for failing to enforce the sanctity of "amateurism." Sportswriters denounce the NCAA for both tyranny and impotence in its quest to "clean up" college sports. Observers on all sides express jumbled emotions about youth and innocence, venting against professional mores or greedy amateurs.

For all the outrage, the real scandal is not that students are getting illegally paid or recruited, it's that two of the noble principles on which the NCAA justifies its existence—"amateurism" and the "student-athlete"—are cynical hoaxes, legalistic confections propagated by the universities so they can exploit the skills and fame of young athletes. The tragedy at the heart of college sports is not that some college athletes are getting paid, but that more of them are not.

Don Curtis, a UNC trustee, told me that impoverished football players cannot afford movie tickets or bus fare home. Curtis is a rarity among those in higher education today, in that he dares to violate the signal taboo: "I think we should pay these guys something."

Fans and educators alike recoil from this proposal as though from original sin. Amateurism is the whole point, they say. Paid athletes would destroy the integrity and appeal of college sports. Many former college athletes object that money would have spoiled the sanctity of the bond they enjoyed with their teammates. I, too, once shuddered instinctively at the notion of paid college athletes.

But after an inquiry that took me into locker rooms and ivory towers across the country, I have come to believe that sentiment blinds us to what's before our eyes. Big-time college sports are fully commercialized. Billions of dollars flow through them each year. The NCAA makes money, and enables universities and corporations to make money, from the unpaid labor of young athletes.

Slavery analogies should be used carefully. College athletes are not slaves. Yet to survey the scene—corporations and universities enriching themselves on the backs of uncompensated young men, whose status as "student-athletes" deprives them of the right to due process guaranteed by the Constitution—is to catch an unmistakable whiff of the plantation. Perhaps a more apt metaphor is colonialism: college sports, as overseen by the NCAA, is a system imposed by well-meaning paternalists and rationalized with hoary sentiments about caring for the well-being of the colonized. But it is, nonetheless, unjust. The NCAA, in its zealous defense of bogus principles, sometimes destroys the dreams of innocent young athletes.

The NCAA today is in many ways a classic cartel. Efforts to reform it—most notably by the three Knight Commissions over the course of 20 years—have, while making changes around the edges, been largely fruitless. The time has come for a major overhaul. And whether the powers that be like it or not, big changes are coming. Threats loom on multiple fronts: in Congress, the courts, breakaway athletic conferences, student rebellion, and public disgust. Swaddled in gauzy clichés, the NCAA presides over a vast, teetering glory.

Founding Myths

From the start, amateurism in college sports has been honored more often in principle than in fact; the NCAA was built of a mixture of noble and venal impulses. In the late 19th century, intellectuals believed that the sporting arena simulated an impending age of Darwinian struggle. Because the United States did not hold a global empire like England's, leaders warned of national softness once railroads conquered the last continental frontier. As though heeding this warning, ingenious students turned variations on rugby into a toughening agent. Today a plaque in New Brunswick, New Jersey, commemorates the first college game, on November 6, 1869, when Rutgers beat Princeton 6–4.

Walter Camp graduated from Yale in 1880 so intoxicated by the sport that he devoted his life to it without pay, becoming "the father of American football." He persuaded other schools to reduce the chaos on the field by trimming each side from 15 players to 11, and it was his idea to paint measuring lines on the field. He conceived functional designations for players, coining terms such as *quarterback*. His game remained violent by design. Crawlers could push the ball forward beneath piles of flying elbows without pause until they cried "Down!" in submission.

In an 1892 game against its archrival, Yale, the Harvard football team was the first to deploy a "flying wedge," based on Napoleon's surprise concentrations of military force. In an editorial calling for the abolition of the play, *The New York Times* described it as "half a ton of bone and muscle coming into collision with a man weighing 160 or 170 pounds," noting that surgeons often had to be called onto the field. Three years later, the continuing mayhem prompted the Harvard faculty to take the first of two votes to abolish football. Charles Eliot, the university's president, brought up other concerns. "Deaths and injuries are not the strongest argument against football," declared Eliot. "That cheating and brutality are profitable is the main evil." Still, Harvard football persisted. In 1903, fervent alumni built Harvard Stadium with zero college funds. The team's first paid head coach, Bill Reid, started in 1905 at nearly twice the average salary for a full professor.

A newspaper story from that year, illustrated with the Grim Reaper laughing on a goalpost, counted 25 college players killed during football season. A fairy-tale version of the founding of the NCAA holds that President Theodore Roosevelt, upset by a photograph of a bloodied Swarthmore College player, vowed to civilize or destroy football. The real story is that Roosevelt maneuvered shrewdly to preserve the sport— and give a boost to his beloved Harvard. After *McClure's* magazine published a story on corrupt teams with phantom students, a muckraker exposed Walter Camp's $100,000 slush fund at Yale. In response to mounting outrage, Roosevelt summoned leaders from Harvard, Princeton, and Yale to the White House, where Camp parried mounting criticism and conceded nothing irresponsible in the college football rules he'd established. At Roosevelt's behest, the three schools issued a public statement that college sports must reform to survive, and representatives from 68 colleges founded a new organization that would soon be called the National Collegiate Athletic Association. A Haverford College official was confirmed as secretary but then promptly resigned in favor of Bill Reid, the new Harvard coach, who instituted new rules that benefited Harvard's playing style at the expense of Yale's. At a stroke, Roosevelt saved football and dethroned Yale.

For nearly 50 years, the NCAA, with no real authority and no staff to speak of, enshrined amateur ideals that it was helpless to enforce. (Not until 1939 did it gain the power even to mandate helmets.) In 1929, the Carnegie Foundation made headlines with a report, "American College Athletics," which concluded that the scramble for players had "reached the proportions of nationwide commerce." Of the 112 schools surveyed, 81 flouted NCAA recommendations with inducements to students ranging from open payrolls and disguised booster funds to no-show jobs at movie studios. Fans ignored the uproar, and two-thirds of the colleges mentioned told *The New York Times* that they planned no changes.

Embarrassed, the NCAA in 1948 enacted a "Sanity Code," which was supposed to prohibit all concealed and indirect benefits for college athletes; any money for athletes was to be limited to transparent scholarships awarded solely on financial need. Schools that violated this code would be expelled from NCAA membership and thus exiled from competitive sports.

This bold effort flopped. Colleges balked at imposing such a drastic penalty on each other, and the Sanity Code was repealed within a few years. The University of Virginia went so far as to call a press conference to say that if its athletes were ever accused of being paid, they should be forgiven, because their studies at Thomas Jefferson's university were so rigorous.

The Big Bluff

In 1951, the NCAA seized upon a serendipitous set of events to gain control of intercollegiate sports. First, the organization hired a young college dropout named Walter Byers as executive director. A journalist who was not yet 30 years old, he was an appropriately inauspicious choice for the vaguely defined new post. He wore cowboy boots and a toupee. He shunned personal contact, obsessed over details, and proved himself a bureaucratic master of pervasive, anonymous intimidation. Although discharged from the Army during World War II for defective vision, Byers was able to see an opportunity in two contemporaneous scandals. In one, the tiny College of William and Mary, aspiring to challenge football powers Oklahoma and Ohio State, was found to be counterfeiting grades to keep conspicuously pampered players eligible. In the other, a basketball point-shaving conspiracy (in which gamblers paid players to perform poorly) had spread from five New York colleges to the University of Kentucky, the reigning national champion, generating tabloid "perp" photos of gangsters and handcuffed basketball players. The scandals posed a crisis of credibility for collegiate athletics, and nothing in the NCAA's feeble record would have led anyone to expect real reform.

But Byers managed to impanel a small infractions board to set penalties without waiting for a full convention of NCAA schools, which would have been inclined toward forgiveness. Then he lobbied a University of Kentucky dean—A. D. Kirwan, a former football coach and future university president—not to contest the NCAA's dubious legal position (the association had no actual authority to penalize the university), pleading that college sports must do something to restore public support. His gambit succeeded when Kirwan reluctantly accepted a landmark precedent: the Kentucky basketball team would be suspended for the entire 1952–53 season. Its legendary coach, Adolph Rupp, fumed for a year in limbo.

The Kentucky case created an aura of centralized command for an NCAA office that barely existed. At the same time, a colossal misperception gave Byers leverage to mine gold. Amazingly in retrospect, most colleges and marketing experts considered the advent of television a dire threat to sports. Studies found that broadcasts reduced live attendance, and therefore gate receipts, because some customers preferred to watch at home for free. Nobody could yet imagine the revenue bonanza that television represented. With clunky new TV sets proliferating, the 1951 NCAA convention voted 161–7 to outlaw televised games except for a specific few licensed by the NCAA staff.

All but two schools quickly complied. The University of Pennsylvania and Notre Dame protested the order to break contracts for home-game television broadcasts, claiming the right to make their own decisions. Byers objected that such exceptions would invite disaster. The conflict escalated. Byers brandished penalties for games televised without approval. Penn contemplated seeking antitrust protection through the courts. Byers issued a contamination notice, informing any opponent scheduled to play Penn that it would be punished for showing up to compete. In effect, Byers mobilized the college world to isolate the two holdouts in what one sportswriter later called "the Big Bluff."

Byers won. Penn folded in part because its president, the perennial White House contender Harold Stassen, wanted to mend relations with fellow schools in the emerging Ivy League, which would be formalized in 1954. When Notre Dame also surrendered, Byers conducted exclusive negotiations with the new television networks on behalf of every college team. Joe Rauh Jr., a prominent civil-rights attorney, helped him devise a rationing system to permit only 11 broadcasts a year—the fabled *Game of the Week*. Byers and Rauh selected a few teams for television exposure, excluding the rest. On June 6, 1952, NBC signed a one-year deal to pay the NCAA $1.14 million for a carefully restricted football package. Byers routed all contractual proceeds through his office. He floated the idea that, to fund an NCAA infrastructure, his organization should take a 60 percent cut; he accepted 12 percent that season. (For later contracts, as the size of television revenues grew exponentially, he backed down to 5 percent.) Proceeds from the first NBC contract were enough to rent an NCAA headquarters, in Kansas City.

Only one year into his job, Byers had secured enough power and money to regulate all of college sports. Over the next decade, the NCAA's power grew along with television revenues. Through the efforts of Byers's deputy and chief lobbyist. Chuck Neinas, the NCAA won an important concession in the Sports Broadcasting Act of 1961, in which Congress made its granting of a precious antitrust exemption to the National Football League contingent upon the blackout of professional football on Saturdays. Deftly, without even mentioning the NCAA, a rider on the bill carved each weekend into protected broadcast markets: Saturday for college, Sunday for the NFL. The NFL got its antitrust exemption. Byers, having negotiated the NCAA's television package up to $3.1 million per football season—which was higher than the NFL's figure in those early years—had made the NCAA into a spectacularly profitable cartel.

"We Eat What We Kill"

The NCAA's control of college sports still rested on a fragile base, however: the consent of the colleges and universities it governed. For a time, the vast sums of television money delivered to these institutions through Byers's deals made them willing to submit. But the big football powers grumbled about the portion of the television revenue diverted to nearly a thousand NCAA member schools that lacked major athletic programs. They chafed against cost-cutting measures—such as restrictions on team size—designed to help smaller schools. "I don't want Hofstra telling Texas how to play football," Darrell Royal, the Longhorns coach, griped. By the 1970s and '80s, as college football games delivered bonanza ratings—and advertising revenue—to the networks, some of the big football schools began to wonder: Why do we need to have our television coverage brokered through the NCAA? Couldn't we get a bigger cut of that TV money by dealing directly with the networks?

Byers faced a rude internal revolt. The NCAA's strongest legions, its big football schools, defected en masse. Calling the NCAA a price-fixing cartel that siphoned every television dollar through its coffers, in 1981 a rogue consortium of 61 major football schools threatened to sign an independent contract with NBC for $180 million over four years.

With a huge chunk of the NCAA's treasury walking out the door, Byers threatened sanctions, as he had against Penn and Notre Dame three decades earlier. But this time the universities of Georgia and Oklahoma responded with an antitrust suit. "It is virtually impossible to overstate the degree of our resentment … of the NCAA," said William Banowsky, the president of the University of Oklahoma. In the landmark 1984 *NCAA v. Board of Regents of the University of Oklahoma* decision, the U.S. Supreme Court struck down the NCAA's latest football contracts with television— and any future ones—as an illegal restraint of trade that harmed colleges and viewers. Overnight, the NCAA's control of the television market for football vanished. Upholding Banowsky's challenge to the NCAA's authority, the *Regents* decision freed the football schools to sell any and all games the markets would bear. Coaches and administrators no longer had to share the revenue generated by their athletes with smaller schools outside the football consortium. "We eat what we kill," one official at the University of Texas bragged.

A few years earlier, this blow might have financially crippled the NCAA—but a rising tide of money from basketball concealed the structural damage of the *Regents* decision. During the 1980s, income from the March Madness college basketball tournament, paid directly by the television networks to the NCAA, grew tenfold. The windfall covered and then far exceeded—what the organization had lost from football.

Still, Byers never forgave his former deputy Chuck Neinas for leading the rebel consortium. He knew that Neinas had seen from the inside how tenuous the NCAA's control really was, and how diligently Byers had worked to prop up its Oz-like façade. During Byers's tenure, the rule book for Division I athletes grew to 427 pages of scholastic detail. His NCAA personnel manual banned conversations around water coolers, and coffee cups on desks, while specifying exactly when drapes must be drawn at the NCAA's 27,000-square-foot headquarters near Kansas City (built in 1973 from the proceeds of a 1 percent surtax on football contracts). It was as though, having lost control where it mattered, Byers pedantically exerted more control where it didn't.

After retiring in 1987, Byers let slip his suppressed fury that the ingrate football conferences, having robbed the NCAA of television revenue, still expected it to enforce amateurism rules and police every leak of funds to college players. A lethal greed was "gnawing at the innards of college athletics," he wrote in his memoir. When Byers renounced the NCAA's pretense of amateurism, his former colleagues would stare blankly, as though he had gone senile or, as he wrote, "desecrated my sacred vows." But Byers was better positioned than anyone else to argue that college football's claim to amateurism was unfounded. Years later, as we will see, lawyers would seize upon his words to do battle with the NCAA.

Meanwhile, reformers fretted that commercialism was hurting college sports, and that higher education's historical balance between academics and athletics had been distorted by all the money sloshing around. News stories revealed that schools went to extraordinary measures to keep academically incompetent athletes eligible for competition, and would vie for the most-sought-after high-school players by proffering under-the-table payments. In 1991, the first Knight Commission report, "Keeping Faith With the Student Athlete," was published; the commission's "bedrock conviction" was that university presidents must seize control of the NCAA from athletic directors in order to restore the preeminence of academic values over athletic or commercial ones. In response, college presidents did take over the NCAA's governance. But by 2001, when the second Knight Commission report ("A Call to Action: Reconnecting College Sports and Higher Education") was issued, a new generation of reformers was admitting that problems of corruption and commercialism had "grown rather than diminished" since the first report. Meanwhile the NCAA itself, revenues rising, had moved into a $50 million, 116,000-square-foot headquarters in Indianapolis. By 2010, as the size of NCAA headquarters increased yet again with a 130,000-square-foot expansion, a third Knight Commission was groping blindly for a hold on independent college-athletic conferences that were behaving more like sovereign pro leagues than confederations of universities. And still more money continued to flow into NCAA coffers. With the basketball tournament's 2011 television deal, annual March Madness broadcast revenues had skyrocketed 50-fold in less than 30 years.

The Myth of the "Student-Athlete"

Today, much of the NCAA's moral authority—indeed much of the justification for its existence—is vested in its claim to protect what it calls the "student-athlete." The term is meant to conjure the nobility of amateurism, and the precedence of scholarship over athletic endeavor. But the origins of the "student-athlete" lie not in a disinterested ideal but in a sophistic formulation designed, as the sports economist Andrew Zimbalist has written, to help the NCAA in its "fight against workmen's compensation insurance claims for injured football players."

"We crafted the term *student-athlete*," Walter Byers himself wrote, "and soon it was embedded in all NCAA rules and interpretations." The term came into play in the 1950s, when the widow of Ray Dennison, who had died from a head injury received while playing football in Colorado for the Fort Lewis A&M Aggies, filed for workmen's-compensation death benefits. Did his football scholarship make the fatal collision a "work-related" accident? Was he a school employee, like his peers who worked part-time as teaching assistants and bookstore cashiers? Or was he a fluke victim of extracurricular pursuits? Given the hundreds of incapacitating injuries to college athletes each year, the answers to these questions had enormous consequences. The Colorado Supreme Court ultimately agreed with the school's contention that he was not eligible for benefits, since the college was "not in the football business."

The term *student-athlete* was deliberately ambiguous. College players were not students at play (which might understate their athletic obligations), nor were they just athletes in college (which might imply they were professionals). That they were high-performance athletes meant they could be forgiven for not meeting the academic standards of their peers; that they were students meant they did not have to be compensated, ever, for anything more than the cost of their studies. *Student-athlete* became the NCAA's signature term, repeated constantly in and out of courtrooms.

Using the "student-athlete" defense, colleges have compiled a string of victories in liability cases. On the afternoon of October 26, 1974, the Texas Christian University Horned Frogs were playing the Alabama Crimson Tide in Birmingham, Alabama. Kent Waldrep, a TCU running back, carried the ball on a "Red Right 28" sweep toward the Crimson Tide's sideline, where he was met by a swarm of tacklers. When Waldrep regained consciousness, Bear Bryant, the storied Crimson Tide coach, was standing over his hospital bed. "It was like talking to God, if you're a young football player," Waldrep recalled.

Waldrep was paralyzed: he had lost all movement and feeling below his neck. After nine months of paying his medical bills, Texas Christian refused to pay any more, so the Waldrep family coped for years on dwindling charity.

Through the 1990s, from his wheelchair, Waldrep pressed a lawsuit for workers' compensation. (He also, through heroic rehabilitation efforts, recovered feeling in his arms, and eventually learned to drive a specially rigged van. "I can brush my teeth," he told me last year, "but I still need help to bathe and dress.") His attorneys haggled with TCU and the state worker-compensation fund over what constituted employment. Clearly, TCU had provided football players with equipment for the job, as a typical employer would—but did the university pay wages, withhold income taxes on his financial aid, or control work conditions and performance? The appeals court finally rejected Waldrep's claim in June of 2000, ruling that he was not an employee because he had not paid taxes on financial aid that he could have kept even if he quit football. (Waldrep told me school officials "said they recruited me as a student, not an athlete," which he says was absurd.)

The long saga vindicated the power of the NCAA's "student-athlete" formulation as a shield, and the organization continues to invoke it as both a legalistic defense and a noble ideal. Indeed, such is the term's rhetorical power that it is increasingly used as a sort of reflexive mantra against charges of rabid hypocrisy.

Last Thanksgiving weekend, with both the FBI and the NCAA investigating whether Cam Newton had been lured onto his team with illegal payments, Newton's Auburn Tigers and the Alabama Crimson Tide came together for their annual game, known as the Iron Bowl, before 101,821 fans at Bryant-Denny Stadium. This game is always a highlight of the football season because of the historic rivalry between the two schools, and the 2010 edition had enormous significance, pitting the defending national champion Crimson Tide against the undefeated Tigers, who were aiming for their first championship since 1957. I expected excited fans; what I encountered was the throbbing heart of college sports. As I drove before daybreak toward the stadium, a sleepless caller babbled over WJOX, the local fan radio station, that he "couldn't stop thinking about the coin toss." In the parking lot, ticketless fans were puzzled that anyone need ask why they had tailgated for days just to watch their satellite-fed flat screens within earshot of the roar. All that morning, pilgrims packed the Bear Bryant museum, where displays elaborated the misery of Alabama's 4–24 run before the glorious Bryant era dawned in 1958.

Finally, as Auburn took the field for warm-ups, one of Alabama's public-address-system operators played "Take the Money and Run" (an act for which he would be fired). A sea of signs reading $CAM taunted Newton. The game, perhaps the most exciting of the season, was unbearably tense, with Auburn coming from way behind to win 28–27, all but assuring that it would go on to play for the national championship. Days later, Auburn suspended Newton after the NCAA found that a rules violation had occurred: his father was alleged to have marketed his son in a pay-for-play scheme; a day after that, the NCAA reinstated Newton's eligibility because investigators had not found evidence that Newton or Auburn officials had known of his father's actions. This left Newton conveniently eligible for the Southeastern Conference championship game and for the postseason BCS championship bowl. For the NCAA, prudence meant honoring public demand.

"Our championships," NCAA President Mark Emmert has declared, "are one of the primary tools we have to enhance the student-athlete experience."

"Whoremasters"

NCAA V. Regents left the NCAA devoid of television football revenue and almost wholly dependent on March Madness basketball. It is rich but insecure. Last year, CBS Sports and Turner Broadcasting paid $771 million to the NCAA for television rights to the 2011 men's basketball tournament alone. That's three-quarters of a billion dollars built on the backs of amateurs—on unpaid labor. The whole edifice depends on the players' willingness to perform what is effectively volunteer work. The athletes, and the league officials, are acutely aware of this extraordinary arrangement. William Friday, the former North Carolina president, recalls being yanked from one Knight Commission meeting and sworn to secrecy about what might happen if a certain team made the NCAA championship basketball game. "They were going to dress and go out on the floor," Friday told me, "but refuse to play," in a wildcat student strike. Skeptics doubted such a diabolical plot. These were college kids—unlikely to second-guess their coaches, let alone forfeit the dream of a championship. Still, it was unnerving to contemplate what hung on the consent of a few young volunteers: several hundred million dollars in television revenue, countless livelihoods, the NCAA budget, and subsidies for sports at more than 1,000 schools. Friday's informants exhaled when the suspect team lost before the finals.

Cognizant of its precarious financial base, the NCAA has in recent years begun to pursue new sources of revenue. Taking its cue from member schools such as Ohio State (which in 2009 bundled all its promotional rights—souvenirs, stadium ads, shoe deals—and outsourced them to the international sports marketer IMG College for a guaranteed $11 million a year), the NCAA began to exploit its vault of college sports on film. For $29.99 apiece, NCAA On Demand offers DVDs of more than 200 memorable contests in men's ice hockey alone. Video-game technology also allows nostalgic fans to relive and even participate in classic moments of NCAA Basketball. NCAA Football, licensed by the NCAA through IMG College to Electronic Arts, one of the world's largest video-game manufacturers, reportedly sold 2.5 million copies in 2008. Brit Kirwan, the chancellor of the Maryland university system and a former president at Ohio State, says there were "terrible fights" between the third Knight Commission and the NCAA over the ethics of generating this revenue.

All of this money ultimately derives from the college athletes whose likenesses are shown in the films or video games. But none of the profits go to them. Last year, Electronic Arts paid more than $35 million in royalties to the NFL players union for the underlying value of names and images in its pro football series—but neither the NCAA nor its affiliated companies paid former college players a nickel. Naturally, as they have become more of a profit center for the NCAA, some of the vaunted "student-athletes" have begun to clamor that they deserve a share of those profits. You "see everybody getting richer and richer," Desmond Howard, who won the 1991 Heisman Trophy while playing for the Michigan Wolverines, told *USA Today* recently. "And you walk around and you can't put gas in your car? You can't even fly home to see your parents?"

Some athletes have gone beyond talk. A series of lawsuits quietly making their way through the courts cast a harsh light on the absurdity of the system—and threaten to dislodge the foundations on which the NCAA rests. On July 21, 2009, lawyers for Ed O'Bannon filed a class-action antitrust suit against the NCAA at the U.S. District Court in San Francisco. "Once you leave your university," says O'Bannon, who won the John Wooden Award for player of the year in 1995 on UCLA's national-championship basketball team, "one would think your likeness belongs to you." The NCAA and UCLA continue to collect money from the sales of videos of him playing. But by NCAA rules, O'Bannon, who today works at a Toyota dealership near Las Vegas, alleges he is still not allowed to share the revenue the NCAA generates from his own image as a college athlete. His suit quickly gathered co-plaintiffs from basketball and football, ex-players featured in NCAA videos and other products. "The NCAA does not license student-athlete likenesses," NCAA spokesperson Erik Christianson told *The New York Times* in response to the suit, "or prevent former student-athletes from attempting to do so. Likewise, to claim the NCAA profits off student-athlete likenesses is also pure fiction."

The legal contention centers on Part IV of the NCAA's "Student-Athlete Statement" for Division I, which requires every athlete to authorize use of "your name or picture … to promote NCAA championships or other NCAA events, activities or programs." Does this clause mean that athletes clearly renounce personal interest forever? If so, does it actually undermine the NCAA by implicitly recognizing that athletes have a property right in their own performance? Jon King, a lawyer for the plaintiffs, expects the NCAA's core mission of amateurism to be its "last defense standing."

In theory, the NCAA's passion to protect the noble amateurism of college athletes should prompt it to focus on head coaches in the high-revenue sports—basketball and football—since holding the top official accountable should most efficiently discourage corruption. The problem is that the coaches' growing power has rendered them, unlike their players, ever more immune to oversight. According to research by Charles Clotfelter, an economist at Duke, the average compensation for head football coaches at public universities, now more than $2 million, has grown 750 percent (adjusted for inflation) since the *Regents* decision in 1984; that's more than 20 times the cumulative 32 percent raise for college professors. For top basketball coaches, annual contracts now exceed $4 million, augmented by assorted bonuses, endorsements, country-club memberships, the occasional private plane, and in some cases a negotiated percentage of ticket receipts. (Oregon's ticket concessions netted former football coach Mike Bellotti an additional $631,000 in 2005.)

The NCAA rarely tangles with such people, who are apt to fight back and win. When Rick Neuheisel, the head football coach of the Washington Huskies, was punished for petty gambling (in a March Madness pool, as it happened), he sued the NCAA and the university for wrongful termination, collected $4.5 million, and later moved on to UCLA. When the NCAA tried to cap assistant coaches' entering salary at a mere $16,000, nearly 2,000 of them brought an antitrust suit, *Law V. NCAA,* and in 1999 settled for $54.5 million. Since then, salaries for assistant coaches have commonly exceeded $200,000, with the top assistants in the SEC averaging $700,000. In 2009, Monte Kiffin, then at the University of Tennessee, became the first assistant coach to reach $1 million, plus benefits.

The late Myles Brand, who led the NCAA from 2003 to 2009, defended the economics of college sports by claiming that they were simply the result of a smoothly functioning free market. He and his colleagues deflected criticism about the money saturating big-time college sports by focusing attention on scapegoats; in 2010, outrage targeted sports agents. Last year *Sports Illustrated* published "Confessions of an Agent," a firsthand account of dealing with high-strung future pros whom the agent and his peers courted with flattery, cash, and tawdry favors. Nick Saban, Alabama's head football coach, mobilized his peers to denounce agents as a public scourge. "I hate to say this," he said, "but how are they any better than a pimp? I have no respect for people who do that to young people. None."

Saban's raw condescension contrasts sharply with the lonely penitence from Dale Brown, the retired longtime basketball coach at LSU. "Look at the money we make off predominantly poor black kids," Brown once reflected. "We're the whoremasters."

"Picayune Rules"

NCAA officials have tried to assert their dominion—and distract attention from the larger issues—by chasing frantically after petty violations. Tom McMillen, a former member of the Knight Commission who was an All-American basketball player at the University of Maryland, likens these officials to traffic cops in a speed trap, who could flag down almost any passing motorist for prosecution in kangaroo court under a "maze of picayune rules." The publicized cases have become convoluted soap operas. At the start of the 2010 football season, A. J. Green, a wide receiver at Georgia, confessed that he'd sold his own jersey from the Independence Bowl the year before, to raise cash for a spring-break vacation. The NCAA sentenced Green to a four-game suspension for violating his amateur status with the illicit profit generated by selling the shirt off his own back. While he served the suspension, the Georgia Bulldogs store continued legally selling replicas of Green's No. 8 jersey for $39.95 and up.

A few months later, the NCAA investigated rumors that Ohio State football players had benefited from "hook-ups on tatts"—that is, that they'd gotten free or underpriced tattoos at an Ohio tattoo parlor in exchange for autographs and memorabilia—a violation of the NCAA's rule against discounts linked to athletic personae. The NCAA Committee on Infractions imposed five-game suspensions on Terrelle Pryor, Ohio State's tattooed quarterback, and four other players (some of whom had been found to have sold their Big Ten championship rings and other gear), but did permit them to finish the season and play in the Sugar Bowl. (This summer, in an attempt to satisfy NCAA investigators, Ohio State voluntarily vacated its football wins from last season, as well as its Sugar Bowl victory.) A different NCAA committee promulgated a rule banning symbols and messages in players' eye black—reportedly aimed at Pryor's controversial gesture of support for the pro quarterback Michael Vick, and at Bible verses inscribed in the eye black of the former Florida quarterback Tim Tebow.

The moral logic is hard to fathom: the NCAA bans personal messages on the bodies of the players, and penalizes players for trading their celebrity status for discounted tattoos—but it codifies precisely how and where commercial insignia from multinational corporations can be displayed on college players, for the financial benefit of the colleges. Last season, while the NCAA investigated him and his father for the recruiting fees they'd allegedly sought, Cam Newton compliantly wore at least 15 corporate logos—one on his jersey, four on his helmet visor, one on each wristband, one on his pants, six on his shoes, and one on the headband he wears under his helmet—as part of Auburn's $10.6 million deal with Under Armour.

"Restitution"

Obscure NCAA rules have bedeviled Scott Boras, the preeminent sports agent for Major League Baseball stars, in cases that may ultimately prove more threatening to the NCAA than Ed O'Bannon's antitrust suit. In 2008, Andrew Oliver, a sophomore pitcher for the Oklahoma State Cowboys, had been listed as the 12th-best professional prospect among sophomore players nationally. He decided to dismiss the two attorneys who had represented him out of high school, Robert and Tim Baratta, and retain Boras instead. Infuriated, the Barattas sent a spiteful letter to the NCAA. Oliver didn't learn about this until the night before he was scheduled to pitch in the regional final for a place in the College World Series, when an NCAA investigator showed up to question him in the presence of lawyers for Oklahoma State. The investigator also questioned his father, Dave, a truck driver.

Had Tim Baratta been present in their home when the Minnesota Twins offered $390,000 for Oliver to sign out of high school? A *yes* would mean trouble. While the NCAA did not forbid all professional advice—indeed, *Baseball America* used to publish the names of agents representing draft-likely underclassmen—NCAA Bylaw 12.3.2.1 prohibited actual negotiation with any professional team by an adviser, on pain of disqualification for the college athlete. The questioning lasted past midnight.

Just hours before the game was to start the next day, Oklahoma State officials summoned Oliver to tell him he would not be pitching. Only later did he learn that the university feared that by letting him play while the NCAA adjudicated his case, the university would open not only the baseball team but all other Oklahoma State teams to broad punishment under the NCAA's "restitution rule" (Bylaw 19.7), under which the NCAA threatens schools with sanctions if they obey any temporary court order benefiting a college athlete, should that order eventually be modified or removed. The baseball coach did not even let his ace tell his teammates the sad news in person. "He said, 'It's probably not a good idea for you to be at the game,'" Oliver recalls.

The Olivers went home to Ohio to find a lawyer. Rick Johnson, a solo practitioner specializing in legal ethics, was aghast that the Baratta brothers had turned in their own client to the NCAA, divulging attorney-client details likely to invite wrath upon Oliver. But for the next 15 months, Johnson directed his litigation against the two NCAA bylaws at issue. Judge Tygh M. Tone, of Erie County, came to share his outrage. On February 12, 2009, Tone struck down the ban on lawyers negotiating for student-athletes as a capricious, exploitative attempt by a private association to "dictate to an attorney where, what, how, or when he should represent his client," violating accepted legal practice in every state. He also struck down the NCAA's restitution rule as an intimidation that attempted to supersede the judicial system. Finally, Judge Tone ordered the NCAA to reinstate Oliver's eligibility at Oklahoma State for his junior season, which started several days later.

The NCAA sought to disqualify Oliver again, with several appellate motions to stay "an unprecedented Order purporting to void a fundamental Bylaw." Oliver did get to pitch that season, but he dropped into the second round of the June 2009 draft, signing for considerably less than if he'd been picked earlier. Now 23, Oliver says sadly that the whole experience "made me grow up a little quicker." His lawyer claimed victory. "Andy Oliver is the first college athlete ever to win against the NCAA in court," said Rick Johnson.

Yet the victory was only temporary. Wounded, the NCAA fought back with a vengeance. Its battery of lawyers prepared for a damages trial, ultimately overwhelming Oliver's side eight months later with an offer to resolve the dispute for $750,000. When Oliver and Johnson accepted, to extricate themselves ahead of burgeoning legal costs, Judge Tone was compelled to vacate his orders as part of the final settlement. This freed NCAA officials to reassert the two bylaws that Judge Tone had so forcefully overturned, and they moved swiftly to ramp up rather than curtail enforcement. First, the NCAA's Eligibility Center devised a survey for every drafted undergraduate athlete who sought to stay in college another year. The survey asked whether an agent had conducted negotiations. It also requested a signed release waiving privacy rights and authorizing professional teams to disclose details of any interaction to the NCAA Eligibility Center. Second, NCAA enforcement officials went after another Scott Boras client.

The Toronto Blue Jays had made the left-handed pitcher James Paxton, of the University of Kentucky, the 37th pick in the 2009 draft. Paxton decided to reject a reported $1 million offer and return to school for his senior year, pursuing a dream to pitch for his team in the College World Series. But then he ran into the new NCAA survey. Had Boras negotiated with the Blue Jays? Boras has denied that he did, but it would have made sense that he had—that was his job, to test the market for his client. But saying so would get Paxton banished under the same NCAA bylaw that had derailed Andrew Oliver's career. Since Paxton was planning to go back to school and not accept their draft offer, the Blue Jays no longer had any incentive to protect him—indeed, they had every incentive to turn him in. The Blue Jays' president, by telling reporters that Boras had negotiated on Paxton's behalf, demonstrated to future recruits and other teams that they could use the NCAA's rules to punish college players who wasted their draft picks by returning to college. The NCAA's enforcement staff raised the pressure by requesting to interview Paxton.

Though Paxton had no legal obligation to talk to an investigator, NCAA Bylaw 10.1(j) specified that anything short of complete cooperation could be interpreted as unethical conduct, affecting his amateur status. Under its restitution rule, the NCAA had leverage to compel the University of Kentucky to ensure obedience.

As the 2010 season approached, Gary Henderson, the Kentucky coach, sorely wanted Paxton, one of *Baseball America's* top-ranked players, to return. Rick Johnson, Andrew Oliver's lawyer, filed for a declaratory judgment on Paxton's behalf, arguing that the state constitution—plus the university's code of student conduct—barred arbitrary discipline at the request of a third party. Kentucky courts deferred to the university, however, and Paxton was suspended from the team. "Due to the possibility of future penalties, including forfeiture of games," the university stated, it "could not put the other 32 players of the team and the entire UK 22-sport intercollegiate athletics department at risk by having James compete." The NCAA appraised the result with satisfaction. "When negotiations occur on behalf of student-athletes,"

Erik Christianson, the NCAA spokesperson, told *The New York Times* in reference to the Oliver case, "those negotiations indicate that the student-athlete intends to become a professional athlete and no longer remain an amateur."

Paxton was stranded. Not only could he not play for Kentucky, but his draft rights with the Blue Jays had lapsed for the year, meaning he could not play for any minor-league affiliate of Major League Baseball. Boras wrangled a holdover job for him in Texas with the independent Grand Prairie Air-Hogs, pitching against the Pensacola Pelicans and Wichita Wingnuts. Once projected to be a first-round draft pick, Paxton saw his stock plummet into the fourth round. He remained unsigned until late in spring training, when he signed with the Seattle Mariners and reported to their minor-league camp in Peoria, Arizona.

"You Might as Well Shoot Them in the Head"

"When you dream about playing in college," Joseph Agnew told me not long ago, "you don't ever think about being in a lawsuit." Agnew, a student at Rice University in Houston, had been cut from the football team and had his scholarship revoked by Rice before his senior year, meaning that he faced at least $35,000 in tuition and other bills if he wanted to complete his degree in sociology. Bereft of his scholarship, he was flailing about for help when he discovered the National College Players Association, which claims 7,000 active members and seeks modest reforms such as safety guidelines and better death benefits for college athletes. Agnew was struck by the NCPA scholarship data on players from top Division I basketball teams, which showed that 22 percent were not renewed from 2008 to 2009—the same fate he had suffered.

In October 2010, Agnew filed a class action antitrust suit over the cancellation of his scholarship and to remove the cap on the total number of scholarships that can be awarded by NCAA schools. In his suit, Agnew did not claim the right to free tuition. He merely asked the federal court to strike down an NCAA rule, dating to 1973, that prohibited colleges and universities from offering any athletic scholarship longer than a one-year commitment, to be renewed or not, unilaterally, by the school—which in practice means that coaches get to decide each year whose scholarships to renew or cancel. (After the coach who had recruited Agnew had moved on to Tulsa, the new Rice coach switched Agnew's scholarship to a recruit of his own.) Agnew argued that without the one-year rule, he would have been free to bargain with all eight colleges that had recruited him, and each college could have decided how long to guarantee his scholarship.

Agnew's suit rested on a claim of an NCAA antitrust violation combined with a laudable academic goal—making it possible for students to finish their educations.

Around the same time, lawyers from President Obama's Justice Department initiated a series of meetings with NCAA officials and universities in which they asked what possible educational rationale there was for allowing the NCAA—an organization that did not itself pay for scholarships—to impose a blanket restriction on the length of scholarships offered by colleges. Tidbits leaked into the press. In response, the NCAA contended that an athletic scholarship was a "merit award" that should be reviewed annually, presumably because the degree of "merit" could change. Justice Department lawyers reportedly suggested that a free market in scholarships would expand learning opportunities in accord with the stated rationale for the NCAA's tax-exempt status— that it promotes education through athletics. The one-year rule effectively allows colleges to cut underperforming "student-athletes," just as pro sports teams cut their players. "Plenty of them don't stay in school," said one of Agnew's lawyers, Stuart Paynter. "They're just gone. You might as well shoot them in the head."

Agnew's lawsuit has made him a pariah to former friends in the athletic department at Rice, where everyone identified so thoroughly with the NCAA that they seemed to feel he was attacking them personally. But if the premise of Agnew's case is upheld by the courts, it will make a sham of the NCAA's claim that its highest priority is protecting education.

"They Want to Crush These Kids"

Academic performance has always been difficult for the NCAA to address. Any detailed regulation would intrude upon the free choice of widely varying schools, and any academic standard broad enough to fit both MIT and Ole Miss would have little force. From time to time, a scandal will expose extreme lapses. In 1989, Dexter Manley, by then the famous "Secretary of Defense" for the NFL's Washington Redskins, teared up before the U.S. Senate Subcommittee on Education, Arts, and Humanities, when admitting that he had been functionally illiterate in college.

Within big-time college athletic departments, the financial pressure to disregard obvious academic shortcomings and shortcuts is just too strong. In the 1980s, Jan Kemp, an English instructor at the University of Georgia, publicly alleged that university officials had demoted and then fired her because she refused to inflate grades in her remedial English courses. Documents showed that administrators replaced the grades she'd given athletes with higher ones, providing fake passing grades on one notable occasion to nine Bulldog football players who otherwise would have been ineligible to compete in the 1982 Sugar Bowl. (Georgia lost anyway, 24–20, to a University of Pittsburgh team led by the future Hall of Fame quarterback Dan Marino.) When Kemp filed a lawsuit against the university, she was publicly vilified as a troublemaker, but she persisted bravely in her testimony. Once, Kemp said, a supervisor demanding that she fix a grade had bellowed, "Who do you think is more important to this university, you or Dominique Wilkins?" (Wilkins was a star on the basketball team.) Traumatized, Kemp twice attempted suicide.

In trying to defend themselves, Georgia officials portrayed Kemp as naive about sports. "We have to compete on a level playing field," said Fred Davison, the university president. During the Kemp civil trial, in 1986, Hale Almand, Georgia's defense lawyer, explained the university's patronizing aspirations for its typical less-than-scholarly athlete. "We may not make a university student out of him," Almand told the court, "but if we can teach him to read and write, maybe he can work at the post office rather than as a garbage man when he gets through with his athletic career." This argument backfired with the jurors: finding in favor of Kemp, they rejected her polite request for $100,000, and awarded her $2.6 million in damages instead. (This was later reduced to $1.08 million.) Jan Kemp embodied what is ostensibly the NCAA's reason for being—to enforce standards fairly and put studies above sports—but no one from the organization ever spoke up on her behalf.

ℛℰℭ℃ℰℭ℃ℰℱ

The NCAA body charged with identifying violations of any of the Division I league rules, the Committee on Infractions, operates in the shadows. Josephine Potuto, a professor of law at the University of Nebraska and a longtime committee member who was then serving as its vice chair, told Congress in 2004 that one reason her group worked in secret was that it hoped to avoid a "media circus." The committee preferred to deliberate in private, she said, guiding member schools to punish themselves. "The enforcement process is cooperative, not adversarial," Potuto testified. The committee consisted of an elite coterie of judges, athletic directors, and authors of legal treatises. "The committee also is savvy about intercollegiate athletics," she added. "They cannot be conned."

In 2009, a series of unlikely circumstances peeled back the veil of secrecy to reveal NCAA procedures so contorted that even victims marveled at their comical wonder. The saga began in March of 2007, shortly after the Florida State Seminoles basketball team was knocked out of the NIT basketball tournament, which each spring invites the best teams not selected for the March Madness tournament. At an athletic-department study hall, Al Thornton, a star forward for the team, completed a sports-psychology quiz but then abandoned it without posting his written answers electronically by computer. Brenda Monk, an academic tutor for the Seminoles, says she noticed the error and asked a teammate to finish entering Thornton's answers onscreen and hit "submit," as required for credit. The teammate complied, steaming silently, and then complained at the athletic office about getting stuck with clean-up chores for the superstar Thornton (who was soon to be selected by the Los Angeles Clippers in the first round of the NBA draft). Monk promptly resigned when questioned by FSU officials, saying her fatigue at the time could not excuse her asking the teammate to submit the answers to another student's completed test.

Monk's act of guileless responsibility set off a chain reaction. First, FSU had to give the NCAA preliminary notice of a confessed academic fraud. Second, because this would be its seventh major infraction case since 1968, FSU mounted a vigorous self-investigation to demonstrate compliance with NCAA academic rules. Third, interviews with 129 Seminoles athletes unleashed a nightmare of matter-of-fact replies about absentee professors who allowed group consultations and unlimited retakes of open-computer assignments and tests. Fourth, FSU suspended 61 of its athletes in 10 sports. Fifth, the infractions committee applied the byzantine NCAA bylaws to FSU's violations. Sixth, one of the penalties announced in March of 2009 caused a howl of protest across the sports universe.

Twenty-seven news organizations filed a lawsuit in hopes of finding out how and why the NCAA proposed to invalidate 14 prior victories in FSU football. Such a penalty, if upheld, would doom coach Bobby Bowden's chance of overtaking Joe Paterno of Penn State for the most football wins in Division I history. This was sacrosanct territory. Sports reporters followed the litigation for six months, reporting that 25 of the 61 suspended FSU athletes were football players, some of whom were ruled ineligible retroactively from the time they had heard or yelled out answers to online test questions in, of all things, a music-appreciation course.

When reporters sought access to the transcript of the infractions committee's hearing in Indianapolis, NCAA lawyers said the 695-page document was private. (The NCAA claimed it was entitled to keep all such records secret because of a landmark Supreme Court ruling that it had won in 1988, in *NCAA V. Tarkanian,* which exempted the organization from any due-process obligations because it was not a government organization.) Media outlets pressed the judge to let Florida State share its own copy of the hearing transcript, whereupon NCAA lawyers objected that the school had never actually "possessed" the document; it had only seen the transcript via a defendant's guest access to the carefully restricted NCAA website. This claim, in turn, prompted intercession on the side of the media by Florida's attorney general, arguing that letting the NCAA use a technical loophole like this would undermine the state's sunshine law mandating open public records. After tumultuous appeals, the Florida courts agreed and ordered the NCAA transcript released in October of 2009.

News interest quickly evaporated when the sports media found nothing in the record about Coach Bowden or the canceled football victories. But the transcript revealed plenty about the NCAA. On page 37, T. K. Wetherell, the bewildered Florida State president, lamented that his university had hurt itself by cooperating with the investigation. "We self-reported this case," he said during the hearing, and he later complained that the most ingenuous athletes—those who asked "What's the big deal, this happens all the time?"—received the harshest suspensions, while those who clammed up on the advice of lawyers went free. The music-appreciation professor was apparently never questioned. Brenda Monk, the only instructor who consistently cooperated with the investigation, appeared voluntarily to explain her work with learning-disabled athletes, only to be grilled about her credentials by Potuto in a pettifogging inquisition of remarkable stamina.

In January of last year, the NCAA's Infractions Appeals Committee sustained all the sanctions imposed on FSU except the number of vacated football victories, which it dropped, ex cathedra, from 14 to 12. The final penalty locked Bobby Bowden's official win total on retirement at 377 instead of 389, behind Joe Paterno's 401 (and counting). This carried stinging symbolism for fans, without bringing down on the NCAA the harsh repercussions it would have risked if it had issued a television ban or substantial fine.

Cruelly, but typically, the NCAA concentrated public censure on powerless scapegoats. A dreaded "show cause" order rendered Brenda Monk, the tutor, effectively unhirable at any college in the United States. Cloaking an old-fashioned blackball in the stately language of law, the order gave notice that any school hiring Monk before a specified date in 2013 "shall, pursuant to the provisions of Bylaw 19.5.2.2(1), show cause why it should not be penalized if it does not restrict the former learning specialist [Monk] from having any contact with student-athletes." Today she works as an education supervisor at a prison in Florida.

CRITICS

The Florida State verdict hardly surprised Rick Johnson, the lawyer who had represented the college pitchers Andrew Oliver and James Paxton. "All the NCAA's enforcements are random and selective," he told me, calling the organization's appeals process a travesty. (Johnson says the NCAA has never admitted to having wrongly suspended an athlete.) Johnson's scalding experience prompted him to undertake a law-review article on the subject, which in turn sent him trawling through NCAA archives. From the summary tax forms required of nonprofits, he found out that the NCAA had spent nearly $1 million chartering private jets in 2006. "What kind of nonprofit organization leases private jets?," Johnson asks. It's hard to determine from tax returns what money goes where, but it looks as if the NCAA spent less than 1 percent of its budget on enforcement that year. Even after its plump cut for its own overhead, the NCAA dispersed huge sums to its 1,200 member schools, in the manner of a professional sports league. These annual payments are universal—every college gets something—but widely uneven. They keep the disparate shareholders (barely) united and speaking for all of college sports. The payments coerce unity within the structure of a private association that is unincorporated and unregulated, exercising amorphous powers not delegated by any government.

Searching through the archives, Johnson came across a 1973 memo from the NCAA general counsel recommending the adoption of a due-process procedure for athletes in disciplinary cases. Without it, warned the organization's lawyer, the association risked big liability claims for deprivation of rights. His proposal went nowhere. Instead, apparently to limit costs to the universities, Walter Byers had implemented the year-by-year scholarship rule that Joseph Agnew would challenge in court 37 years later. Moreover, the NCAA's 1975 convention adopted a second recommendation "to discourage legal actions against the NCAA," according to the minutes. The members voted to create Bylaw 19.7, Restitution, to intimidate college athletes in disputes with the NCAA. Johnson recognized this provision all too well, having won the temporary court judgment that the rule was illegal if not downright despotic. It made him nearly apoplectic to learn that the NCAA had deliberately drawn up the restitution rule as an obstacle to due process, contrary to the recommendation of its own lawyer. "They want to crush these kids," he says.

The NCAA, of course, has never expressed such a desire, and its public comments on due process tend to be anodyne. At a congressional hearing in 2004, the infractions committee vice chair, Josephine Potuto, repeatedly argued that although the NCAA is "not bound by any judicial due process standards," its enforcement, infractions, and hearing procedures meet and "very likely exceed" those of other public institutions. Yet when pressed, Potuto declared that athletes would have no standing for due process even if the Supreme Court had not exempted the NCAA in the 1988 *Tarkanian* decision. "In order to reach due-process issues as a legal Constitutional principle, the individual challenging has to have a substantive property or liberty interest," she testified. "The opportunity to play intercollegiate athletics does not rise to that level."

To translate this from the legal jargon, Potuto used a circular argument to confine college athletes beneath any right to freedom or property in their own athletic effort. They have no stake to seek their rights, she claimed, because they have no rights at stake.

Potuto's assertion might be judged preposterous, an heir of the *Dred Scott* dictum that slaves possessed no rights a white person was bound to respect. But she was merely being honest, articulating assumptions almost everyone shares without question. Whether motivated by hostility for students (as critics like Johnson allege), or by noble and paternalistic tough love (as the NCAA professes), the denial of fundamental due process for college athletes has stood unchallenged in public discourse. Like other NCAA rules, it emanates naturally from the premise that college athletes own no interest in sports beyond exercise, character-building, and good fun. Who represents these young men and women? No one asks. The debates and commissions about reforming college sports nibble around the edges—trying to reduce corruption, to prevent the "contamination" of athletes by lucre, and to maintain at least a pretense of concern for academic integrity. Everything stands on the implicit presumption that preserving amateurism is necessary for the well-being of college athletes. But while amateurism—and the free labor it provides—may be necessary to the preservation of the NCAA, and perhaps to the profit margins of various interested corporations and educational institutions, what if it doesn't benefit the athletes? What if it hurts them?

"The Plantation Mentality"

"Ninety percent of the NCAA revenue is produced by 1 percent of the athletes," Sonny Vaccaro says. "Go to the skill positions"—the stars. "Ninety percent African Americans." The NCAA made its money off those kids, and so did he. They were not all bad people, the NCAA officials, but they were blind, Vaccaro believes. "Their organization is a fraud."

Vaccaro retired from Reebok in 2007 to make a clean break for a crusade. "The kids and their parents gave me a good life," he says in his peppery staccato. "I want to give something back." Call it redemption, he told me. Call it education or a good cause. "Here's what I preach," said Vaccaro. "This goes beyond race, to human rights. The least educated are the most exploited. I'm probably closer to the kids than anyone else, and I'm 71 years old."

Vaccaro is officially an unpaid consultant to the plaintiffs in *O'Bannon v. NCAA*. He connected Ed O'Bannon with the attorneys who now represent him, and he talked to some of the additional co-plaintiffs who have joined the suit, among them Oscar Robertson, a basketball Hall of Famer who was incensed that the NCAA was still selling his image on playing cards 50 years after be left the University of Cincinnati.

Jon King, an antitrust lawyer at Hausfeld LLP in San Francisco, told me that Vaccaro "opened our eyes to massive revenue streams hidden in college sports." King and his colleagues have drawn on Vaccaro's vast knowledge of athletic-department finances, which include off-budget accounts for shoe contracts. Sonny Vaccaro and his wife, Pam, "had a mountain of documents," he said. The outcome of the 1984 *Regents* decision validated an antitrust approach for O'Bannon, King argues, as well as for Joseph Agnew in his continuing case against the one-year scholarship rule. Lawyers for Sam Keller—a former quarterback for the University of Nebraska who is featured in video games—are pursuing a parallel "right of publicity" track based on the First Amendment. Still other lawyers could revive Rick Johnson's case against NCAA bylaws on a larger scale, and King thinks claims for the rights of college players may be viable also under laws pertaining to contracts, employment, and civil rights.

Vaccaro had sought a law firm for O'Bannon with pockets deep enough to withstand an expensive war of attrition, fearing that NCAA officials would fight discovery to the end. So far, though, they have been forthcoming. "The numbers are off the wall," Vaccaro says. "The public will see for the first time how all the money is distributed."

Vaccaro has been traveling the after-dinner circuit, proselytizing against what he sees as the NCAA's exploitation of young athletes. Late in 2008, someone who heard his stump speech at Howard University mentioned it to Michael Hausfeld, a prominent antitrust and human-rights lawyer, whose firm had won suits against Exxon for Native Alaskans and against Union Bank of Switzerland for Holocaust victims' families. Someone tracked down Vaccaro on vacation in Athens, Greece, and he flew back directly to meet Hausfeld. The shoe salesman and the white-shoe lawyer made common cause.

Hausfeld LLP has offices in San Francisco, Philadelphia, and London. Its headquarters are on K Street in Washington, D.C., about three blocks from the White House. When I talked with Hausfeld there not long ago, he sat in a cavernous conference room, tidy in pinstripes, hands folded on a spotless table that reflected the skyline. He spoke softly, without pause, condensing the complex fugue of antitrust litigation into simple sentences. "Let's start with the basic question," he said, noting that the NCAA claims that student-athletes have no property rights in their own athletic accomplishments. Yet, in order to be eligible to play, college athletes have to waive their rights to proceeds from any sales based on their athletic performance.

"What right is it that they're waiving?," Hausfeld asked. "You can't waive something you don't have. So they had a right that they gave up in consideration to the principle of amateurism, if there be such." (At an April hearing in a U.S. District Court in California, Gregory Curtner, a representative for the NCAA, stunned O'Bannon's lawyers by saying: "There is no document, there is no substance, that the NCAA ever takes from the student-athletes their rights of publicity or their rights of likeness. They are at all times owned by the student-athlete." Jon King says this is "like telling someone they have the winning lottery ticket, but by the way, it can only be cashed in on Mars." The court denied for a second time an NCAA motion to dismiss the O'Bannon complaint.)

The waiver clause is nestled among the paragraphs of the "Student-Athlete Statement" that NCAA rules require be collected yearly from every college athlete. In signing the statement, the athletes attest that they have amateur status, that their stated SAT scores are valid, that they are willing to disclose any educational documents requested, and so forth. Already, Hausfeld said, the defendants in the Ed O'Bannon case have said in court filings that college athletes thereby transferred their promotional rights forever. He paused. "That's ludicrous," he said. "Nobody assigns rights like that. Nobody can assert rights like that." He said the pattern demonstrated clear abuse by the collective power of the schools and all their conferences under the NCAA umbrella—"a most effective cartel."

The faux ideal of amateurism is "the elephant in the room," Hausfeld said, sending for a book. "You can't get to the bottom of our case without exposing the hypocrisy of amateurism, and Walter Byers says it eloquently." An assistant brought in Byers's memoir. It looked garish on the shiny table because dozens of pink Post-its protruded from the text. Hausfeld read to me from page 390:

> The college player cannot sell his own feet (the coach does that) nor can he sell his own name (the college will do that). This is the plantation mentality resurrected and blessed by today's campus executives.

He looked up. "That wasn't me," he said. "That was the NCAA's architect." He found a key recommendation on page 388:

> Prosecutors and the courts, with the support of the public, should use antitrust laws to break up the collegiate cartel—not just in athletics but possibly in other aspects of collegiate life as well.

Could the book become evidence? Might the aged Byers testify? (He is now 89.) Was that part of the plaintiffs' strategy for the O'Bannon trial? Hausfeld smiled faintly. "I'd rather the NCAA lawyers not fully understand the strategy," he said.

He put the spiny book away and previewed what lies ahead. The court soon would qualify his clients as a class. Then the Sherman Antitrust Act would provide for thorough discovery to break down exactly what the NCAA receives on everything from video clips to jerseys, contract by contract. "And we want to know what they're carrying on their books as the value of their archival footage," he concluded. "They say it's a lot of money. We agree. How much?"

The work will be hard, but Hausfeld said he will win in the courts, unless the NCAA folds first. "Why?" Hausfeld asked rhetorically. "We know our clients are foreclosed: neither the NCAA nor its members will permit them to participate in any of that licensing revenue. Under the law, it's up to them [the defendants] to give a precompetitive justification. They can't. End of story."

CRISOCRISOCRISO

In 2010 the third Knight Commission, complementing a previous commission's recommendation for published reports on academic progress, called for the finances of college sports to be made transparent and public—television contracts, conference budgets, shoe deals, coaches' salaries, stadium bonds, everything. The recommendation was based on the worthy truism that sunlight is a proven disinfectant. But in practice, it has not been applied at all. Conferences, coaches, and other stakeholders resisted disclosure; college players still have no way of determining their value to the university.

"Money surrounds college sports," says Domonique Foxworth, who is a cornerback for the NFL's Baltimore Ravens and an executive-committee member for the NFL Players Association, and played for the University of Maryland. "And every player knows those millions are floating around only because of the 18-to-22-year-olds." Yes, he told me, even the second-string punter believes a miracle might lift him into the NFL, and why not? In all the many pages of the three voluminous Knight Commission reports, there is but one paragraph that addresses the real-life choices for college athletes. "Approximately 1 percent of NCAA men's basketball players and 2 percent of NCAA football players are drafted by NBA or NFL teams," stated the 2001 report, basing its figures on a review of the previous 10 years, "and just being drafted is no assurance of a successful professional career." Warning that the odds against professional athletic success are "astronomically high," the Knight Commission counsels college athletes to avoid a "rude surprise" and to stick to regular studies. This is sound advice as far as it goes, but it's a bromide that pinches off discussion. Nothing in the typical college curriculum teaches a sweat-stained guard at Clemson or Purdue what his monetary value to the university is. Nothing prods students to think independently about amateurism—because the universities themselves have too much invested in its preservation. Stifling thought, the universities, in league with the NCAA, have failed their own primary mission by providing an empty, cynical education on college sports.

The most basic reform would treat the students as what they are—adults, with rights and reason of their own—and grant them a meaningful voice in NCAA deliberations. A restoration of full citizenship to "student-athletes" would facilitate open governance, making it possible to enforce pledges of transparency in both academic standards and athletic finances. Without that, the NCAA has no effective checks and balances, no way for the students to provide informed consent regarding the way they are governed. A thousand questions lie willfully silenced because the NCAA is naturally afraid of giving "student-athletes" a true voice. Would college players be content with the augmented scholarship or allowance now requested by the National College Players Association? If a player's worth to the university is greater than the value of his scholarship (as it clearly is in some cases), should he be paid a salary? If so, would teammates in revenue sports want to be paid equally, or in salaries stratified according to talent or value on the field? What would the athletes want in Division III, where athletic budgets keep rising without scholarships or substantial sports revenue? Would athletes seek more or less variance in admissions standards? Should non-athletes also have a voice, especially where involuntary student fees support more and more of college sports? Might some schools choose to specialize, paying players only in elite leagues for football, or lacrosse? In athletic councils, how much would high-revenue athletes value a simple *thank you* from the tennis or field-hockey players for the newly specified subsidies to their facilities?

University administrators, already besieged from all sides, do not want to even think about such questions. Most cringe at the thought of bargaining with athletes as a general manager does in professional sports, with untold effects on the budgets for coaches and every other sports item. "I would not want to be part of it," North Carolina Athletic Director Dick Baddour told me flatly. After 44 years at UNC, he could scarcely contemplate a world without amateur rules. "We would have to think long and hard," Baddour added gravely, "about whether this university would continue those sports at all."

I, too, once reflexively recoiled at the idea of paying college athletes and treating them like employees or professionals. It feels abhorrent—but for reasons having to do more with sentiment than with practicality or law. Not just fans and university presidents but judges have often found cursory, non-statutory excuses to leave amateur traditions intact. "Even in the increasingly commercial modern world," said a federal-court judge in *Gaines v. NCAA* in 1990, "this Court believes there is still validity to the Athenian concept of a complete education derived from fostering the full growth of both mind and body." The fact that "the NCAA has not distilled amateurism to its purest form," said the Fifth Circuit Court of Appeals in 1988, "does not mean its attempts to maintain a mixture containing some amateur elements are unreasonable."

But one way or another, the smokescreen of amateurism may soon be swept away. For one thing, a victory by the plaintiffs in O'Bannon's case would radically transform college sports. Colleges would likely have to either stop profiting from students or start paying them. The NCAA could also be forced to pay tens, if not hundreds, of millions of dollars in damages. If O'Bannon and Vaccaro and company win, "it will turn college sports on its ear," said Richard Lapchick, the president of the National Consortium for Academics and Sports, in a recent interview with *The New York Times*.

Though the O'Bannon case may take several years yet to reach resolution, developments on other fronts are chipping away at amateurism, and at the NCAA. This past summer, *Sports Illustrated* editorialized in favor of allowing college athletes to be paid by non-university sources without jeopardizing their eligibility. At a press conference last June, Steve Spurrier, the coach of the South Carolina Gamecocks football team (and the winner of the 1966 Heisman Trophy as a Florida Gator), proposed that coaches start paying players $300 a game out of their own pockets. The coaches at six other SEC schools (Alabama, Florida, Ole Miss, Mississippi State, LSU, and Tennessee) all endorsed Spurrier's proposal. And Mark Emmert, the NCAA president, recently conceded that big changes must come. "The integrity of collegiate athletics is seriously challenged today by rapidly growing pressures coming from many directions," Emmert said in July. "We have reached a point where incremental change is not sufficient to meet these challenges. I want us to act more aggressively and in a more comprehensive way than we have in the past. A few new tweaks of the rules won't get the job done."

Threats to NCAA dominion also percolate in Congress. Aggrieved legislators have sponsored numerous bills. Senator Orrin Hatch, citing mistreatment of his Utah Utes, has called witnesses to discuss possible antitrust remedies for the Bowl Championship Series. Congressional committees have already held hearings critical of the NCAA's refusal to follow due process in disciplinary matters; other committees have explored a rise in football concussions. Last January, calls went up to investigate "informal" football workouts at the University of Iowa just after the season-ending bowl games—workouts so grueling that 41 of the 56 amateur student-athletes collapsed, and 13 were hospitalized with rhabdomyolysis, a life-threatening kidney condition often caused by excessive exercise.

The greatest threat to the viability of the NCAA may come from its member universities. Many experts believe that the churning instability within college football will drive the next major change. President Obama himself has endorsed the drumbeat cry for a national playoff in college football. This past spring, the Justice Department questioned the BCS about its adherence to antitrust standards. Jim Delany, the commissioner of the Big Ten, has estimated that a national playoff system could produce three or four times as much money as the existing bowl system does. If a significant band of football schools were to demonstrate that they could orchestrate a true national playoff, without the NCAA's assistance, the association would be terrified—and with good reason. Because if the big sports colleges don't need the NCAA to administer a national playoff in football, then they don't need it to do so in basketball. In which case, they could cut out the middleman in March Madness and run the tournament themselves. Which would deprive the NCAA of close to $1 billion a year, more than 95 percent of its revenue. The organization would be reduced to a rule book without money—an organization aspiring to enforce its rules but without the financial authority to enforce anything.

Thus the playoff dreamed of and hankered for by millions of football fans haunts the NCAA. "There will be some kind of playoff in college football, and it will not be run by the NCAA," says Todd Turner, a former athletic director in four conferences (Big East, ACC, SEC, and Pac-10). "If I'm at the NCAA, I have to worry that the playoff group can get basketball to break away, too."

This danger helps explain why the NCAA steps gingerly in enforcements against powerful colleges. To alienate member colleges would be to jeopardize its own existence. Long gone are television bans and the "death penalty" sentences (commanding season-long shutdowns of offending teams) once meted out to Kentucky (1952), Southwestern Louisiana (1973), and Southern Methodist University (1987). Institutions receive mostly symbolic slaps nowadays. Real punishments fall heavily on players and on scapegoats like literacy tutors.

A deeper reason explains why, in its predicament, the NCAA has no recourse to any principle or law that can justify amateurism. There is no such thing. Scholars and sportswriters yearn for grand juries to ferret out every forbidden bauble that reaches a college athlete, but the NCAA's ersatz courts can only masquerade as public authority. How could any statute impose *amateur* status on college athletes, or on anyone else? No legal definition of amateur exists, and any attempt to create one in enforceable law would expose its repulsive and unconstitutional nature—a bill of attainder, stripping from college athletes the rights of American citizenship.

CRISO CRISO CRISO

For all our queasiness about what would happen if some athletes were to get paid, there is a successful precedent for the professionalization of an amateur sports system: the Olympics. For years, Walter Byers waged war with the NCAA's older and more powerful nemesis, the Amateur Athletic Union, which since 1894 had overseen U.S. Olympic athletes. Run in high-handed fashion, the AAU had infamously banned Jesse Owens for life in 1936—weeks after his four heroic gold medals punctured the Nazi claim of Aryan supremacy—because instead of using his sudden fame to tour and make money for the AAU at track meets across Europe, he came home early. In the early 1960s, the fights between the NCAA and the AAU over who should manage Olympic athletes become so bitter that President Kennedy called in General Douglas MacArthur to try to mediate a truce before the Tokyo Olympic Games.

Ultimately, Byers prevailed and effectively neutered the AAU. In November 1978, President Jimmy Carter signed the bipartisan Amateur Sports Act. Amateurism in the Olympics soon dissolved—and the world did not end. Athletes, granted a 20 percent voting stake on every Olympic sport's governing body, tipped balances in the United States and then inexorably around the world. First in marathon races, then in tennis tournaments, players soon were allowed to accept prize money and keep their Olympic eligibility. Athletes profited from sponsorships and endorsements. The International Olympic Committee expunged the word *amateur* from its charter in 1986. Olympic officials, who had once disdained the NCAA for offering scholarships in exchange for athletic performance, came to welcome millionaire athletes from every quarter, while the NCAA still refused to let the pro Olympian Michael Phelps swim for his college team at Michigan.

This sweeping shift left the Olympic reputation intact, and perhaps improved. Only hardened romantics mourned the amateur code. "Hey, come on," said Anne Audain, a track-and-field star who once held the world record for the 5,000 meters. "It's like losing your virginity. You're a little misty for awhile, but then you realize. *Wow, there's a whole new world out there!*"

Without logic or practicality or fairness to support amateurism, the NCAA's final retreat is to sentiment. The Knight Commission endorsed its heartfelt cry that to pay college athletes would be "an unacceptable surrender to despair." Many of the people I spoke with while reporting this article felt the same way. "I don't want to pay college players," said Wade Smith, a tough criminal lawyer and former star running back at North Carolina. "I just don't want to do it. We'd lose something precious."

"Scholarship athletes are already paid," declared the Knight Commission members, "in the most meaningful way possible: with a free education." This evasion by prominent educators severed my last reluctant, emotional tie with imposed amateurism. I found it worse than self-serving. It echoes masters who once claimed that heavenly salvation would outweigh earthly injustice to slaves. In the era when our college sports first arose, colonial powers were turning the whole world upside down to define their own interests as all-inclusive and benevolent. Just so, the NCAA calls it heinous exploitation to pay college athletes a fair portion of what they earn.

Credit _____

Branch, Taylor. "The Shame of College Sports." *The Atlantic*, Oct 2011:80–110. © 2011 The Atlantic Media Co., as first published in *The Atlantic Magazine*. All rights reserved. Distributed by Tribune Content Agency, LLC.

Unit 3

Urban Growth and Renewal

As Cleveland evolves to accommodate new industries, social realities, and challenges, our conceptualization of both our community and its people must similarly evolve to incorporate these and other developments. Discussions of how the new millennium will change our understanding of the American city must include myriad questions of race, class, policy, sustainability, history, logistics, and economics. The modern perception of America's urban centers is constantly shifting, and yet it is eternally bound to dichotomies between economy and creativity, between personal security and public prosperity, between a philosophy of comfort at any cost and a celebration of diversity, equality, and opportunity for all.

More now than ever before, the role of the citizen is key in shaping the image and forms of city life. Even as Cleveland and other cities have been forced to either advance new policies or be relegated to a long, painful decline into poverty and obsolescence, the rise of "engaged" residents has birthed some of the most influential, significant changes to our city and our way of life. The past organic, industrial growth of downtown Cleveland and its outlying communities has given way to a structured, neighborhood-centric model, and we as engaged members of the public must understand that old models based on the manufacturing boomtowns of the 19th century and the unfettered economic growth of the 20th must give way to novel ideas, new opportunities, and updated definitions of civic responsibility.

In its time, our city has been known by many names—"The Sixth City," "The Mistake on the Lake," "The Comeback City"—yet however one views Cleveland's role in America's past and future, one thing is clear: it is a space, both physical and philosophical, that is always changing, under construction, moving. In order to move through a discourse on the challenges facing urban development both in Northeast Ohio and around the world, together we must redefine metropolitan landscapes and populations to reflect these ever-changing dynamics in innovative and exciting ways.

Engaging the City: Civic Participation and Teaching Urban History

Amy L. Howard

Amy L. Howard, who holds a Ph.D. in American Studies, is Executive Director of the Bonner Center for Civic Engagement at the University of Richmond. Much of Dr. Howard's scholarship focuses on urban history in the United States, especially as it relates to those disenfranchised by public policy and urban renewal. In her most recent book, More Than Shelter: Activism and Community in San Francisco Public Housing, *she sets out to challenge outdated perceptions of those living in urban poverty, arguing that opportunities to improve housing and living experiences can come from within struggling communities. Her article, "Engaging the City: Civic Participation and Teaching Urban History," first published in the* Journal of Urban History *in 2010, considers how urban studies courses can act as a productive bridge between students and the communities that house their universities.*

⊰❧⊱⊱❧⊰

In the last several years, "civic engagement" has become one of the buzzwords of American higher education, yet the notion that U.S. colleges and universities have an obligation to prepare students for lives of active citizenship and to produce knowledge that addresses societal needs is as old as the American academy itself.[1] Colonial colleges were created in part to educate "learned men" to bolster a fledging society. Religiously affiliated colleges worked to provide moral instruction for young citizens. Land-grant universities were founded to improve farming and instruct engineers. "Normal schools" opened their doors to train teachers to staff a growing public education system. Statewide extension services emerged after World War II, linking universities to the social and economic issues facing their states. As the Cold War intensified, universities used federal funds to support research on defense, health, and the sciences. Growing student activism in the 1960s, spurred by the civil rights movement, galvanized college students across the nation to tackle social problems.[2] Two decades later, faculty responded to community needs by starting to incorporate service-learning and community-based research into the curriculum. The quest for higher education institutions to realize their potential for the public good continues.

Through working in a campus-based center focused on local social issues and teaching an urban history course tied to a living-learning community, I have gained insight into the academy's ability to impact social change.

Urban colleges and universities with their proximity to social, cultural, political, economic, and health networks have established a wide range of outreach programs over the years. From the University of Chicago's School of Social Service Administration's work in local neighborhoods in the early twentieth century to Indiana University-Purdue University Indianapolis' creation in 1969 and subsequent outreach efforts, urban higher education institutions have trained professionals, provided applied research, and developed public service opportunities for local communities.[3] In recent years, urban colleges and universities have begun to promote community engagement more intentionally. Building on a history of outreach and student participation, institutions have embraced engaged citizenship—broadly defined—in mission statements, strategic plans, and resource allocation. A number of urban universities have expanded their work into community development. A prominent example of this trend was the University of Pennsylvania's partnership with the neighboring West Philadelphia district beginning in the late 1990s to rebuild the area's "social and economic capacity" by addressing housing, public education, safety, and economic development through research and financial commitment. A showcase of the partnership, a university-assisted public elementary school, opened in 2001.[4] Other colleges and universities have deepened their commitment to their local communities through the creation of new schools and centers. Tufts University launched an interdisciplinary College of Citizenship and Public Service to empower students, faculty, and alumni to be active leaders in their communities in 2000.[5] In 2005, Bates opened the Harward Center for Community Partnership's to support "teaching, research, artistic creation, environmental stewardship and volunteer service—that enrich community life."[6] The Carnegie Foundation for the Advancement of Teaching's addition, in 2006, of community engagement as a category in their elective classification system for higher education institutions registers this growing interest in civic engagement in the academy.[7]

As the emphasis on civic engagement in higher education continues, urban history courses have a central role to play in providing context, creating new knowledge, strengthening campus–community partnerships, and supporting student engagement. Urban historians teaching in or near city settings have myriad opportunities to connect their courses with their institution's local engagement efforts. Courses in urban history linking local and national trends provide an opportunity to leverage student learning and interest in the history of the city students call home for a few years as a means of generating research with impact and educating engaged citizens for the twenty-first century. Student (and faculty) research on the historical context and contours of the local area equips university and community leaders with important knowledge for making informed decisions about community and economic development and public service opportunities. With community-based courses, activities, and programs on the rise, urban historians and other educators have a range of tools to draw from, including literature on community-based research and service-learning, research funds targeted at those projects addressing local issues, and a growing national network of faculty, staff, and administrators committed to blending theory and practice through community-based learning.[8] New scholarship and networks have emerged along with a number of positions within higher education to coordinate and support the myriad ways individuals and campuses are engaging in local, national, and international communities.

Centering Engagement

Five years ago I stumbled into this world by accident. With my dissertation nearing completion, I began looking for positions. For personal reasons related to my family, I confined my job search to central Virginia.[9] After extensive research I applied for a position that stood out for me: working at the newly created Bonner Center for Civic Engagement (CCE) at the University of Richmond. Situated within the university's academic affairs division, and with a mission of connecting faculty, staff, and students to the metropolitan Richmond community to address social issues through action, reflection, and research, the center appealed to me. I was hired and soon jumped into a broad range of activities, including program planning, fellowship creation, and even looking at carpet samples for the center's new space. The collaborative experience of shaping the CCE from the ground up with the founding director has been incredibly rewarding. In this position I have combined my research and teaching interests in the history of cities and civic participation by low-income Americans with administrative duties focused on building sustained campus-community partnerships and educating students to, in the words of the university's mission statement, "live lives of purpose, thoughtful inquiry, and responsible leadership in a global and pluralistic society."[10] In my position I get to think about social change, to learn about the local community, and to work with students inside and outside the classroom. Serendipity landed me a great job.

The CCE grew out of a long tradition of student service at the University of Richmond. Building on community service days and the Bonner Scholars Program, started at the university in 1993 to fund one hundred students to engage in service and related educational and developmental experiences for ten hours a week, the university began talks with the Bonner Foundation about starting a center in 2002.[11] With the support of the president, provost, the Board of Trustees, and the Bonner Foundation, the university allocated a portion of Bonner Foundation endowment funds to support a new center dedicated to integrating civic engagement into a University of Richmond education.

As urban historians have demonstrated, location and design can influence perceptions of people and places.[12] The University of Richmond, located in the tony west end of Richmond with gothic-style buildings surrounded by lush green space and a lake, is fifteen minutes and a world away from the center city, which has a 20 percent poverty rate. A large endowment, high tuition rate, and proximity to a country club have contributed to the perception that the school is divorced from the city and focused on perpetuating class privilege by educating students from wealthy families.[13] While located within the city of Richmond, the university is associated with the upper-class neighborhoods of Henrico County near the campus.[14] In Virginia, state laws prevent annexation and call for separate city and county governments. As a result, regional silos have exacerbated disparities in public schools, housing, and wealth between Richmond and the surrounding counties.[15] Battling community misperceptions that the University of Richmond is insular and isolated, as well as challenging some of our students' assumptions that the city of Richmond is dangerous, impoverished, and uninteresting, comprises a key aspect of the CCE's work. We aim to combat stereotypes with substantive, meaningful, educationally grounded programs. With an urban historical frame undergirding many of our efforts, we have taken on the challenge of bursting the University of Richmond "bubble" by making the city an extension of the classroom.

The CCE has created a number of programs to connect the university with the city, to stimulate engagement, and to address community-identified needs while deepening connections with curricular and cocurricular learning. We have established numerous pathways to cultivate civic involvement. Each fall during orientation, 150 first-year students participate in UniverCity Day. This half-day program includes a bus tour of Richmond that introduces students to the city, past and present. As part of the tour, students stop at a nonprofit agency to hear about a social issue and ways to address it through research, internships, and service. Local leaders and faculty present on major issues facing the region. The discussions that UniverCity Day initiates continue throughout the year at weekly CCE brown bags where students, faculty, staff, and community leaders discuss local, national, and international social issues.

Other students take another step out of the "bubble" by signing on to join Build It, the university's largest community engagement initiative focused on sustained partnerships. The four-year-old program is designed to connect students, staff, and faculty to each other and to the residents of metropolitan Richmond through "community-based experiences that support both students' broad learning goals and local efforts to meet pressing social needs."[16] Participants, a number coming from community-based learning courses with a required service component, commit to work weekly at one of six partner sites in Richmond's Highland Park district as part of a sustained partnership with the community.[17] Other students join because they want to volunteer as part of their college experience, and the program provides a structured way for them to serve. Students in the Build It program attend an orientation session where they learn about the neighborhood's history as a middle-class street car suburb in the late nineteenth century, a white middle-class city district in the early 1940s, an African American middle-class district in the wake of white flight by mid-century, an increasingly poor African American neighborhood neglected by the city in the 1970s and 1980s, and, in recent decades, a community fighting crime, class divisions, and creeping gentrification.[18] The session also addresses issues of privilege, reciprocity, responsibility, and partnership. Throughout the school year, the CCE invites Build It participants (and the university community) to attend educational programs on topics such as public schools in Richmond, affordable housing, and payday lending, all to provide further context for their work and to make intentional links with coursework. During the past two years, the CCE has collaborated with our Build It community partners and other nonprofits on two large-scale projects: a campus-community fair held in Highland Park in 2007 and a four-way partnership to construct a historically accurate Habitat for Humanity house in the neighborhood in 2008.[19] As we continue our relationship with Highland Park, we strive to educate students about the need for building sustained, reciprocal partnerships to work for social change.

In connecting with students interested in "change," the CCE staff stresses the importance of research and understanding social problems in context. We have incentivized the process as well. The CCE offers paid summer fellowships that support independent student research and faculty–student collaborative research projects that address ways to "effect change in social, cultural, legal, environmental or political spheres" with dedicated funding for projects focusing on Richmond.[20] Past fellows have examined gentrification in Richmond, the history of community-building in Highland Park, voting technology and its impact on local elections, global warming in Richmond, and other related topics. Fellows are required to share their work in both academic and community forums for broad impact.

Support for faculty is also a critical component of the CCE's work. In May 2008 we piloted a community-based learning faculty fellows program. Thirteen faculty members from four schools and a wide array of disciplines, including business management, English, political science, and law, were selected to transform or create a new course with a rigorous community-based learning—including service-learning or community-based research—component.[21] Faculty fellows participated in a two-day workshop and continued to work with the CCE community-based learning program manager throughout the school year to connect their courses and pedagogical aims to community needs. The faculty cohort will also participate in a faculty learning community throughout the academic year as part of their fellowship.

In spring 2009, in partnership with the University of Richmond's School of Law, the CCE launched the Richmond Families Initiative (RFI) out of the newly opened University of Richmond Downtown, located in the heart of the city. Equipped with a classroom, community room, and multipurpose gallery, UR Downtown houses the Harry L. Carrico Center for Pro Bono Service, and the Jeanette Lipman Family Law Clinic. The latter partners with Virginia Commonwealth University's psychology and social work graduate programs to provide wraparound programs for clients working with the law clinic. The University of Richmond Downtown also serves as the headquarters for the RFI program aimed at promoting healthy, stable families through undergraduate engagement in research, community-based learning, and service in collaboration with nonprofits and city agencies addressing family needs.[22] The RFI provides another outlet for faculty to connect their courses and research while the University of Richmond Downtown serves as a visual and spatial marker of the university's growing commitment to live up to its name.

Civic Engagement House

The line between the CCE's commitment to Richmond and my own is blurred. My partner and I choose to live in the city rather than the surrounding counties that boast lower property taxes and better schools. I am a resident, student, and teacher of the city. A colleague and I are working on a book proposal on leadership, racial politics, and the city's development since 1970 that will follow on Christopher Silver's *Twentieth-Century Richmond: Planning, Politics, and Race.*[23] In the first history course that I taught at the university, "The American City, 1880-Present," I devoted three weeks to a case study on the city. We read Elsa Barkley Brown and Gregg D. Kimball's article on "Mapping the Terrain of Black Richmond" and took a walking tour of Jackson Ward.[24] The executive director of the Richmond's Valentine History Center spoke eloquently on the city's role in our national history when he visited the class. Students wrote their final papers on a Richmond subject, and I learned more about such topics as the baseball stadium, the history of the Churchill neighborhood, gentrification in the Fan District, and the history and spatial impact of the Medical College of Virginia through their work.

Despite the success of these assignments and the course overall, the students had not really engaged the city where they lived in meaningful ways. Many students in class confessed that their trips off campus were confined to nearby suburban malls and restaurants. The parts of the city I assumed would beckon to students, Carytown with its funky shops and cafes and Shockoe Bottom with its cobblestone streets, restaurants, and bars, were not frequented by the young people in my class, a number of whom felt these areas might be "dangerous." Students were not only socially isolated but intellectually adrift from the city as well: few had knowledge of the city's assets, problems, or political landscape. My course had provided research opportunities and a field trip in the city, but it did not do enough to burst the University of Richmond "bubble."

Around the time I fully began to realize my students' disconnection from the city, I was invited to participate in a pilot living-learning community with a focus on civic engagement. Living-learning communities tied to an academic course had been selected by the university community (through an open voting process) as the Quality Enhancement Plan (QEP) portion of our Southern Association of Colleges and Schools (SACS) reaccreditation review in March 2006. Course-based living-learning communities holistically bring together residence life with coursework in an effort to link curricular and cocurricular learning. Participants sign on to live together in a dormitory, to take a course, and to join in cocurricular programs related to the course content. Because civic engagement was deemed a popular topic by students, I was asked to pilot a course-based living-learning community.[25] The opportunity to create a new urban history course with ties to cocurricular programs sparked my interest. Perhaps I could devise a way to structure the living-learning community to combat student apathy, address the historical roots of urban social issues, and activate students. I signed on to pilot a new living-learning initiative called the Civic Engagement House, a coed residential program supported by student development and the CCE. I sought to better integrate urban history, current urban problems, and community engagement on campus.

In the fall of 2006, I began the pilot year of the Civic Engagement House. Thirteen students were selected through an application process in the spring of 2006 to participate in the program. Students signed on to live together for the year, take my one-unit history course in the fall semester, and participate when they could in related cocurricular activities throughout the academic year. These students, representing a variety of majors, moved into the on-campus house and registered for my history course, "The Urban Crisis in America."[26] The course examines the roots and impact of the urban crisis on metropolitan areas from 1945 to the present. Throughout the semester we investigated racial segregation, poverty, demographic shifts, public housing, urban renewal, deindustrialization, and suburbanization. At different points in the course, I brought in Richmond as a case study to illustrate both the specific challenges the region faced as well as to represent problems that impacted metropolitan regions nationally. Texts included Thomas Sugrue's *The Origins of the Urban Crisis: Race and Inequality in Postwar Detroit*, Peter Medoff and Holly Sklar's *Streets of Hope*, Dolores Hayden's *Building Suburbia: Green Fields and Urban Growth, 1820-2000*, Philippe Bourgois's *In Search of Respect: Selling Crack in El Barrio*, essays from Raymond Mohl and Arnold Hirsch's *Urban Policy in Twentieth-Century America*, and a range of primary documents, essays, and films.[27]

The difference between this course and others I had designed and taught came in the assignments.[28] My aim was for students to understand urban social problems in historical context, to examine an issue nationally and locally, and to produce knowledge that could stimulate others to think about and possibly take action for social change. I explained this process to my students as "learning out," and I used technology at different times to support the process.[29] Students drew on and connected lectures, readings, class discussion, current events, and Civic Engagement House cocurricular activities to write seven blog entries and three comments on their peers' entries. Called the Urban Issues and Action blog, the site described our quest to examine the history of urban policies, problems, and the possibilities for social change. The postings increased in sophistication over the semester as students gained knowledge, and posts and comments from bloggers inside and outside the class fueled their motivation to continue the dialogue. The blog, as a virtual venue, encouraged discussion outside the classroom and provided an alternate format to classroom dialogue for student participation. The assignment also reinforced the concept that students could engage other people at the university and elsewhere in discussing and thinking about urban history, policies, and activism.

The concept of "learning out" played a larger role in the multifaceted individual and group assignment described as an "urban issues and action portfolio." The language from the syllabus sums up my intent:

> Students will form groups to study particular aspects of cities and suburbs after World War II at the beginning of the semester. Each group will work with me to study the historical and current parameters of an urban problem, to account for past attempts to solve the problem, and to pose recommendations for a course of action. Topics for study might include transportation, downtown redevelopment, affordable housing, or the impact of racial segregation on metropolitan regions. This assignment is designed to help you understand urban policy and problems both nationally and locally and *to share what you are learning with others on campus* and in the community. You will have the opportunity to disseminate information on your selected issue and to suggest actions that will affect change.[30]

The portfolio included three different parts designed to build on one another, depending on students' effort and engagement with the assignments. During the second week of class, students formed groups around shared interests they identified. Topics ranged from homelessness to gang violence. Over the next week each group put together a one-page description of the issue they intended to study and an annotated bibliography of sources illuminating the history of the issue. Students met with me to go over their bibliographies and to discuss sources and local resources for them to consider as they moved forward. Students used these shared sources as they began work on their individual research papers related to the group's chosen issue. Due before fall break, these research papers provided an important foundation, along with class materials, for the groups to draw on as they moved forward with the final portfolio assignment: creating a ten- to fifteen-minute documentary film on an urban issue in Richmond.

The preparation for making documentary films, I learned after my pilot year, needs to begin on the first day of the course. My students have had mixed emotions—some excited, some scared—about the prospect the two times I have taught the course. The University of Richmond's Center for Teaching, Learning, and Technology (CTLT) has been a key partner in my efforts to teach students visual literacy skills and the possibilities and limits of historical storytelling through documentary filmmaking. These lessons have come at some cost: I give over two full days of class during the semester so my coeducator from the CTLT can train the students to use the cameras and editing software.[31] I also wrestle with what some of my students call the "beast" of the Institutional Review Board (IRB) requiring each student group, with my assistance, to receive IRB approval before starting their interviews. Receiving IRB approval protects interviewees and allows the students to screen their documentaries widely.[32]

Over the past two years, the benefits of the assignment have outweighed these costs. The documentary has proved to be a powerful engagement tool. Students have toured the city, met and interviewed nonprofit and governmental leaders, and began reading multiple local publications to seek out different perspectives on an issue. They have connected in clear ways urban history to Richmond's present state. They have developed a keener sense of visual literacy. They have started to see themselves as citizens of the city of Richmond, not just as students at the University of Richmond. The range of topics as well as the quality of the documentaries produced over the past two years varies. Film titles include "Homelessness: It Could Be You," "Latinos in Richmond," "Urban Environmental Justice: A Case Study of Battery Park," and "Not Just Sticks and Bricks: Affordable Housing in Richmond." Each film focuses on a social issue in Richmond, within a national historical context, and provides suggestions for change. Public screenings of the films on campus have brought in over one hundred people and students, and I have distributed copies to nonprofits and other citizens to share what we have learned and to galvanize others to think about pressing problems in the city, their historical origins, and possible solutions. The documentaries, as the students have noted, can continue to interest and educate others after the course ends and even after they graduate: these are intellectual artifacts created for—and often reaching—a larger audience than just me, their professor.

Connecting with the City

In addition to the filmmaking assignment, the "learning" part of the Civic Engagement House living-learning community occurred through the portfolio project and other readings and assignments but also through the cocurricular activities connected to the course. Removed from the traditional classroom setting during Civic Engagement House activities, students loosened up and began asking me and each other questions about life, career choices, city politics, pop culture, and even urban history. The "living" part of the Civic Engagement House created a quick familiarity between the students, a shared purpose, and an ease with one another that yielded great gains in and outside the classroom. Students felt a sense of community early on because of their living arrangements and seemed willing and able to tackle difficult issues such as race, class, and inequality, to disagree with one another respectfully, and to challenge one another to think through their opinions and assumptions.

Cocurricular activities for the living-learning community dovetailed with my work at the CCE. In early September, students took part in a Community Action Poverty Simulation with seventy other participants.[33] Many students wrote insightful and reflective blog postings on their experience at the simulation while critiquing their peers, and, at the time, the simulation itself. Later in the month students joined another class in taking a four-hour bus tour of Richmond neighborhoods with local expert Dr. John Moeser. Equipped with census data on twelve Richmond neighborhoods, the students learned about the history of the city and current challenges facing several districts. Stops included a meeting with a city council member to learn more about her district and a tour of a new real estate project with the developer. This Saturday tour, which I required students to attend, provided important context for the course and their portfolio projects. It also generated more interest in Richmond and sparked new answers to the question I posed the first day of class: "What activities do you all want to do this year?"

Building on student interest, with feedback from the resident assistant, I planned other programs, casting a wide net for "engagement." Many students wanted to volunteer for a day, so we spent a Saturday in Highland Park working on a house rehab project with our Build It community partners. Others asked for social outings into the city, which included dining at independently-owned restaurants and introducing students to the best local ice cream shop in town (Bev's). We also went as a group to hear speakers on and off campus and met up for discussion afterwards. My aim in scheduling these activities was to balance what I thought the students should do with what they wanted to do. When green architecture emerged as a popular discussion topic, I brought in a Leadership in Energy and Environmental Design (LEED)-certified architect to discuss the process and to talk about the LEED buildings on campus at students' request. During exam time I coordinated with the resident assistant to host a study break. Funding from the student development division paid for these activities as well as the programs in the spring. Without the class, there were fewer cocurricular programs during the spring semester. The upside for me was to see continued interest in and discussion about the themes we had covered in the fall. The major spring semester program was the premier of the documentary films. Students, faculty, staff, interviewees, nonprofit leaders, and interested citizens turned out to view and discuss the films with the student filmmakers. A culmination of a semester's work, the films impressed the audience and left me scrambling to order more copies from the CTLT. The assignment, and the course, seemed successful, at least to me.

Evaluation

What about the students? How did they evaluate the documentary film project, the course, and the living-learning experience? At the end of the fall semester, I asked the students to write short reflection papers on the process of completing their group documentary film. The paper provided a chance for each student to assess his or her work and to comment on the amount of effort put in by group members. A constant refrain in the papers was that the assignment, on top of the reading load, was "too much work." These comments were not news to me: I had received similar responses in all of my teaching evaluations in past courses. What surprised me was the impact the process of making the documentaries had on students, only one of whom had any experience with a camera and editing software. A star biology student, taking the course as an elective, reflected on her group's project in a paper entitled "Homelessness: Behind the Scenes."

> In retrospect, this project was the most difficult task I have ever tackled simply because it was completely out of my element and because of the sheer amount of work. In spite of that, I will never regret taking this class and making this documentary because the point of it was bigger than just doing an assignment. It was, finally, the kind of class I came to college for.[34]

A student in a group examining youth gang violence in Richmond characterized the documentary filmmaking process as a struggle. "We struggled to meet as a group, we struggled to find relevant information, we struggled to schedule interviews, and we struggled in editing our documentary." Because of, rather than despite, these challenges, she claimed to have "learned more from it than I have from any other school

147

assignment."[35] Other reflection papers included similar comments about frustration with different members of the group, scheduling issues, and the amount of work involved in film production. Overall, though, students indicated that they had a deeper knowledge of the issue they studied and a sense of responsibility toward the city. They also expressed pride in their films and excitement that the documentaries could reach a broad audience.

The course evaluations bear out the themes in the response papers on the documentaries. With a 100 percent response rate, I have strong data to draw from. I learned that the course was hard, there was too much reading, and I had set very high expectations. Good, good, and good. Despite complaints about the intense work load, the evaluations were quite positive. One student noted that the course

> … was one of the most rigorous yet rewarding courses I have taken. … I really enjoyed the integration of activism and engagement with developing a working knowledge of the subject areas over the course of the semester. It really allowed us to apply what we learned in real, meaningful context.

In my estimation, because of the living-learning component, students had a richer learning experience, which they reflected in their evaluations. "This course has been a great eye-opener for me in terms of specific historical decisions and trends that create our urban landscape. I feel more empowered and knowledgeable about how to function within American cities," commented an anonymous student. Another student directly addressed the benefits of living with classmates: "As part of a living and learning community, I think its design aids in the community effect. I also think it incorporates innovative ways to get students involved in the community, making change, and connecting those things to the classroom."[36]

While the strong evaluations reflected well on the course and the living-learning community, it was the comments that came from students after the school year ended that point to the value of engaging the city in different ways as part of an urban history course. In July 2007, a rising senior took time away from her summer internship to write me a two-page email to illuminate the connections she was making between her work and the course. As an intern for the local government in her hometown of Orlando, Florida, the student had the opportunity to work on homeless outreach (after making the documentary on homelessness) and downtown revitalization. The course, she explained, had prepared her well for her work:

> So when I hear about HOPE VI or listen in on a community discussion about the need, lack, or growing partnership and input of citizens, businesses, and the government, I think, "Hey! I already know this!" Pretty much everything from green buildings, transportation, affordable housing, etc., is coming into play in my experience as a summer intern, which has been really neat to see.[37]

In 2007, as the second year of the Civic Engagement House was gearing up, a junior from the pilot year wrote an email with a subject line I smiled to read: "The Urban Crisis applies to everything." The student had worked at Camp Bob, an outreach camp for low-income kids in North Carolina, and she found the course materials provided important context for her duties. She continued:

> [T]he knowledge that I gained in Urban Crisis really added a lot to what I experienced working with the kids. The kids who attended Camp Bob faced issues that we studied every single day. A lot of them lived in housing projects, were homeless, or were in (or had brother and sisters in) gangs. If I had not taken your class and done the documentary on gangs or studied homelessness, I would not have been as well equipped to work with these kids, because I would have had almost no understanding of the situations that they are in. It was so awesome to apply everything that I had learned in class to something practical—helping kids.[38]

These emails, along with conversations with returning students in the hallways and the dining hall and their zeal to recruit more students to participate in the Civic Engagement House, have proved rewarding. I am now a convert to course-based living-learning communities. The pilot year and my second year with the Civic Engagement House in 2007–2008 have been highlights in my teaching career. Students stop me to talk about sprawl; to express frustration about the history of redlining; to discuss local politics; and to complain that they can not drive on the interstate without thinking of transportation technologies and policy. Spending the year together in and outside the classroom created tight bonds between the students and shaped their shared interest in engaging the city.

Next Steps

The future of living-learning programs at the University of Richmond looks bright. In fall 2008 seventeen students participated in the Civic Engagement House. They lived in a new dorm (nicknamed the "the hotel" by students on campus because it is so plush) and take my course in a classroom located on the ground floor of the building. Over thirty students applied to join the community. I applied what I had learned over the past two years as I continued to improve my syllabus. Four other faculty members also taught courses tied to a living-learning community, and all the students in these courses lived together in the new dorm. Themes included Literature of the Heart, Election 2008, the Earth Lodge, and Spanish in the Community. These programs generated more interest in living-learning communities and provided a basis of support for the development of the university's new Sophomore Scholars in Residence Program (SSIR), the final evolution of the QEP tied to reaccreditation.

Four faculty members, selected through an application process to serve as the first cohort for the SSRI, designed or revised their courses as living-learning communities with a one-unit (four-credit) class in the fall and a half-unit in the spring, plus cocurricular programs for the 2009–2010 school year. After the initial year the number of programs will grow to ten over five years. Targeted at sophomores in an effort to provide a variety of communities for students to join and to improve retention, the four programs have substantial budgets to engage students in a range of educational experiences. As a faculty participant, I revised my course based on past lessons. The biggest changes have come with the addition of a half-unit in the spring and a large budget to spend. I envision adding a comparative element during the spring semester. My aim is to take the students to New York, Philadelphia, and Washington D.C. during spring break. I hope to tap (and pay) colleagues who teach urban history in these cities to provide educational tours with a focus on the main themes studied in the fall including urban renewal, public housing, poverty, transportation, and downtown development. Along with the tours and discussions with local faculty members, students will meet with political and nonprofit leaders to discuss the topics they covered in their documentary films in the fall. They may consider the following questions: How did the issue play out historically in New York, Philadelphia, and Washington, D.C.? What is the current state of affairs? What steps have leaders and citizens taken to address these issues? Students will also share what they have learned about Richmond, including their documentaries. After the trip, students will write a comparative paper integrating their historical knowledge with the information they learned during the fall and the spring semesters. The comparative framework and spring break trip provide new opportunities for examining urban history, engaging students in active learning, and building community among participants.

As colleges and universities continue to prioritize civic engagement, urban historians are poised to become leaders in thoughtful, rigorous, place-based, community-based learning courses. The elements are in place, including excellent secondary and primary sources to lay out the context for how and why cities and suburbs look and function as they do; eager community partners waiting to build or strengthen relationships with university faculty to foster student learning; seemingly endless research questions; and a growing number of students asking for "real world" experiences as part of their college education. Whether through an individual class, administrative work focused on community engagement, or the further development of informal networks of urbanists committed to creative, meaningful campus-community partnerships, we have untold possibilities to leverage our intellectual and institutional resources for engaged student learning and the slow process of social change.

Acknowledgments

Special thanks to Lisa Krissoff Boehm, Jennifer Blanchard, and Robert K. Nelson for their comments and suggestions on this article.

Notes

1   Kenneth P. Gonzalez and Raymond V. Padilla, "Latina/o Faculty Perspectives on Higher Education for the Public Good," in *Doing the Public Good: Latina/o Scholars Engage Civic Participation* (Sterling, VA: Stylus, 2008), 1.

2   Tony C. Chambers, "The Special Role of Higher Education in Society: As a Public Good for the Public Good," in *Higher Education for the Public Good*, ed. Adrianna J. Kezar, Tony C. Chambers, John C. Burkhardt, and Associates (San Francisco: Jossey-Bass, 2005).

3   The University of Chicago School of Social Service Administration was called the Chicago School of Civics and Philanthropy when it started in 1908. See http://ssacentennial.uchicago.edu/history/ for more information on the history of the school. In "The Impact of an Urban University on Community Development," George Hampton and David Higham outline the categories of contributions urban universities have made to local communities and discuss the emerging role of urban higher education institutions in community development. See www.umdnj.edu/comreweb/pdf/The_Impact_of_an_Urban%20University.PDF (accessed June 24, 2008). For information on IUPUI, see Ralph D Gray, *IUPUI: The Making of an Urban University* (Bloomington and Indianapolis: Indiana University Press, 2003).

4   From http://www.upen.edu/campus/westphilly/index.html (accessed on May 15, 2008). The Penn Alexander School, a collaboration between parents, neighborhood organizations, and the university, opened for kindergarteners and first-graders in 2001. In September 2002, the new building for students in grades K–8 opened. For more information on the history behind the Penn-West Philadelphia partnership, see David J. Maurrasse, *Beyond the Campus: How Colleges and Universities Form Partnerships with Their Communities* (Routledge: New York, 2001), 29–64.

5   The University College of Citizenship and Public Service launched in 2000. The school became the Jonathan M. Tisch College of Citizenship and Public Service after Tisch gave a $40 million gift to endow the school in 2006. See http://www.tufts.edu/home/feature/?p=tisch_gift (accessed May 2, 2008) for information on the gift and http://activecitizen.tufts.edu/?pid=1 for information on the college.

6   Bates announced a $1.7 million endowment to fund the center named in honor of former president Donald Harward and his wife, Ann. David Scobey, the former director of the Arts of Citizenship Program and associate professor of architecture and urban planning at the University of Michigan, was named as the first director of the Harward Center in 2005. See http://www.bates.edu/x166253.xml accessed on May 2, 2008.

7   Schools are selected for the elective classification through a competitive application process. Audrey Williams June, "Carnegie Foundation Offers Community–Engagement Classification," *Chronicle of Higher Education*, April 2006, http://chronicle.com/weekly/v52/i32/32a03003.htm (accessed on May 2, 2008), and Amy Driscoll, "Carnegie's Community–Engagement Classification: Intentions and Insights," *Change*, January/February 2008, http://www.carnegiefoundation.org/files/elibrary/Driscoll.pdf (accessed on May 2, 2008). For more information on the classification and application process, see http://www.carnegiefoundation.org/classifications/index.asp?key=1213.

8   There are a range of networks including the National Service-Learning Clearinghouse (http://www.servicelearning.org/), Campus Compact (http://www.compact.org/), Project Pericles (http://www.projectpericles.org/), Imagining America (http://www.imaginingamerica.org/), and others. Colleges and universities with Bonner Scholars and Bonner Leader programs connect through the Bonner Foundation network (http://www.bonner.org/).

9   I earned my PhD in American studies from the College of William and Mary, where I focused on twentieth-century cultural, social, and urban history, and film.

10 From the University of Richmond mission statement; see http://provost.richmond.edu/.

11 The founding director of the CCE, Dr. Douglas A. Hicks, ably led the center until August 2009 when he returned to full-time teaching in the Jepson School of Leadership Studies. The Bonner Foundation in Princeton University supports the Bonner Scholars Program at twenty-seven colleges and universities across the country. The Foundation seeks to "transform the lives of students … campuses, local communities, and the nation by providing access to education and opportunities to serve." To this end, the Foundation provides four-year scholarships to 1,500 students—Bonner Scholars—annually who have "high financial need and a commitment to service." For more information, see http://www.bonner.org/campus/bsp/ home.htm.

12 See, for example, Thomas J. Sugrue, *The Origins of the Urban Crisis: Race and Inequality in Postwar Detroit* (Princeton, NJ: Princeton University Press, 1996).

13 In 2007, the University of Richmond had over $1 billon in endowment funds. In 2007–2008, tuition, room, board, and fees totaled $44,810. The university uses a need-blind admission process for applicants and has a program that offers full tuition, room, and board to admitted Virginia applicants whose parents earn less than $40,000 a year. The new strategic plan focuses on access and affordability, integrated academic and student experiences, community engagement, and diversity and inclusion.

14 The University of Richmond apartments are located in Henrico County. The rest of the campus is in the city of Richmond. Chesterfield County also abuts the city.

15 The former capital of the Confederacy with a high poverty rate and a majority African American population, Richmond's political landscape has been further complicated by a unique trio of Virginia state laws. Cities in Virginia are independent from counties, forbidden to annex, and constrained by the Dillon Rule that mandates that all local charter changes must be approved by the General Assembly.

16 From http://buildit.richmond.edu/ (accessed May 5, 2008). Text written by Betsy Kelly.

17 The CCE has partnered with the Highland Park community and the following partners since 2005: Overby-Sheppard Elementary School, Chandler Middle School, Hotchkiss Field Community Center, Reach Out and Read Virginia, Boaz and Ruth (a nonprofit dedicated to successful prisoner reentry), and the William Byrd Community House's youth program in Highland Park. These partnerships were established through asset-mapping, dialogue, and relationship building with the goal of forming sustained partnerships to address community-identified needs while educating students. In 2005–2006 approximately eighty students participated in ongoing service, many through service-learning courses. The numbers increased to 150 participants in 2006–2007. During the 2007–2008 school year, one hundred students participated in the program.

18 See Christopher Silver, *Twentieth-Century Richmond: Planning, Politics, and Race* (Knoxville: University of Tennessee Press, 1984), and Danielle Amarant, "The Redevelopment of Highland Park and the Role of the Residents," undergraduate research paper, http://research.richmond.edu/students/Dani_Amarant.htm, for more information on Highland Park's history.

19 The campus-community fair was held at the Hotchkiss Community Field in April 2007. Over three hundred neighbors came out to the event that included a number of booths with social and legal services information, college admissions information, and other services requested by community members, as well as music, food, games, and readings circles for kids. In 2008, the collaborative efforts of four community partners made possible the building of an affordable house in Highland Park. Richmond Redevelopment and Housing Authority donated the land for the project; Richmond Metropolitan Habitat for Humanity offered supplemental funding and logistical support; Boaz and Ruth catered the lunches for the volunteers and provided some volunteers; and University of Richmond provided significant funding and many volunteers, drawn from the ranks of students, faculty, staff, alumni, and friends of the university, for the eight-week build. Two graduates of the Boaz and Ruth program are the owners of the Habitat house.

20 For more information on these ten-week fellowships, see http://engage.richmond.edu/programs/fellowships/research.html.

21 The University of Richmond has five schools: the School of Arts and Sciences, the Jepson School of Leadership Studies, the T. C. Williams School of Law, the Robins School of Business, and the School of Continuing Studies. Selected faculty fellows receive $1,800 to transform a course and $3,000 to create a new course with a community-based learning component. They also receive a stipend for participating in the faculty learning community during the academic year. Faculty fellows, with the support of their department chair or dean, commit to teach the course within three semesters.

22 For more information on the RFI program and the University of Richmond Downtown see http://downtown.richmond.edu/.

23 Thad Williamson, assistant professor of leadership studies, and I have recently begun working on this project. We presented a conference paper at the Urban Affairs Association entitled "Richmond, Doug Wilder, and the Move to a Strong Mayor System: A Report on a Political Experiment in Progress" in April 2008. An excerpt from this paper appeared in the May 14, 2008 edition of *Style Weekly*, Richmond, Virginia. Christopher Silver, *Twentieth-Century Richmond: Planning, Politics, and Race* (Knoxville: University of Tennessee Press, 1984).

24 Elsa Barkley Brown and Gregg D. Kimball, "Mapping the Terrain of Black Richmond," *Journal of Urban History* (March 1995): 296–345. Thanks to Kelly Quinn for recommending this article.

25 My colleague Lee Carlton piloted the first course-based learning community in 2006–2007 called the Outdoor House. Students enrolled in the program lived together, took a course on the environment in literature, and participated in a range of outdoor offerings.

26 My course draws from a rich syllabus put together by Joseph Heathcott. Joseph is currently an associate professor of urban studies at the New School and a leader of the school's civic engagement efforts.

27 Readers interested in a copy of the syllabus can email the author at ahoward3@richmond.edu.

28 I have now taught the course three times and I have included the changes I have made—through trial and error—in this article. I would be remiss not to offer special thanks to Andy Gurka and the Richmond College Dean's Office staff for their support of the Civic Engagement House.

29 "Learning out" is a phrase I came up with in talking with my students.

30 Amy L. Howard, Syllabus, "The Urban Crisis in America," University of Richmond, Fall 2006.

31 Special thanks to Hil Scott in the CTLT.

32 Over the past two years I have developed a template for students to work off of as they put together their IRB forms. The first year, my students' requests were expedited. Last year, with a new person running IRB, the students' requests went to the full committee. I put the IRB deadline on the syllabus and worked with students to submit their forms on time. For an engaging discussion on the debates around IRB in the social sciences and humanities see Zachary Schrag's blog at http://www.institutionalreviewblog. com. While students have learned about the importance of protecting vulnerable populations through the IRB process, they complain and question it.

33 See http://www.communityaction.org/Poverty%20Simulation.htm for more information on the simulation.

34 Kay Holstein, "Homelessness: Behind the Scenes," reflection paper submitted on December 8, 2006.

35 Lindsey Foss, "Youth, Gangs, and Violence Reflection," reflection paper submitted on December 8, 2006.

36 Comments from course evaluations, December 2007.

37 Dominique Thomas, email to author, July 24, 2007.

38 Lindsey Foss, email to author, September 18, 2007. Lindsey went on to say that her experience working at Camp Bob combined with what she learned in the Civic Engagement House led her to "completely change her career path. … from international work, to work with at-risk kids."

Credit _____

Amy L. Howard. "Engaging the City: Civic Participation and Teaching Urban History." *Journal of Urban History* 36 (1)1 Jan. 2010: 42–55, © 2010. by SAGE Publications Reprinted by Permission of SAGE Publications.

Cities Mobilize to Help Those Threatened by Gentrification

Timothy Williams

Timothy Williams is a former staff writer for The Los Angeles Times *and current freelance writer whose work has appeared in* The New York Times, The Huffington Post, *and* National Post, *among other publications. He has written extensively about police brutality and increased oversight, gun control legislation, and the politics of prison reform. In "Cities Mobilize to Help Those Threatened by Gentrification," published in* The New York Times, *Williams reports on a recent initiative in many large American cities to curb the negative impacts of gentrifying neighborhoods on long-time residents: specifically, the freezing of property taxes for homeowners.*

❧❀❧❀❧❀

Cities that have worked for years to attract young professionals who might have once moved to the suburbs are now experimenting with ways to protect a group long deemed expendable—working- and lower-middle class homeowners threatened by gentrification.

The initiatives, planned or underway in Boston, Philadelphia, Washington, Pittsburgh and other cities, are centered on reducing or freezing property taxes for such homeowners in an effort to promote neighborhood stability, preserve character, and provide a dividend of sorts to those who have stayed through years of high crime, population loss, and declining property values, officials say.

Newcomers, whose vitality is critical to cities, are hardly being turned away. But officials say a balance is needed, given the attention and government funding being spent to draw young professionals—from tax breaks for luxury condominium buildings to new bike lanes, dog parks, and athletic fields.

"We feel the people who toughed it out should be rewarded," said Darrell L. Clarke, president of the Philadelphia City Council, which last year approved legislation to limit property tax increases for longtime residents. "And we feel it is incumbent upon us to protect them."

In doing so, cities are turning urban redevelopment policy on its head and shunning millions in property tax revenue that could be used to restore municipal services that were trimmed during the recession because of budget cuts, including rehiring police officers.

A decision to reduce property taxes can be risky because such levies account for at least 50 percent of operating budgets in most American cities and sometimes provide as much as 80 percent of a city's revenue.

But even Detroit, where a declining tax base has been at the core of the bankrupt city's troubles, recently announced plans to cut property tax rates.

Last month, Mike Duggan, Detroit's new mayor, said property taxes would be cut by up to 20 percent to levels that more accurately represent the value of homes in the city. The reduction could cost Detroit as much as $15 million annually in revenue.

The tax adjustments are part of a broader strategy by cities to aid homeowners—who continue to struggle financially since the home mortgage crisis. In Richmond, Calif., lawmakers are attempting to use eminent domain to seize underwater mortgages to try to help homeowners keep their houses.

Housing experts say the arrival of newcomers to formerly working-class areas—from the Mission District in San Francisco to the Shaw neighborhood in Washington—is distinct from previous influxes over the past 30 years because new residents are now far more likely to choose to move into new condominiums or lofts instead of into existing housing, making the changes more disruptive.

"This latest wave of gentrification has happened very quickly, and cities are cognizant to keep from turning over entirely," said Lisa Sturtevant, executive director of the Center for Housing Policy, a nonprofit research group. "And cities where property values are up and budgets are generally more stable have the wherewithal to provide tax breaks."

Ms. Sturtevant said that given that many of the younger, newer arrivals do not necessarily plan to stay for long, cities are making a sensible economic choice.

"There's less personal investment and less incentive to stay, so cities are saying, 'Let's invest in the stayers,' " she said.

In Boston, which an analysis by the Federal Reserve Bank of Cleveland last year found had the highest gentrifying pressure in the nation—followed by Seattle, New York, San Francisco, Washington and Atlanta—concluded that about one-fourth the city's population lived in gentrifying neighborhoods.

"Property values are increasing exponentially, and longtime homeowners are victims of the success story," said Stephen J. Murphy, a city councilor in Boston who co-introduced legislation allowing residents who have owned homes for more than 10 years and whose property taxes have increased by 10 percent or more to defer property tax payments until they sell their home. The bill, approved by the City Council, is pending the approval of the state legislature.

But Philadelphia, undergoing a resurgence during which the city has had its first population increase since the 1950s, appears to have enacted the most comprehensive measures to safeguard longtime homeowners.

The first, the Homestead Exemption, allows most homeowners to reduce the assessed value of their house by $30,000 for tax purposes, while a second law, called Gentrification Protection or LOOP, short for Longtime Owner Occupants Program, is more narrowly focused on protecting homeowners from increases to their property tax bills because of gentrification.

The program generally allows homeowners who have lived in homes for 10 years or more and whose household income is less than about $110,000 annually to cap and freeze their assessments for 10 years if the assessments increased by 300 percent or more as part of the city's new property tax formula.

"Philadelphia is a city of neighborhoods, and the reason people want to move to our neighborhoods is because of the character they have," said Mark Squilla, a council member who said it had been common in his district for home assessments to surge by as much as 10 times in a single year. "Gentrification is a great thing. But we have to keep a handle on it."

Rene Goodwin, who lives in the same South Philadelphia neighborhood her grandparents lived in during the 1920s, has seen the value of her home rise to $281,000 from $90,000 in a single year.

"To keep an urban area vital, there has to be an infusion of new people and buildings, but that doesn't mean you destroy people who have kept up the neighborhood, who've swept the sidewalk," she said. "It's that commitment that has made developers interested in the neighborhood—and then you're going to penalize the people who've stayed?"

Jacy Webster, 56, who lives on what had until recently been an Italian-American block in South Philadelphia, said he had come to feel like a stranger.

The new arrivals, mostly young families, seem to move a step faster than he does or to not see him. Old courtesies like waving hello and casual chats have become rare.

"I don't belong anymore," he said.

The changes have meant that the assessment on his house has more than quintupled during the past year—to $250,000 from $45,000—which he said might force him to move and perhaps rent his home out if he does not qualify for LOOP. The Feb. 17 deadline to apply has passed, and he is waiting to hear from the city.

Mr. Webster said, however, that there was at least one advantage to being surrounded by wealthier neighbors: "It's actually safer than it's ever been."

Is Gentrification All Bad?

Justin Davidson

Justin Davidson, a staff writer for both Newsday and the New York Magazine, *has had an illustrious career writing predominantly about music and architecture. A classically trained composer, he studied at both Harvard and Columbia, and won a Pulitzer Prize in 2002 for his music criticism. Much of his writing on architecture considers innovative approaches to affordable housing. Similarly, in his article, "Is Gentrification All Bad?" he argues that an influx of wealthier neighbors—along with their investments in the local economy—can actually curb displacement and improve the experiences of residents over time, but only if a "sweet spot" is reached that meets the needs of both groups.*

෬෨ও෨ও෨

Gentrification: New Yorkers can sense it immediately. It plumes out of Darling Coffee, on Broadway and 207th Street, and mingles with the live jazz coming from the Garden Café next door. Down the block, at Dichter Pharmacy, it's visible on the shelf of Melissa & Doug toys. An algae bloom of affluence is spreading across the city, invading the turf of artists and ironworkers, forming new habitats for wealthy vegans.

It's an ugly word, a term of outrage. Public Advocate Letitia James sounded the bugle against it in her inauguration speech on New Year's Day: "We live in a gilded age of inequality where decrepit homeless shelters and housing developments stand in the neglected shadow of gleaming multimillion-dollar condos," she cried, making it clear that she would love to fix up the first two and slam the brakes on the third. In this moral universe, gentrification is the social equivalent of secondhand smoke, drifting across class lines.

Yet gentrification can be either a toxin or a balm. There's the fast-moving, invasive variety nourished by ever-rising prices per square foot; then there's a more natural, humane kind that takes decades to mature and lives on a diet of optimism and local pride. It can be difficult to tell the two apart. "The things that low-income people think are nice are the same as what wealthy people want," says Nancy Biberman, who runs the Women's Housing and Economic Development Corporation in the Bronx.

Communities fight for basic upgrades in quality of life, and when they're successful, their food options and well-kept streets attract neighbors (and developers). It also works the other way: Richer, more entitled parents can lift up weak schools, says Biberman. "They're more aggressive, and they empower other parents."

Gentrification doesn't need to be something that one group inflicts on another; often it's the result of aspirations everybody shares. All over the city, a small army of the earnest toils away, patiently trying to sluice some of the elitist taint off neighborhoods as they grow richer. When you're trying to make a poor neighborhood into a nicer place to live, the prospect of turning it into a racially and economically mixed area with thriving stores is not a threat but a fantasy. As the cost of basic city life keeps rising, it's more important than ever to reclaim a form of urban improvement from its malignant offshoots. A nice neighborhood should be not a luxury but an urban right.

Somewhere, a mournful bugle sounds for every old shoe-repair place that shutters to make way for a gleaming cookie boutique. And yet some old-school businesses, if they're flexible enough, can do more than survive: They can help nudge a neighborhood into the right kind of change.

"I'm a corner druggist," says Manny Ramirez, the stocky, genial owner of Dichter Pharmacy. You can feel the pleasure he gets from pronouncing the phrase—the same retro jolt he gets from saying *stickball*, *soda shop*, and *candy store*. But he is hardly living in the past. He's a canny businessman, Inwood-born, and bilingual in English and Spanish, who has known some of his customers from his own childhood and keeps his antennae tuned to the tastes of those he hasn't even met. Keenly conscious of his low-income neighborhood, he undersells the chain stores on basics like Tylenol and keeps the prices of most items at his lunch counter below $5. But he also stocks expensive lotions, organic moisturizers, and those Melissa & Doug toys. "Now we have people who will buy that stuff," he says, sounding a little amused. "The idea of a new group of people with disposable income is excellent."

The drugstore doubles as an ad hoc performance center, where Ramirez hosts chamber-music concerts, "Shakespeare Saturdays," and poetry slams. "I'm big on social media, and I read the comments," he says. "Among the people who have migrated here, there's a large vegetarian and vegan group, so we have veggie chili on Wednesdays and Sundays. If you're listening, however the neighborhood changes, that's how you stay in business."

Ramirez's optimistic realism contrasts with a common perception of neighborhoods that remain unchanged for generations—at least until the gentrifiers roar in. A few areas where the change is that stark do exist, but far more typical are enclaves that each dominant ethnic group cedes to the next. Of course Inwood is changing; it always was. Right now, it's a neighborhood of immigrants. Nearly half of its residents were born abroad, most in the Dominican Republic. Yet that "old Inwood" isn't the one Ramirez grew up in. The year he was born, 1968, a TV station in Ireland aired a documentary, *Goodbye to Glocamorra*, which chronicled a neighborhood that could have passed for a city in County Mayo. "Five years ago, these apartment buildings were Irish to the last man, woman, and child," the narrator says mournfully. "Today, their defenses have begun to crumble. The first Puerto Ricans have moved in. The first Negroes have moved in. And more will certainly follow."

Ramirez was one of those Puerto Ricans, and he grew up acutely conscious of his bifurcated world. "I was too Spanish for the white community and too white for the Spanish community," he recalls. When he was 10, his family moved from the mostly Hispanic east side of Broadway to the still whitish west side. In the early nineties, he moved to a New Jersey suburb. But Ramirez kept roots in the neighborhood, commuting to work for the district Rite Aid office and attending Good Shepherd. One day, he heard the checkout girls at a Dominican bakery grumbling in Spanish about how the neighborhood was changing. "I remembered when I was a kid and the white people were talking about the neighborhood changing—only they were speaking English." Same complaint, different language.

Ramirez detected an opening. "I saw that there was an antiques store now, and a Moroccan restaurant, and I thought, *This is something I need to jump on.*" He bought the 100-year-old Dichter Pharmacy, where he had worked as a teenager. At times, it looked like a bad call. The recession hit the neighborhood hard. The Moroccan restaurant and the antiques store closed. In 2012, a fire destroyed the block. But Ramirez moved the business a few dozen yards up the street. Soon, the Badger Balm and apple-crumb muffins started to sell, and his poetry slams built a following— mostly from the west side of Broadway, though he's trying to recruit some Dominican bards too.

With strong feelings about the past and an eye on the future, Ramirez is a one-man neighborhood-improvement center. He knows that the change he's helping to nurture could one day turn on him, though he draws comfort from the fact that his lease won't expire (so his rent can't soar) for another twenty years. He keeps a fatherly eye on local kids and notes the low-margin stores that close and the new bars that force up rents. It pains him to see how few Latinos from the east side of Broadway welcome the new stores, and he knows that goodwill extends only so far. "If they're a low-income family and they're walking up the hill, past three or four other pharmacies, to buy Tylenol from me, are they going to go next door to Darling for a $4 cup of coffee?

Probably not." That doesn't stop Ramirez from steering occasional customers there—until the day when he can feed their soy-latte cravings himself.

Nothing symbolizes the abyss between plenty and deprivation more than their physical proximity. The rapid gilding of Brooklyn has, in places, produced a grotesque companionship of vintage-clothing boutiques and Goodwill stores. Even as Bedford-Stuyvesant real estate approaches Manhattan prices, nearly a third of its residents—47 percent of its children—live below the poverty line. The neighborhood remains a bastion of unemployment, public assistance, and crime, moated by great ramparts of public housing. The old inner-city anxieties—that poor people who know only other poor people are more likely to remain that way—have not disappeared. Only now, instead of being stranded in sprawling ghettos, the poor are confined to islands of deprivation, encircled by oceans of prosperity.

Yet those Dickensian juxtapositions are actually a sign of a city that is doing something right. Subsidized housing helps preserve neighborhoods from a uniform wash of affluence. Chelsea and the Upper West Side—two of the wealthiest districts in the nation—still make room for low-income residents in nycha projects. "Those are neighborhoods where gentrification has been meaningfully tempered," says Brooklyn city councilman Brad Lander, a staunchly progressive ally of Bill de Blasio's. And all over the city, developers reap tax benefits by erecting luxury buildings and earmarking 20 percent of the apartments for renters who pay far less than their neighbors. A group of visiting developers from Mumbai was thunderstruck by that custom: They couldn't imagine why well-off New Yorkers would voluntarily share their enclaves with the poor.

The fact that single-family townhouses and public housing often share the same few blocks gives community organizers a versatile set of tools. Colvin Grannum, the president of the Bedford-Stuyvesant Restoration Corporation, arrives at his offices the morning after the city has announced a $50,000 grant to help restore a small ice rink that's been sitting idle for years near the corner of Fulton and Marcy Streets. He had been hoping for a more robust infusion; now he has to raise nine times as much as he's getting. A staffer greets him with a shot of ambivalence: "Congratulations, I guess."

Robert F. Kennedy's children went skating on the Bed-Stuy rink in the seventies, when the area was an encyclopedia of urban decline. "It looked like a war zone," Grannum says—"a desolate and blighted community." In the summer of 1964, riots fared at the corner of Fulton Street and Nostrand Avenue, and mounted police shot at looters. Three years later, RFK and Senator Jacob Javits founded Restoration, the country's first comprehensive community-development organization. Kennedy envisioned a fusion of public funds and private investment that would nurture local, self-reliant businesses: "What is given or granted can be taken away," he said. "What you do for yourselves and for your children can never be taken away ... We must combine the best of community action with the best of the private-enterprise system."

That principle forms the foundation of nonprofit community-building groups all over the country and motivates private do-gooder developers like Jonathan Rose. "Can you create models of gentrification in which the benefits are spread out through the community?" Rose asks. The key, he says, is to make sure that residents and shopkeepers in low-income neighborhoods have equity and a political voice—before a real-estate surge. African-American residents of Bed-Stuy who managed to cling to their brownstones through the misery of the sixties, the heroin and crack years, and the devastating epidemic of foreclosures can finally reap the benefit that any longtime homeowner takes for granted: selling the house for a profit. "Development can be a positive force," Rose says.

Today, Grannum has inherited the dream of healing through business. "I see our job as trying to create a healthy commercial corridor and capture as many retail dollars as we can," he says. It's not as if he's got his eye on Tiffany and Per Se, but he would like the dollar stores and pawnbrokers to be joined by some slightly more genteel options. He mentions Island Salad, a Caribbean-themed place just across Fulton Street from his office, where $6.99 will buy an Asian Rasta (romaine, roasted teriyaki chicken, mandarin oranges, cucumbers, sliced almonds, crispy chow mein noodles, and "island sesame ginger"). It's the sort of place a couple of young Park Slopers in search of an extra bedroom might wander into and think: *Yes! I could live here.*

Grannum is unapologetic about trying to bring a better life to Bed-Stuy's poor by attracting the very outsiders who are supposedly making things worse. "We need affluent and middle-income people," he insists. "We need a healthy community, and we need services that are first-rate. I just came from a meeting, and someone said, 'Go to Seventh Avenue in Park Slope and recruit some of those stores!' And I tell them: Businesses don't bring affluence; they follow affluence."

To the residents of East Harlem, a neighborhood ribbed with nycha towers and dotted with new condos, almost any change seems ominous. Andrew Padilla's 2012 documentary *El Barrio Tours: Gentrification in East Harlem* ends with a group of conga players on a patch of sidewalk at Lexington Avenue and East 108th Street, with a tenement building on one corner and the DeWitt Clinton Houses on the other. Padilla's film traces the creep of generic luxury and residents' tenacious desire to hang on. The conga players' impromptu jam session encapsulates both the history and the fragility of East Harlem's identity: All it takes for it to vaporize is for the musicians to pick up their drums and walk away. And they have. According to the Center for Urban Research, Hispanics made up 52.9 percent of southeastern Harlem's population in 2000; a decade later, that figure had fallen to 47.5. Whites took their place (11.5 percent before, 17.5 percent after).

But trend lines are not destiny. Who does the gentrifying, how, and how quickly—these variables separate an organically evolving neighborhood from one that is ruthlessly replaced. A trickle of impecunious artists hungry for space and light is one thing; a flood of lawyers with a hankering to renovate is quite another. The difference may be just a matter of time—but when it comes to gentrification, time is all.

Gus Rosado, a deceptively mild-mannered activist with a brush cut and a graying Clark Gable mustache, runs El Barrio's Operation Fightback, which rehabs vacant buildings for affordable housing, and his latest undertaking is a huge gothic hulk at the far end of East 99th Street. Surrounded by public housing and the Metropolitan Hospital, it used to be P.S. 109, closed by the Department of Education in 1995 and badly decayed since then. After years of scrounging for some way to convert the school into living space, Rosado teamed up with the nationwide organization Artspace for a $52 million overhaul that will yield PS109 Artspace, 90 affordable live-work studios, half of them set aside for artists who live nearby. "The only way we were able to get this done was because of the arts," Rosado recently said. "Suddenly, there was a whole other set of funding sources."

Leveraging the moneyed art world to provide low-cost housing in a creative community seems like the perfect revitalization project. It promotes stability, fosters local culture, recycles unused real estate, and brings in philanthropic dollars rather than predatory investors. Artspace's website makes the link between creativity and urban improvements plain: "Artists are good for communities. The arts create jobs and draw tourists and visitors. Arts activities make neighborhoods livelier, safer, and more attractive."

At the same time, Rosado's P.S. 109 project triggers a spray of explosive hypotheticals. Who should get preference: a white filmmaker from Yale who moved to East Harlem a few years ago and therefore qualifies as a resident, or a Dominican-born muralist who grew up in El Barrio but has since left for cheaper quarters in the South Bronx? Or: If East Harlem's new Artspace incubates a nascent gallery scene, will its cash and snobbery help the neighborhood or ruin it? Will the Lexington Avenue conga players find a place in the neighborhood's new arts hub?

Artists are like most people: They think gentrification is fine so long as it stops with them. They are pioneers, all-accepting enthusiasts, and they wish to change nothing about their new home turf (although a halfway decent tapas place would be nice). The next arrivals, though, will be numerous and crass. Interlopers will ruin everything. As artists migrate across the boroughs, from the East Village to Williamsburg, Red Hook, Bushwick, and Mott Haven, surfing a wave of rising rents, they are simultaneously victims and perpetrators of gentrification.

Rosado understands these dynamics well, but he believes that a little local involvement can go a long way toward shaping the subtleties of neighborhood change. "You can't stop development and growth, but we'd like to have a say in how that transition takes place." Lurking in that plain statement is the belief that gentrification happens not because a few developers or politicians foist it on an unwilling city but because it's a medicine most people want to take. The trick is to minimize the harmful side effects.

In the popular imagination, gentrification and displacement are virtually synonymous, the input and output of a zero-sum game. One professional couple's $2 million brownstone renovation in Bedford-Stuyvesant equals three families drifting toward Bayonne in search of barely adequate shelter. And so a sense of grievance and shame permeates virtually all discussions of neighborhood change. Even gentrifiers themselves are convinced they are doing something terrible. Young professionals whose moving trucks keep pulling up to curbs in Bushwick and Astoria carry with them trunkfuls of guilt.

The link between a neighborhood's economic fortunes and the number of people being forced to move away, while anecdotally obvious, is difficult to document. Everyone's heard stories of brutally coercive landlords forcing low-income tenants out of rent-controlled apartments in order to renovate them and triple the rent. But it's difficult to know how often that takes place. Between 2009 and 2011, about 7 percent of New York households—around 200,000 of them—moved within the city in each year. Others left town altogether. Yet we know little about where they went, or why, or whether their decisions were made under duress.

Among experts, a furor continues to swirl over whether gentrification and displacement are conjoined. What qualifies as displacement, anyway? Forcible eviction by a rapacious landlord, obviously, but what about a rent that creeps up while a household's income doesn't? How about the intangible, dispiriting feeling of being out of place, or a young person's knowledge that leaving the family home means living in another borough? Or the dislocation that comes when an industry flees, taking its jobs along?

These pressures can affect investment bankers and nurses, as well as busboys and the unemployed, and it's not always easy to distinguish coerced departure from a fresh opportunity, or gentrifies from the displaced.

In 2005, Lance Freeman, a professor of urban planning at Columbia, examined national housing statistics to see whether low-income residents move more often once their neighborhoods start to gentrify. His conclusion was that they don't. Mobility, he suggested, is a fact of American life, and he could find no evidence to suggest that gentrification intensifies it. Instead, it appears that many low-income renters stay put even as their rents go up. "It may be that households are choosing to stay in these neighborhoods because quality of life is improving: They're more satisfied, but they're dedicating a larger slice of their income to housing," says Ingrid Gould Ellen, co-director of NYU's Furman Center for Real Estate and Urban Policy. There is an exception: Poor homeowners who see the value of their properties skyrocket often do cash out. Freeman garnished his findings with caveats and qualifications, but his charged conclusion fueled an outbreak of headlines that have dogged him ever since.

Eight years after he lit the gentrification-is-good-for-everyone match, Freeman sits in his office at Columbia, more resigned than rah-rah about the implications of his work. He doesn't doubt that displacement occurs, but he describes it as an inevitable consequence of capitalism. "If we are going to allow housing to be a market commodity, then we have to live with the downsides, even though we can blunt the negative effects to some extent. It's pretty hard to get around that."

That infuriates the British scholar Tom Slater, who sees Freeman's data studies as largely irrelevant because, he has written, they "cannot capture the struggles low-income and working-class people endure *to remain where they are*." Freeman waves away the binary rhetoric. "You can't boil gentrification down to good-guy-versus-bad-guy. That makes a good morality play, but life is a lot messier than that." In the days when RFK was helping to launch Restoration, an ideological split divided those who wrote cities off as unlivable relics from those who believed they must be saved. Today, a similar gulf separates those who fear an excess of prosperity from those who worry about the return of blight. Economic flows can be reversed with stunning speed: Gentrification can nudge a neighborhood up the slope; decline can roll it off a cliff. Somewhere along that trajectory of change is a sweet spot, a mixed and humming street that is not quite settled or sanitized, where Old Guard and new arrivals coexist in equilibrium. The game is to make it last.

Credit _____

Davidson, Justin. "Is Gentrification All Bad?" *New York Magazine* 2 Feb. 2014. Print.

Gentrification's Insidious Violence: The Truth about American Cities

Daniel José Older

A former paramedic in New York City, Daniel José Older has gained notoriety as a widely-respected writer of fantasy and young-adult fiction. His first novel, Half-Resurrection Blues, *was published by Penguin Books in 2015. That same year a production company optioned for the film and television rights to both the debut novel and two more in his anticipated series. Based in Brooklyn, a city whose issues with gentrification have been well-documented, Older has commented frequently in articles and interviews about the racial and socioeconomic tensions in his city. In his op-ed piece, "Gentrification's Insidious Violence," Older addresses Justin Davidson's rosy portrait of gentrification in New York City neighborhoods directly, arguing that the feature Davidson ignores—the inevitable displacement of poorer, long-standing residents—is its most pressing problem. He calls this displacement a kind of cultural "erasure," and "a slow, dirty war" perpetuated by the privileged white optimism echoed in Davidson's article.*

গ৶৹৻৶৹৻৶৹

Too many claim white people are at risk in communities of color. Really, it's those communities that are threatened.

গ৶৹৻৶৹৻৶৹

A few years back, when I was still a paramedic, we picked up a white guy who had been pistol whipped during a home invasion in Williamsburg. "I can't believe this happened to me," he moaned, applying the ice pack I'd given him to a small laceration on his temple. "It's like a movie!"

Indeed.

While film narratives of white folks in low-income neighborhoods tend to focus on how endangered they are by a gangland black or brown menace, this patient was singular in that he was literally the only victim of black on white violence I encountered in my entire 10-year career as a medic.

"What is distinctively 'American' is not necessarily the amount or kind of violence that characterizes our history," Richard Slotkin writes, "but the mythic significance we have assigned to the kinds of violence we have actually experienced, the forms of symbolic violence we imagine or invent, and the political uses to which we put that symbolism." Slotkin was talking about the American frontier as a symbolic reference point for justifying expansionist violence throughout history. Today, we can see the mytho-political uses of symbolic violence in mainstream media portrayals of the "hood."

It's easy to fixate on physical violence. Movies sexualize it, broadcasters shake their heads as another fancy graphic whirs past sensationalizing it, politicians build careers decrying it with one side of their mouths and justifying it with the other. But institutionalized violence moves in far more insidious and wide-reaching patterns. "Gentrification," Suey Park and Dr. David J. Leonard wrote in a recent post at Model View Culture, "represents a socio-historic process where rising housing costs, public policy, persistent segregation, and racial animus facilitates the influx of wealthier, mostly white, residents into a particular neighborhood. Celebrated as 'renewal' and an effort to 'beautify' these communities, gentrification results in the displacement of residents."

Gentrification is violence. Couched in white supremacy, it is a systemic, intentional process of uprooting communities. It's been on the rise, increasing at a frantic rate in the last 20 years, but the roots stretch back to the disenfranchisement that resulted from white flight and segregationist policies. Real estate agents dub changing neighborhoods with new, gentrifier-friendly titles that designate their proximity to even safer areas: Bushwick becomes East Williamsburg, parts of Flatbush are now Prospect Park South. Politicians manipulate zoning laws to allow massive developments with only token nods at mixed-income housing.

Beyond these political and economic maneuvers, though, the thrust of gentrification takes place in our mythologies of the hood. It is a result, as Park and Leonard explain, of a "discourse that imagines neighborhoods of color as pathological and criminal, necessitating outside intervention for the good of all." Here's where my pistol-whipped patient's revelation about his cinematic experience kicks in. The dominant narrative of the endangered white person barely making it out of the hood alive is, of course, a myth. No one is safer in communities of color than white folks. White privilege provides an invisible force field around them, powered by the historically grounded assurance that the state and media will prosecute any untoward event they may face.

With gentrification, the central act of violence is one of erasure. Accordingly, when the discourse of gentrification isn't pathologizing communities of color, it's erasing them. *Girls*, for example, reimagines today's Brooklyn as an entirely white community. Here's a show that places itself in the epicenter of a gentrifying city with gentrifiers for characters—it is essentially a show about gentrification that refuses to address gentrification. After critics lambasted Season 1 for its lack of diversity, the show brought in Donald Glover to play a black Republican and still managed to avoid the more pressing and relevant question of displacement and racial disparity that the characters are, despite their self-absorption, deeply complicit with. What's especially frustrating about *Girls* not only dodging the topic entirely but pushing back—often with snark and defensiveness against calls for more diversity—is that it's a show that seems to want to bring a more nuanced take on the complexities of modern life.

In an appallingly overwritten *New York Magazine* article with the (I guess) provocative title "Is Gentrification All Bad?," Justin Davidson imagines a first wave of gentrifiers much the way I've heard it described again and again: "A trickle of impecunious artists hungry for space and light." This is the standard, "first it was the artists" narrative of gentrification, albeit a little spruced up, and the unspoken but the understood word here is "white." Because, really, there have always been artists in the hood. They aren't necessarily recognized by the academy or using trust funds supplementing coffee shop tips to fund their artistic careers, but they are still, in fact, artists. The presumptive, unspoken "white" in the first round of artists gentrification narrative is itself an erasure of these artists of color.

"In the popular imagination, gentrification and displacement are virtually synonymous," Davidson writes without giving any actual data to back up his claim. And, he adds, "a sense of grievance and shame permeates virtually all discussions of neighborhood change." Davidson's euphemistic, maybe-it's-this-but-probably-it's-that take on gentrification is precisely the type of reporting we hear on WNYC and other media outlets on a regular basis. The standard frame for a story on gentrification pits the upside of "urban renewal" against what's painted as a necessary byproduct of this renewal: some folks have to move out. The underlying premise is, are these bakeries and coffee shops worth a few people having to move? And the underlying answer is, of course! The entirety of Bloomberg's tenure as mayor was a continuous stream of bring-in-the-rich schemes, openly flaunted and always at the cost of New York's poor. What's missing from this analysis is that the forced displacement of peoples and dispersal of communities, whether through economic, political or cultural policies, is a long-term human rights violation.

For groups facing economic and cultural marginalization in the U.S., community means much more than just a residential area. In a country whose institutions historically fail or deliberately erase us, community constitutes a central pillar in surviving hetero-patriarchal white supremacy. Technology has brought new possibilities for collective action and resistance, but the centrality of physical community remains crucial. What becomes of community organizing, which is responsible for our continued survival here, when communities are increasingly uprooted and scattered?

The shifting power dynamics of today's urban neighborhoods are reflected even in issues of food and nutrition. "Once-affordable ingredients have been discovered by trendy chefs," cultural critic Mikki Kendall writes, "and have been transformed into haute cuisine. Food is facing gentrification that may well put traditional meals out of reach for those who created the recipes. Despite the hype, these ingredients have always been delicious, nutritious and no less healthy than other sources of protein." Writing about this phenomenon at Bitch Media, Soleil Ho stated that food gentrification takes "the form of a curious kind of reacharound logic wherein economic and racial minorities are castigated for eating 'primitively' and 'unhealthily' while their traditional foods are cherry picked for use by the upper class as 'exotic' delicacies."

"Even gentrifiers themselves are convinced they are doing something terrible," Davidson continues. "Young professionals whose moving trucks keep pulling up to curbs in Bushwick and Astoria carry with them trunkfuls of guilt." It's an odd and eloquent assumption about the mind of a gentrifier, but really, it's irrelevant what they think or what Davidson thinks they think. The gears are all already in place, the mechanisms of white supremacy and capitalism poised to make their moves. Davidson talks of a "sweet spot": some mythical moment of racial, economic harmony where the neighborhood stays perfectly diverse and balanced. There is no "sweet spot," as Andrew Padilla at El Barrio Tours points out in his excellent point-by-point takedown, just fleeting moments of harmony in the midst of an ongoing legacy of forced displacement.

Here's a refrain you'll hear a lot in conversations about gentrifications: "Well, it's really a class issue." Davidson's piece manages to avoid any race analysis whatsoever. Of course economics plays a huge role in this. But race and class are inseparably entwined. Rising rents, along with institutionally racist policies like stop-and-frisk, have forced black people to leave New York and urban areas around the country at historic rates. And yes, there are many layers at play: When non-black people of color with class privilege, like myself, move into a historically black and lower-income neighborhood, the white imagination reads our presence as making the area a notch safer for them.

The mythology of safety and racial coding regards our presence as a marker of change; the white imagination places higher value on anything it perceives as closer to itself, further from blackness. We become complicit in the scam; the cycle continues.

These power plays—cultural, political, economic, racial—are the mechanics of a city at war with itself. It is a slow, dirty war, steeped in American traditions of racism and capitalism. The participants are often wary, confused, doubtful. Macklemore summarized the attitudes of many young white wealthy newcomers in his fateful text to Kendrick Lamar on Grammy night: "It's weird and sucks that I robbed you." But as with Macklemore, being surprised about a system that has been in place for generations is useless. White supremacy is nothing if not predictable. To forge ahead, we require an outrageousness that sees beyond the tired tropes and easy outs that mass media provides. This path demands we organize with clarity about privilege and the shifting power dynamics of community. It requires foresight, discomfort and risk-taking. It will be on the Web and in the streets, in conversations, rants and marches.

We need a new mythology.

Credit _____

Older, Daniel José. "Gentrification's Insidious Violence: The Truth about American Cities." This article first appeared in Salon.com, at *http://www.Salon.com*. An online version remains in the Salon archives. Reprinted with permission.

Go Forth and Gentrify?

Dashka Slater

Dashka Slater is a novelist, children's author, and award-winning journalist whose work has appeared in Newsweek, Salon, The New York Times Magazine, *and* Mother Jones. *In 2004, she received a creative writing fellowship from the National Endowment for the Arts. In her article, "Go Forth and Gentrify," first published in* Mother Jones, *Slater acknowledges both the historic and existing displacement gentrification causes, but wonders if current, negative predictions about the trend are not, in part, perception. She goes on to defend the role "[u]pscale newcomers" can play in a struggling neighborhood, bringing, as she sees it, an enterprising energy toward improving local businesses and schools for all who live there.*

⋘⋙⋘⋙⋘⋙

Eighteen years ago my husband and I bought our first house in what real estate agents termed an "up and coming" neighborhood in Oakland, California. We didn't think of ourselves as gentrifiers. We were paying more than we could afford, hoping that someday our neighborhood would have more cafés and fewer car thefts. We eventually bailed, but today the pawnshops and porn theater have indeed been replaced by boutiques and bakeries, and the house we sold at a loss has tripled in value.

So are "transitional" homebuyers guilty of class warfare? It's easy to talk about the downside of gentrification—high housing prices, evictions, and a creeping nimbyism that elbows out social services. But there are benefits, too. When the white middle class left America's cities in the 1950s and '60s, they took the tax base with them, leaving behind concentrated pockets of poverty and powerlessness. Upscale newcomers bring investment, jobs, and tax revenue to neighborhoods that desperately need them, as well as intangibles like the political know-how required to extract money and services from urban bureaucracies.

There's also the environmental benefit. Renovating a house in the urban core is far more sustainable than commuting to a newly built subdivision. A University of Toronto study found that residents of low-density suburbs consumed twice as much energy and produced twice as much greenhouse gases as those living in the city centers.

Whether the costs outweigh the benefits is a tough call, partly because some of what we think we know about gentrification isn't exactly right. Take displacement. A 2005 study by Lance Freeman, a professor of urban planning at Columbia University, found the chances that a poor resident of a gentrifying neighborhood would be forced to move were only 1.5 percent—compared to a 1 percent chance of that same resident being displaced in a nongentrifying neighborhood. This is partly because poor people tend to be transient anyway, and partly because poor neighborhoods tend to have high vacancy rates. Maureen Kennedy, a Clinton administration housing official who coauthored a study of gentrification for the Brookings Institution, found that in one Cleveland neighborhood, city residents believed there had been an enormous displacement of blacks by whites, although census data revealed that there had been only a "modest inflow" of white residents. But, she adds, "perception becomes reality."

That's in part because blacks are moving to the suburbs at twice the rate of whites, an exodus driven as much by high crime as it is by high housing prices. "At least 50 percent have left because of poor education and poor public safety," says housing activist Charlene Overshown, who two years ago moved back into the West Oakland neighborhood where she grew up and has been astonished by the rise in rents and the increase in white residents.

It's true, though, that gentrifiers often exist in a kind of parallel universe. They live behind locked gates, send their kids to private schools, shop outside the neighborhood, and avoid the parks. As Freeman observes, their only interaction with the neighbors may come when they call the cops because the music's too loud.

The problem, says John A. Powell, a leading scholar of race at Ohio State University, stems from making choices based solely on your own costs and benefits. For example, should you send your kid to the local public school? "If I decide to send my kid to a school that's dysfunctional, I feel bad. If I decide not to send my kid to a school that's dysfunctional, I also feel bad. Regardless of my choice, the school remains the same. The question is, how can I transform the system not just for me but for the people who don't have the choices?"

Get involved, suggests Nancy Gapasin Gnass, a high school history teacher who bought into San Francisco's Mission district during the final days of the dot-com boom. She sends her daughter to a local school where 79 percent of the students receive free or subsidized lunches and 80 percent are Latino or black; she volunteers at the school, sits on the PTA and the school site council, and has organized a group that revitalized the local park. When Gnass' daughter turned six this year, she invited the entire class. Eighteen out of twenty children came to the party and brought their families. "We all walk to school together," says Gnass, who is Filipina. "My Spanish is horrible, but I try."

Newcomers elsewhere have helped their neighbors fight evictions, taught at the local school, and started businesses that hired locals. Make sure to patronize local businesses and help the owners figure out how to "ride the wave" of new customers, adds Kennedy. Most important, urges Overshown, "Help us fight for more affordable housing. If you say this is the only place you can afford to live, well, let's all fight so that at least some of the folks, the folks who *want* to stay, can stay here."

Credit _____

Slater, Dashka. "Go Forth and Gentrify?" *Mother Jones* 1 July 2007: Web.

Unit 4

Cultures and Identities

In the opening article of this unit, "Race, Wealth, and Intergenerational Poverty" by Darrick Hamilton and William Darity Jr., the authors establish one of the overarching themes of Unit 4: that a person's relationship to power more often than not correlates with his or her access to privilege. And while what is privileged by a society shifts across decades, certain disparities persist: specifically, power dynamics between races, genders, sexual identities, and socioeconomic strata. The United States of the 21st century, a solid 50 years after the seismic convulsions of the 1960s Civil Rights Movement and second wave feminism, is still grappling with these disparities in arguably more subtle and psychologically complex ways. For example, Sheryl Sandberg, the first female COO of Facebook, in a selection from her book *Lean In*, demands that women be more assertive in a system where women continue to contend with a lack of societal and institutional support for their most ambitious professional goals. And in his article, "When Race Disappears", David Theo Goldberg charts the distressing ways in which Trayvon Martin's murder has illuminated archaic, yet deeply held inequities in our culture regarding "unacceptable" and "suspicious" behaviors in young black men.

This chapter aims to illustrate the difficult play between those who believe that the privileges they have are self-evident rights and those who challenge the very systems and policies that limit access to privilege in the first place. In a particularly modern spin, the article "Standing Up for the Rights of New Fathers" recounts one man's pursuit of a more generous and equitable paternity leave policy for working fathers. That more men wish to have comparable time off to be with their newborns also indicates a larger societal shift in the redefinition of family roles and responsibilities; in other words, our various pursuits of privilege intersect. And in order to understand our own, nuanced relationships to privilege, we must consider the varying perspectives that others have about whether privilege is achieved or withheld, about whether privilege is a national inheritance grounded in our Bill of Rights, or a crooked race to an elusive top.

What Happened to Post-Racial America?

Ward Connerly

Ward Connerly is the president of the American Civil Rights Coalition, a national, non-profit organization, as well as an author. He wrote Creating Equal: My Fight Against Race Preferences *(2007) and* Lessons from My Uncle James: Beyond Skin Color to the Content of Our Character *(2008). His article, "What Happened to Post-Racial America," was originally published in* The Wall Street Journal *on October 4, 2011. In the essay, Connerly adds a conservative voice to the discussion concerning affirmative action or policies that provide equal opportunities to underrepresented persons. He feels that affirmative action makes Americans "content with mediocrity" and argues that President Obama's Executive Order promoting "Diversity and Inclusion in the Federal Workforce" should be rescinded.*

⚜⚜⚜

Few government policies have had the reach, immortality, and consequences of affirmative action. A policy that could be justified at its start, affirmative action has now become yesterday's solution to yesterday's problem. Yet it endures as if nothing has happened in the past 50 years.

There is an interracial man—although self-identified "African-American"— occupying the White House, blacks are on our courts, including the highest court in the land, blacks are mayors of major cities and heads of American corporations.

Notwithstanding all this, President Barack Obama, who was elected largely because Americans thought he would lead the nation to a Promised Land of post-racialism, recently signed Executive Order 13583 "to promote Diversity and Inclusion in the Federal Workforce." The irony is that few institutions in America are more "diverse" and "inclusive" than the federal government, where the workforce is 17% black while blacks are roughly 13% of the U.S population.

In addition to the president's executive order, the Dodd-Frank financial-reform law included Section 342, promoted by Rep. Maxine Waters (D., Calif.), which should be called the "White Male Exclusion Act." It establishes in all federal financial regulatory agencies an "Office of Minority and Women Inclusion" with responsibility for "diversity in management, employment and business activities."

It is doubtful that anyone can name a government agency that does not include an affirmative-action office or "diversity" department in its structure. The infrastructure of the diversity network is vast.

More than anything else, the pursuit of diversity overshadows and subordinates excellence and competence and often makes us content with mediocrity. The late economist Milton Friedman once told me that "Freedom to compete fairly for university admissions, jobs, and contracts is central to all that America professes to be."

In a recent column on these pages, Stanford's Shelby Steele observed that "the values that made us exceptional have been smeared with derision. ... Talk of 'merit' or 'a competition of excellence' in the admissions office of any Ivy League university today and then stand by for the howls of academic laughter." As a former regent of the University of California, I can confirm that these howls, and worse, are not confined to the Ivy League.

When former Supreme Court Justice Sandra Day O'Connor ruled in the 2003 Grutter v. Bollinger decision that the use of race preferences was constitutional while in the pursuit of diversity, she offered the hope that such preferences would no longer be necessary by 2028. Eight years later, the federal government is moving further away from Justice O'Connor's goal, not closer.

The longer we allow preferences to endure in the guise of diversity, the more damage will be done to the nation. If the President is serious about America rededicating itself to our ideals—which are liberty, economic opportunity for all, individual merit, and the principle of equality—then he should begin with rescinding his executive order on affirmative action, calling on Congress to repeal Section 342 of Dodd-Frank, and paring back the burdensome and redundant diversity network that exists within the federal government.

Finally, he should urge Americans to embrace the color-blind vision of John F. Kennedy, who said that "race has no place in American life or law," and of Martin Luther King Jr., who dreamed of the day when the color of his children's skin would be subordinate to the content of their character.

Credit _____

Connerly, Ward. "What Happened to Post-Racial America?" *Wall Street Journal* 4 October 2011: A–19. Print. The *Wall Street Journal* is published by News Corporation's Dow Jones & Co. Reproduced with permission of Dow Jones & Company via Copyright Clearance Center.

When Race Disappears

David Theo Goldberg

David Theo Goldberg was born in South Africa and earned his Ph.D. in philosophy in 1985. Since then, he has written numerous books including The Threat of Race *(2009),* Racist Culture: Philosophy and the Politics of Meaning *(1993), and* Racial Subjects: Writing on Race in America *(1997). He is the director of the University of California Humanities Research Institute as well as a founding co-editor of* Social Identities: Journal for the Study of Race, Nation and Culture. *His article, "When Race Disappears," was published in the international journal* Comparative American Studies *in August 2012. In it, Goldberg argues that racism is still prevalent in America even though some believe that America has become "post-racial" since electing President Barack Obama. Goldberg presents various cases where race played a major role, beginning with the Trayvon Martin case, to illustrate the persistence of racism in contemporary America.*

⊶⊶⊷⊷⊶⊷

Trayvon Martin was a seventeen-year-old African-American boy visiting his father's fiancée who lived in a mostly white housing development in Florida. He was shot to death by a neighbourhood watch vigilante, George Zimmerman, while returning to his father's house after purchasing sweets and a soft drink early one evening at a neighbourhood store. (For a detailed account of events surrounding the Martin killing, see Barry et al., 2012.)

In a sense, Trayvon Martin was (at least potentially) every black teenage boy in America. Just about every young black American male has been stopped under a cloud of suspicion by police, neighbourhood watchmen or, in more extreme cases, by self-appointed vigilantes. George Zimmerman gravitated in the no-man's land between the latter two modes of identification. In 2011 alone, the New York City Police Department, under an orchestrated policy of racial profiling, stopped over 643,000 people on the city's streets. Eighty-seven percent of those stopped were black or Latino, far outstripping their proportional representation in the urban population, which amounts to a combined third of the city's make-up. Nine percent of the accosted were white (while making up 65 percent of the city's population).

Only 12 percent of those stopped were arrested or issued summonses as a result of these stoppages. Clearly, a very large number of black and brown people are being stopped and harassed, on the pretext, as Zimmerman put it, that they are "up to no good," that is, for no reason other than that they are not white.

Paul Haggis's film *Crash* (2004) tugged at the knotted impacts of these intrusions on black lives in the context of Los Angeles. Seek and the police shall find. Highway patrolmen on the main east–west highway that runs past St. Louis regularly pull over black drivers on "suspicion" of drug running and often confiscate their property—cars, cash—even when no wrongdoing has been established (Balko, 2012). If almost three times as many whites were stopped as their population proportion and treated with similar suspicion, you can be sure that their percentage of the criminalized would spiral upwards also.

The case of Trayvon Martin has filled the airwaves and blogosphere across the United States. The widespread community protests both in Florida—an initial gathering of 30,000 people in the town of Sanford, where he was killed—and around the country have prompted vigorous debate across local and national radio and television as well as on the internet. All this has elicited calls by politicians for thorough investigation of the events that led to his killing. In addition, it has renewed calls to reconsider laws that have encouraged police profiling of men of colour and their all too quick stereotyping-induced targeting by whites claiming self-defence. Even President Obama and the Republican presidential candidates have seen fit to weigh in.

In a relatively rare reference to race, President Obama poignantly pointed out that if he had a son, he would look like Trayvon Martin. What he failed to add is that his nominal son would also likely have been suspended from school at one time or another for fairly trivial behavioural infractions. Both Newt Gingrich and Rick Santorum, Republican presidential candidates at the time, chided Obama for invoking race, explicitly stressing that justice should be colour-blind. So in the face of staggering statistics about young black men being subjected to police harassment, racial profiling, and, to an unsettling degree, to white vigilante violence, some of the highest scales of political representation seem committed to placing racial reference outside the frame of reference for justice.

Trayvon Martin's killing, then, set off another one of those intermittent nationwide conversations about the racially inspired violence and threats faced especially by pretty much all young black men in America. (For a biting critique of the Martin case in the context of the war on America's youth, see Giroux, 2012.) In the wake of the Martin case, reports of racial profiling in police enforcement have proliferated. It has also raised, yet again if less obviously, concerns about blackness in the white imagination, and whiteness in the black imagination, as bell hooks insightfully responded some years ago.

In the white imagination blackness has prevailingly conjured the threat of criminality and violence, of laziness and the lack of self-reliance, as state beneficiaries and, in the body of the president now, as socialist, as the "racial hand-out" president. For whites, in short, blacks are slackers, no-gooders, takers. The question has been less pressed among whites, at least, about what their whiteness might signify for blacks. "Whites" as idea and as lived condition, as hooks suggested more than a decade ago, continues to represent a set of complex concerns for blacks, and for those taken not to be white more generally: the terror of harassment and police suspicion, of being stopped frequently even for minding one's own business or simply walking home, of being socially abandoned, evicted, and—in global political terms—more or less randomly bombed, of seeming to be out of place even in one's place. Whiteness, in short, signals to those supposedly not qualifying as white as a form of terrorism by the self-proclaimed guardians against it (hooks, 1992: 338–42).

A recent *Newsweek/Daily Beast* national poll in the wake of the Martin killing reveals stark divisions—and, by implication, dramatically different experiences—in America's racial experience. A solid majority of whites (65 percent) think there is either racial equality or close to racial equality between whites and blacks in the U.S. Only 16 percent of blacks claim to have achieved racial equality, and 47 percent showed scepticism that they would achieve racial equality in their lifetimes. Seventy percent of whites think blacks face no more challenges than whites do in securing affordable housing or landing a job. Among blacks, only 35 percent agree about housing, and 25 percent about securing work. And while close to all agree that racial profiling occurs, far fewer whites (less than 25 percent) than blacks (63 percent) think it happens regularly. And roughly 85 percent of whites think the police and courts treat blacks and whites equally, while over 50 percent of blacks think they are never treated equally in the criminal justice system. Two contrasting worlds, with very different life experiences, then (Schoen, 2012).

The Trayvon Martin case is far from an isolated incident regarding racial consideration in America. It needs to be read against a landscape of racially charged sociality. A recent poll in the state of Mississippi indicated that 21 percent of residents believe that racial intermarriage should be illegal, and another 29 percent are not sure whether it should be. A whopping 46 percent of Republican voters in that state think it should be illegal, while another 11 percent are unsure (Frayer, 2011). So in 2012 fully half the total population of Mississippi, recently identified as the most religious in the U.S., consider there to be something at the very least questionable about racial mixing. This, in a state that has recently created "The Mississippi Freedom Trail" to bolster tourism. The "Freedom Trail" marks approximately 30 key landmarks in Mississippi that figured prominently in the 1950s and 1960s civil rights struggles.

These include the Greyhound Bus where civil rights activists were brutally beaten by bigots as Mississippi police made sure no one would intervene during the Freedom Rides of 1963. Other tour sights include the driveway of Medgar Evers' home where he was shot to death by Klansmen in front of his family, and the firebombed tomb of NAACP leader, Vernon Dahmer. Haley Barbour, then Mississippi governor, one time Republican presidential candidate, head of the Republican National Committee and keen supporter of the white and by all accounts racially exclusionary Citizens Councils, committed $20 million to establishing the trail at a time when employment, education, living standards, and criminalization of black Mississippians in the state continue to rank as or among the worst in the U.S. (Trillin, 2011). Civil rights may be good enough for historic tourism while it is clearly in remission for contemporary civic expectation and experience.

In 2011, in Mississippi also, a white teenager, Daryl Dedmon, and four of his friends, all well known for their racial bigotry and bullying violence, one evening went seeking black men to pick on. They found James Craig Anderson, a 49-year-old Nissan car mechanic, walking to his car in a mall parking lot. They beat him repeatedly and then ran him over and killed him with Dedmon's truck in a chilling display of utter disregard for human life. Dedmon and his friends had a history of harassing black youth at school, were known to refer to black people in openly and only derogatory terms, and had been reported repeatedly to the school principal and local police for their terrorizing actions. Yet police in the case denied they had previously ignored the group's violence towards African-Americans even though they had done little to address the concerns.

These pernicious and violent sensibilities around socialities of the racial are hardly restricted to Mississippi. In El Cajon, a suburban town of San Diego close to the Mexican border, an Iraqi woman was bludgeoned to death in her home in March 2012, the assailant leaving a note by the bleeding body that read "Terrorist go home." A similar note had been posted on the family's front door a couple of months earlier. El Cajon is home to the largest Iraqi population in the United States, though still a significant minority relative to the local largely white, middle-class, and English-speaking population of the town. In November 2011, in White Plains, a town outside New York City, the heart device of a 68-year-old former marine and correctional officer, Kenneth Chamberlain, Sr., accidentally set off a medical alert. The alert sent ten police officers to his housing project apartment at 5 a.m. From behind the closed front door, Chamberlain indicated it was a false alarm. The police insisted he open the door, he demurred, they broke down the door, found him in only a pair of briefs, allegedly hurled a racial epithet at him before tasering him and shooting him to death for apparently resisting their intrusion. It appears that a 68-year-old black man suffering a heart condition is potentially Trayvon Martin too.

In Louisiana, a woman followed Republican presidential candidate Rick Santorum into a shooting gallery where, of all places, he was holding a campaign event. As Santorum was taking aim at the shooting target, the woman shouted out, "Pretend it is Obama." To his credit Santorum later decried the outburst, and the woman was detained for questioning by the Secret Service (Edwards-Levy, 2012). A bumper sticker store in Scottsdale, Arizona, has published for sale a series of stickers that read "2012 Don't Re-Nig," some scripted over the Confederate flag, others alongside a crossed out decal of the Obama campaign.

A national website called "Niggermania" is dedicated in its own terms "to spreading the truth and presenting facts about n------s." The landing page reads: "We also have many pages of n----r jokes and racist humour. Please join our forum where the word n----r is not only allowed but encouraged. All races and religions are welcome to join but n-----s and n----r sympathizers are not allowed." The website's loudly proclaimed name perhaps best represents the broader social sentiment, if mostly less loudly at play in the examples I have been citing here. The site provides just some among thousands of degrading online images, pernicious jokes and crude representations of the Obamas. While all presidents have been subject in public forums to opposition derision, none prior has remotely had to endure this level of completely demeaning and racially prompted disrespect for the man, his family, and the office.

This culture of derogation is underpinned by a proliferating public ecology of racial disrespect on the part of political representatives at pretty much all levels of representation. Earlier this year a federal judge in Montana forwarded an email to friends that characterized African-Americans as dogs and implied President Obama's mother had sexual intercourse with animals. The judge, Richard Cebull, made clear in the accompanying note that the email expressed sentiments he himself harboured about African-Americans and the president. Republican Congressman Doug Lamborn of Colorado called President Obama "tar baby." The Speaker of the Kansas State House, Mike O'Neal, forwarded an email referring to Michelle Obama as "YoMama" while "praying for the President's death." During his nationally televized State of the Union address a couple of years ago, South Carolina congressman Joe Wilson interrupted President Obama's speech in an unprecedented outburst, calling the president "a liar." A libertarian politician, Jules Manson, supporting Ron Paul's presidential campaign, called on Facebook to "assassinate the fucken n----r and his monkey children." Ron Paul had no comment in response. The head of the Texas College Republicans at the University of Texas tweeted that "My President is black, he snorts a lot of crack." A Republican newsletter in California in 2008 represented then-candidate Obama among fried chicken, watermelons, and food stamps. And current Republican presidential candidate Newt Gingrich has called Obama the "food stamp president."

The examples are pretty much endless. What sort of representation, before courts of justice and from elected officials, can black Americans expect to receive from those harbouring such views?

Social commentators tend to see not a trend or a pattern so much as "instances," which are then mostly waved aside on two grounds. First, they may be thought to individualize racist expression, for the most part to the persona of the current president. America seemed to be coming to terms with its racist legacy, largely by ignoring it, until a counter-stereotypical black man was "imposed" upon the country. This not only trivializes racial conditionality by reducing it to anomalous racial expression, it also initiates the trend of racial reversal, turning the object of racial aggression into the perpetrating subject. An editorial in the conservative *Washington Times* newspaper late in 2011 characterized the Obama re-election campaign as "stupid, evil, crazy, racist" (Golub 2011). There is an irony at work here. Racist characterization tends to objectify, to denude subjecthood into objectification. Here, however, in characteristic post-racial reversibility the objectified black man is made subject so as to relegate him—and by extension his "kind"—to the racist perpetrator.

But, second, these instances of racist expression tend to be trivialized by restricting them to jokes, innuendo, individualized expression. This draws attention away from the structural arrangements constituting socialities of the skin, from those that fix in place social subjects into positions of privilege and disprivilege, power and powerlessness. Black Americans continue to suffer unemployment at twice the rate of Americans at large. Today, black family wealth is one-twentieth of white family wealth (for Latinos, the ratio is one-eighteenth), up from one-twelfth three decades ago. Until March 2012, the Federal Bureau of Investigation training manual urged trainees never to stare at or shake hands with Asians, and to beware of Arabs, who have "Jekyll and Hyde personalities" increasing their likelihood of demonstrating "outbursts and loss of control" (Schmidt and Savage, 2012). A Hollywood screenwriter wouldn't be believed if writing this nonsense into a screenplay. Noted African-American national journalist, Juan Williams (author of the award-winning *Eyes on the Prize*, 1988), and Fox News commentator, sparked a heated debate when he claimed that he gets nervous when boarding a plane with "visibly Islamic" passengers. The coterminous public political attacks on stereotyped women and gay folk, in this sense, should not be read as unrelated. As Frantz Fanon and Jean-Paul Sartre both pointed out, when public attacks on one or another class of social pariahs proliferate, all others should pay attention for the attackers are threatening all those taken to be strangers, holding estranged social views, pariahs, outsiders, second-class citizens.

This, then, is America in the age of Obama. What to make of it? It is a state of being and social arrangement in which pernicious racial characterization proliferates, stereotypes readily circulate, and debilitating structures of racial differentiation are deepened. Trayvon Martin's killing evidences that young black men are more likely to have their lives violently foreshortened than are whites, no matter whether or not there is any explicit racist intentionality on the part of the killer. A black teenager wearing a hoodie instantaneously becomes a hoodlum, a gangbanger, while the abiding whiteness of swimmers, surfers, tennis players, and snowboarders who keep warm by keeping their heads covered in hoods are simply looking after their health as they make a fashion statement.

We are nowhere near the promise of a raceless America, or of a post-racial one. Indeed, the claim to post-raciality or racelessness itself is misleading, a sort of malapropism, serving rather to express states of raciality in the name of their erasure or evaporation. So, today's America is one in which blacks can be dismissed, beaten up, degraded, pulled over by police, and incarcerated in record numbers while the language for characterizing such expression as racially implicated has been denuded, trivialized, rubbed out, or denied.

The emptiness those denials effect—the neutralizing of the traditional racial charge— is filled now with racial reversal. Any attempt to characterize and criticize such expression as racist itself is reversed, and itself quickly becomes charged as racist. Family and friends supporting Zimmerman, Martin's admitted killer, are now claiming as much. Joe Oliver, an African-American friend of Zimmerman's, declared in a television interview that "if we weren't sitting here today talking about George shooting Trayvon, we'd be talking about Trayvon shooting George" (Christopher, 2012). Fearful self-defence by a man ten years the teenager's senior, shorter but weighing a good deal more, justifies black death. Conservative pundits have posted to websites reports of Martin's behavioural trouble at school (actually quite minor in the scheme of things), his tattoos (irrelevant), and stereotypical gangster style images of gold-capped teeth (completely fabricated). No questions to be further posed. The accusation of racism is misguided, except when you are doing it to me. Zimmerman's father blurted out in public, "I never foresaw so much hate coming from the President, the Black Congressional Caucus, the NAACP …" (Zimmerman, 2012), as though the trouble in which his son finds himself is a product of black power. Fifty years on, here is the civil rights struggle redux, only now stripped even of the conceptual terms to name the object of concern.

CRSOCRSOCRSO

The above range of examples suggests that buried in the vernacular of racial terms in denial are signals, if not judgements, about social fitness and unfitness, of reliability and unreliability, predictability and uncertainty, objects of fear but also, counterfactually, of fascination. Implicit judgements about social belonging and contribution are made in terms of racial insinuation, if not attribution, at once denied: the president wasn't born here, rendering him ineligible; he is a socialist, rendering him un-American; he is a power-grabbing wannabe monarch in a republic supposedly constitutionally committed to individual liberty and limited government; he is un-American, making his policies unrepresentative; he is Muslim, meaning not Christian, and so not acting on properly American values or with American wellbeing at heart.

There is a racial politics of corrigibility regarding Trayvon Martin, too. He was "inappropriately" dressed; on the street on a rainy night when he should have been home (it was all of 7 p.m.); stalking a neighbourhood not his, even if his father's fiancée lived there. In racially predictable, predictably racial fashion, Trayvon was "characteristically" suspended from school for bad behaviour (traces of marijuana were found in his backpack). He is made culpable for his own demise in "viciously" attacking Zimmerman, breaking his nose and banging his head repeatedly on the kerb side, even though a police video of Zimmerman's initial arrest after the killing shows him to have at most minor signs of the supposed beating, and he declined medical assistance when police showed up at the scene of the killing. No signs of a skirmish producing commensurable injuries with those being claimed were found on the teenager's dead body. Voice analysis of the screams for help during the scuffle leading up to the shooting, and heard on tape as a neighbourhood woman called 911 from her adjacent home, strongly suggest the screams emanated from Martin, not Zimmerman. The scuffle—there is disagreement about who of the two started it—seems to have taken place between a well-grassed lawn, where Martin's dead body was found by the police, and a cement sidewalk, which Zimmerman claimed had produced his own injuries.

Just as President Obama supposedly is unfit to be American, doesn't fit in America, is not fit to lead the country, so Trayvon Martin fails to belong in a gated community in suburban middle-class residential Florida. Explicit racial reference is deemed improperly invoked to reference social arrangements: when used by critical analysts of racial inequality it is dismissed by conservative critics as being just as out of place as Trayvon Martin was that night in Florida, or as a black couple is found "inappropriately" to "occupy" the White House (where black folk historically have been more likely to be fed in the kitchen than in the state dining room) (Lusane, 2011). It doesn't help that Sanford, Florida, was founded in the late nineteenth century by

Henry Sanford, a white segregationist and supremacist who served as emissary and lobbyist for King Leopold II of Belgium in the latter's drive to get recognition from the United States Congress for Leopold's colonization of the Congo. Sanford himself supported the exportation of America's black population to Africa (Daly, 2012). The deathly implications of history's racial symbolics are haunting here.

When surrogate terms for race are invoked disparagingly to dismiss the efforts or actions of people of colour, those condemned for using the terms deny intention or significance, decry over-sensitivity or "double standards." And when they might be forced, usually because they represent a public office, to issue an apology, invariably the apology is for the discomfort anyone may have suffered, never an embracing of one's own responsibility for having done something wrong, thus shifting responsibility from offender to target. Racial denial, in both senses, is the quid pro quo of racial accusation. And the denial of the denial is reflexive reaction when charges of insensitivity are levelled at the proponents of deniability. At the heart of racial signification is the prolific intensification of its fungibility.

It would help to speak here of *disappointment*. Barack Obama and his electioneering team ran for president in 2007–08 on the mantra of "Hope" and the mandate of "Change (we can believe in)." There has been profound disappointment especially but not only among some of President Obama's most vocal election supporters who at his election were deeply hopeful of a more progressive agenda and a genuine transcendence of American racial making. The hope conjured was capacious in its multiple meanings: hope for a more civil political engagement in the wake of civility's trampling; hope for a more equitable body politic regarding access to possibility and the promise of a decent life; hope in decency and the reinstitution of respect for and among global others; and hope in a post-raciality represented in the appealing figure of a mixed-race man for whom race seemed so little a burden.

Hopefulness—perhaps even if only half-justified giddiness at his election—has given way to dolefulness. The disappointment has been directed at the centrism of Obama's political achievement through his first term, all the challenges notwithstanding, and at the extension of some of the Bush policies, especially concerning claims to state security (Goldberg, 2012). There is an attendant disappointment, veering between sometime melancholia and indignation, both in the intensification of raciality rather than its *Aufhebung*, its overcoming, and in Obama's sometime evasions and silences regarding raciality in the face of calls for critical leadership. Black Americans decry his general silence, while applauding his occasional embrace of his own racial experience, as in his Trayvon comments. Whites decry any reference he makes to race, comfortable in his general silence about American raciality. The above-cited *Newsweek* poll revealed blacks to be overwhelmingly appreciative of the president's intervention, while whites found it "unhelpful" (Frayer, 2011).

Here, racial calculation becomes complexly configured as representative of power and its modes of negotiated domination. There tends to be a failure of recognition in this regard that raciality has never been uniformly singular. Raciality is characteristically multiplicitous, shifting in social arrangement and significance, never reducible to one thing or sensibility or social arrangement. And its multiplicity makes it precisely available to power's representation and calculability. The "incidentality" I mentioned above regarding race is a factor here: for whites, race comes in incidents, in "eventfulness"; for people of colour, it is the stuff of persistent everyday experience.

This incidentality, however, speaks to another dimension of contemporary raciality. Considered in terms of "eventfulness," raciality is reduced to "race": the everyday to the occasional; the wearisome weight of everyday baggage to the momentary and fleeting; the ubiquitous threat to the passing and ephemeral; ontological condition to the apparent; constitutive condition to mash-up and make believe.

This speaks to another, less affective sense of disappointment that I suggest is especially illuminating in this context. There are socialities, as Ackbar Abbas (1997) has put it, which are *dis-appointing*. They are dis-appointing in failing to comply or live up to pre-ordained expectations. They are dis-appointments in the non-standard sense of failing or really refusing to conform to their appointed places, to appointed modes of comprehension, of being and doing, to conventional social arrangements. It may be better to understand these manifestations as creases or tremors, warps or, more readily, foldings in on itself in the structure of contemporary sociality and politics. At once apparently states of ordinariness with recognizable everyday markers—residential, recreational, resourceful, socially containable, exploitable—they nevertheless are out of the ordinary. They refuse their *appointed* and so anticipated sites or roles, unrecognizable as and in their everydayness. They are dis-appointments in the sense of being out of place, dis-locations. But they also prompt different ways of speaking about the socialities they conjure, and in that sense they are dis-locutions as much as dislocations. They manifest where least anticipated and express themselves in unexpected and unpredictable ways.

These dis-appointing socialities seem to lack location, or more precisely locatedness. They cast adrift their signifying sources and so also any recognizable touchstone as the stabilizing basis for their comprehensibility. The unpredictability and prolific heterogeneity of "Occupy" sites, at least when they first emerged, exemplify this sense of dis-appointment. And one could say the same thing about Obama's initial run for the presidency. His first presidential term, by contrast, has sewn together these dual meanings, creating a mash-up of these contrasting senses of disappointment. While his policy achievements may have been disappointing in the first sense to supporters and detractors alike, the presidency of a man of many mixtures has been profoundly unsettling, dislocating—dis-appointing—to many, and in some ways to American society more generally. The recourse to renewed expressions of racial attribution and derogation across portions of the population has been one of the significant and significantly alienating responses to this unsettlement.

The *dis*-appointedness at work here is the source and expression of the sometime illegibility at play concerning the social conditions marked by a set of racial configurations no longer so readily nameable. This illegibility spawns a crisis of social representation and control. The social conditions of everyday life in these instances, as more generally, are no longer predictable, can no longer be taken for granted. What these dislocations and dislocutions now point to is the proliferation of the conditions of precariousness, conceptual and material, that we now increasingly and increasingly prolifically face. While there is still no guarantee that justice will be served for Trayvon Martin—what could that be in any case, having lost his life through no fault of his own?—George Zimmerman can no longer so readily assume, as he once might have been able to, that the whiteness of his relatively privileged family connections and influence would protect him from prosecution for shooting an unarmed black teenager.

So, raciality—racial characterization and structuration—invariably disappoints. It fails always to live up to expectation, to deliver (fully) on its premises and promise. The premises are belied by the facts of life. The promises of sustaining privilege and power are always relative to the extension of domination and subjugation. Their targets ultimately refuse, resist, rise up. Raciality accordingly fails as it succeeds. It takes away as it provides. In undercutting the values and virtues of heterogeneities, it projects easiness, simplicity, predictability, and profitability. But it produces always difficulty, complexity, fear, and fabricated danger; ultimately social loss. George Zimmerman is now paying the price of a sociality of the skin, as he sacrificed the life of an innocent to its projection, its misdirecting premises and false promise.

These logics of dis-appointment suggest related insights conjured by the concept of racial *dis-appearance*. In the more straightforward and so obvious sense, the commitment to racelessness is conceptually predicated. Racial differentiation should be rendered obsolete first and foremost by the erasure—the disappearance from social life—of racial conception. When race disappears, so too supposedly will racial arrangement. But numerous commentators have detailed recently how unjustifiable racial inequities are cemented into the social fabric now no longer identifiable because the terms by which they could be recognized through their nomination have been made to disappear. Racial disappearance in this sense signals both the conceptual evaporation and the material unrecognizability of racial matters (Goldberg, 2009).

As with racial dis-appointment, so racial *dis-appearance* speaks to the ways in which racialities re-appear in sometimes unexpected, perhaps unpredictable and less noticeable ways once race conceptually disappears. Consider the euphoria with which the first black president of the U.S. is greeted only to be dismissed quickly on the most pernicious of racist grounds. Racial identification is supposed to be unacceptable in matters of state but profiling proliferates in policing. Racial reference is supposed to evaporate but derogatory references, jokes, and insults become more voluble, more privately public as they are rendered publicly privatized. Invocation of race to invigorate formal distribution of public privilege or positions of power is outlawed but privately mobilized racial differentiation professionally, politically or recreationally spirals upward with considerable material impact. And indeed, as the language of race disappears from the formal sphere of public administration, the newly abstracted facelessness that follows in its wake seems to make drone bombing at a human distance easier to stomach, more readily unquestioned.

So when race disappears, the racial dis-appears. Racial arrangements pop up elsewhere, less readily marked and so not so easily categorized or identifiable. Raciality re-appears in other ways, in newly formulated if less explicit terms in the renewal of contemporary social fabrication, the reweaving of the social in the wake of racial privatization. George Zimmerman could initially get away with murder, and the still anonymous White Plains policemen might yet get away with execution, precisely because the alleged aggression on the part of the killed in both cases fits a longstanding presumption about black men across almost all periods of the life cycle, even where much, if not all of the material evidence evidently belies the allegations.

Racial dis-appearance, then, reveals the effects of a culture of neoliberalizing privatization. It illustrates the sorts of implications that follow when privilege and power are hidden from scrutiny behind the walls of privately structured social arrangements. *Citizens United,* the 2008 U.S. Supreme Court case that enabled private individuals to anonymously donate limitless funding to political action committees so as to impact any election campaign they deemed beneficial to their privately architected interests, represents dis-appearance at the level of political economy. The logic of this sort of politico-economic dis-appearance finds its expression well articulated in the raciality I have been revealing here.

There is an acute awkwardness at work, accordingly, as race disappears from the official administrative lexicon. Presumptions like those concerning the aggression of black men can neither be recognized nor socially sustained without their informal persistence and insistence in privatized settings, supposedly outside the reach of the state. Non-racialists find themselves caught between the insistence that the state not categorize racially, on the one hand, and the recognition, on the other, that the right to free private expression and individualized self-defence "by any means necessary" includes the unhindered possibility of even the most pernicious racist expression. This is directed at a racial group at large even if individualized to only some members of the targeted group when circumstances call for the opportunity. It is enough, even necessary, that only a subset of the targeted racial group bear the "characteristic" traits or exhibit the behaviour in question. After all, that some of the accuser's best friends are group members becomes the defence of first and last resort against charges of racism, and, as it turns out, accusations of racially prompted murder.

For want of a better category, let's call this the "Obama effect." This is a structural condition, not reducible simply to Barack Obama's individualized responsibility, even if his own non-racialism has sometimes helped to shore up the structural formation underlying the tensions at play. Structurally, then, a sociality predicated on nonracialism necessarily entails that racial disappearance will continue to sustain what I have characterized above as dis-appearing raciality. A robust social commitment to critical anti-racism, by contrast, is unlikely to suffer the "Obama effect." Racial disappearance/dis-appearance has made the effectiveness of anti-racist commitments more difficult to achieve because the objects are more nebulous. The "machinic architecture" of racial states has been displaced by the interactions between what Ash Amin (2010) insightfully characterizes as the "vernacular" and "biopolitical regimes," between everyday expression and newly fashioned modes of racially ordered securitization and dispersed control. A critical anti-racism, nevertheless, finds disappearing race deeply knotted with dis-appearing raciality in ways I have attempted to lay out above. The focus for a critical anti-racism is neither simply public racial erasure nor the privatizing dis-appearing of raciality. It is unswervingly the demeaning and potentially deadly effects of that interplay between the vernacular and biopolitical regimes to which, as the Trayvon Martin case so painfully reminds us, both give rise.

Acknowledgments

I am grateful to my colleagues Ackbar Abbas, Nisha Kapoor and Diren Valayden, conversations with whom inspired various conceptual insights included in this article.

Works Cited

Abbas, A. *1997. Hong Kong: Culture and the Politics of Disappearance.* Minneapolis: University of Minnesota Press.

Amin, A. 2010. "The Remainders of Race." *Theory, Culture & Society*, 27(1): 1–23.

Christopher, T. 2012. Lawrence O'Donnell's Interview of "Joe Oliver Didn't Just Make Fireworks, It Made News." *Mediaite.* Available at: <http://www.mediaite.com/tv/lawrence-odonnells-interview-of-joe-oliver-didnt-justmake-fireworks–it-made-news/>.

Balko, R. 2012. "Illinois Traffic Stop of Star Trek Fans Raises Concerns About Drug Searches, Police Dogs, Bad Cops." *Huffington Post*, 31 March. Available at: <http://www.huffingtonpost.com/2012/03/31/drug-searchtrekies-stopped-searched-illinois_n_1364087.html>.

Barry, D. et al. 2012. "In the Eye of a Firestorm: In Florida, an Intersection of Tragedy, Race and Outrage." *New York Times,* 2 April. Available at: <http://www.msnbc.msn.com/id/46922042/ns/us_news-the_new_york_times/#.T3vNto4Vm_g>.

Daly, M. 2012. "Sanford's Racist Past." *Daily Beast,* 4 April. Available at: <http://www.thedailybeast.com/articles/2012/04/04/the-city-of-sanford-s-racist-past.html>.

Edwards-Levy, A. 2012. "Rick Santorum Shoots Gun at Firing Range, Condemns 'Pretend It's Obama' Comment." *Huffington Post*, 23 March. Available at: <http://www.huffingtonpost.com/2012/03/23/rick-santorum-gunfiring-range-obama_n_1375756.html>.

Frayer, L. 2011. "46 Percent of Mississippi Republicans Want Interracial Marriage Banned." *Aol.news.com,* 8 April. Available at: <http://www.aolnews.com/2011/04/08/46-percent-of-mississippi-republicans-wantinterracial- marriage/>.

Giroux, H. 2012. "Hoodie Politics: Trayvon Martin and Racist Violence in Post-Racial America." *Truthout,* 2 April. Available at: <http://truth-out.org/news/item/8203-hoodie-politics-and-the-death-of-trayvon-martin>.

Goldberg, D. T. 2009. *The Threat of Race: Reflections on Racial Neoliberalism.* Oxford: Wiley-Blackwell.

Goldberg, D. T. 2012. "The Tale of Two Obamas." *Qualitative Sociology.* Available at: <http://www.springerlink. com/content/965u7351124770k7/?MUD=MP>.

Golub, E. 2011. "Barack Obama's Stupid, Evil, Crazy, Racist 2012 Campaign." *Washington Times*, 5 October. Available at: <http://communities.washingtontimes.com/neighborhood/tygrrrr-express/2011/oct/5/barack-obamasstupid-evil-crazy-racist-2012-campai/>.

hooks, bell. 1992. "Representing Whiteness in the Black Imagination." In: L. Grossberg et al., eds. *Cultural Studies.* New York and London: Routledge, pp. 338–42.

Lusane, C. 2011. *The Black History of the White House.* San Francisco, CA: City Lights Books.

Schmidt, M. & Savage, C. 2012. "Language Deemed Offensive Is Removed from F.B.I. Training Materials." *New York Times*, 29 March.

Schoen, D. 2012. "Newsweek/Daily Beast Poll Finds Majorities of Americans Think Country Divided by Race." *Daily Beast*, 7 April. Available at: <http://www.thedailybeast.com/articles/2012/04/07/newsweek-daily-beastpoll-finds-majorities-of-americans-think-country-divided-by-race.html>.

Trillin, C. 2011. "Back on the Bus: Remembering the Freedom Riders." *The New Yorker*, 25 July, pp. 36–42.

Williams, J. 1988. *Eyes on the Prize: America's Civil Rights Years, 1954–1965.* Harmondsworth: Penguin.

Zimmerman, G. 2012. Interview. Fox 35 News, 29 March. Available at: <http://www.youtube.com/watch?v= LnEQQnj7eXo>.

Credit

Goldberg, David Theo. "When Race Disappears." *Comparative American Studies*, 10.2. Aug. 2012: 116–27. Print. www.maneyonline.com/cas.

Facts and Fallacies about Paycheck Fairness

Phyllis Schlafly

Phyllis Schlafly is a social and political conservative as well as a retired constitutional lawyer, conservative activist, author, speaker, and founder of the Eagle Forum, a conservative interest group focused mostly on social issues. In the 1970s, she organized a group of women to oppose the Equal Rights Amendment, which was considered instrumental in the eventual non-ratification of the amendment. Her article "Facts and Fallacies about Paycheck Fairness" was originally published in 2014 by the Christian Post, *a "comprehensive Christian news website." In her article, Schlafly continues to battle modern feminist ideals by claiming the pay gap is virtually non-existent and what remains of the gap is caused by choices made by women.*

CR80CR80CR80

President Barack Obama and his feminist friends have been trotting out their tiresome slogan that women are paid only 77 cents for every dollar a man earns. Every reputable scholar who has commented has proved that this is a notorious falsehood that anyone should be embarrassed to use.

U.S. law calls for equal pay for equal work, but the feminist slogan is not based on equal work. Women work fewer hours per day, per week, per year. They spend fewer years as full-time workers outside the home, avoid jobs that require overtime, and choose jobs with flexibility to take time off for personal reasons. According to the Bureau of Labor Statistics, men are twice as likely as women to work more than 40 hours a week.

Women place a much higher value on pleasant working conditions: a clean, comfortable, air-conditioned office with congenial co-workers. Men, on the other hand, are more willing to endure unpleasant working conditions to earn higher pay, doing dirty, dangerous outside work. In 2012, men suffered 92 percent of work-related deaths.

If a man is supporting his family at the peak of his career, he often works longer hours to maximize his earnings. By contrast, a successful woman who reaches a high rank in her career is more likely to reduce her working hours.

All these reasons for women voluntarily choosing lower pay are now beyond dispute among those who have looked at the facts. But even those explanations for the alleged pay "gap" are still only part of the story.

Perhaps an even more important reason for women's lower pay is the choices women make in their personal lives, such as having children. Women with children earn less, but childless women earn about the same as men.

Another fact is the influence of hypergamy, which means that women typically choose a mate (husband or boyfriend) who earns more than she does. Men don't have the same preference for a higher-earning mate.

While women prefer to HAVE a higher-earning partner, men generally prefer to BE the higher-earning partner in a relationship. This simple but profound difference between the sexes has powerful consequences for the so-called pay gap.

Suppose the pay gap between men and women were magically eliminated. If that happened, simple arithmetic suggests that half of women would be unable to find what they regard as a suitable mate.

Obviously, I'm not saying women won't date or marry a lower-earning man, only that they probably prefer not to. If a higher-earning man is not available, many women are more likely not to marry at all.

In colleges, there are no gender separations in courses of study, and students can freely choose their majors. There are no male and female math classes. But women generally choose college courses that pay less in the labor market.

Those are the choices that women themselves make. Those choices contribute to the pay gap, just as much as the choice of a job with flexible hours and pleasant working conditions.

The pay gap between men and women is not all bad because it helps to promote and sustain marriages. Since husband and wife generally pool their incomes into a single economic unit, what really matters is the combined family income, not the pay gap between them.

In two segments of our population, the pay gap has virtually ceased to exist. In the African-American community and in the millennial generation (ages 18 to 32), women earn about the same as men, if not more.

It just so happens that those are the two segments of our population in which the rate of marriage has fallen the most. Fifty years ago, about 80 percent of Americans were married by age 30; today, less than 50 percent are.

Just a coincidence? I think not. The best way to improve economic prospects for women is to improve job prospects for the men in their lives, even if that means increasing the so-called pay gap.

The real economic story of the past 30 years is that women's pay has effectively risen to virtual parity, but men's pay has stagnated and thousands of well-paid blue-collar jobs have been shipped to low-wage countries. Nobody should be surprised that the marriage rate has fallen, the age of first marriage has risen, and marriage, in general, has become unstable.

Credit

Schlafly, Phyllis. "Facts and Fallacies About Paycheck Fairness." *The Christian Post* 15 Apr. 2014: Web.

Why I Want Women to Lean In

An exclusive excerpt from *Lean In: Women, Work, and the Will to Lead*
Sheryl Sandberg

Sheryl Sandberg is a technology executive, author, activist, and the Chief Operating Officer at Facebook. Prior to her COO position at Facebook, she worked as Vice President of Global Online Sales and Operations at Google and as Chief of Staff for the United States Secretary of the Treasury. She and Nell Scovell, a television and magazine writer, wrote Lean In: Women, Work and the Will to Lead, *published in 2013. "Why I Want Women to Lean In" is an excerpt from her book and was originally published in Time in 2013. The excerpt provides professional women with three pieces of advice to help them "lean in" and "dismantle the internal barriers" holding women back.*

CRISORCRISORCRISOR

Today in the United States and the developed world, women are better off than ever before. But the blunt truth is that men still run the world. While women continue to outpace men in educational achievement, we have ceased making real progress at the top of any industry. Women hold around 14% of Fortune 500 executive-officer positions and about 17% of board seats, numbers that have barely budged over the last decade. This means that when it comes to making the decisions that most affect our world, our voices are not heard equally.

It is time for us to face the fact that our revolution has stalled. A truly equal world would be one where women ran half of our countries and companies, and men ran half of our homes. The laws of economics and many studies of diversity tell us that if we tapped the entire pool of human resources and talent, our performance would improve.

Throughout my career, I was told over and over about inequalities in the workplace and how hard it would be to have a career and a family. I rarely, however, heard anything about the ways I was holding myself back. From the moment they are born, boys and girls are treated differently. Women internalize the negative messages we get throughout our lives—the messages that say it's wrong to be outspoken, aggressive, more powerful than men—and pull back when we should lean in.

We must not ignore the real obstacles women face in the professional world, from sexism and discrimination to a lack of flexibility, access to child care and parental leave. But women can dismantle the internal barriers holding us back today. Here are three examples of how women can lean in.

Don't Leave Before You Leave

A few years ago, a young woman at Facebook began asking me lots of questions about how I balance work and family. I inquired if she and her partner were considering having a child. She replied that she did not have a husband, then added with a little laugh, "Actually, I don't even have a boyfriend."

From an early age, girls get the message that they will likely have to choose between succeeding at work and being a good wife and mother. By the time they are in college, women are already thinking about the trade-offs. In a survey of Princeton's class of 2006, 62% of women said they anticipated work/family conflict, compared with 33% of men—and of the men who expected a conflict, 46% expected that their wives would step away from their career track. These expectations yield predictable results: among professional women who take time off for family, only 40% return to work full time.

But women rarely make one big decision to leave the workforce. Instead, they make a lot of small decisions along the way. A law associate might decide not to shoot for partner because someday she hopes to have a family. A sales rep might take a smaller territory or not apply for a management role. A teacher might pass on leading curriculum development for her school. Often without even realizing it, women stop reaching for new opportunities. By the time a baby actually arrives, a woman is likely to be in a drastically different place than she would have been had she not leaned back. Before, she was a top performer on par with her peers in responsibility, opportunity, and pay. But by not finding ways to stretch herself in the years leading up to motherhood, she has fallen behind. When she returns to the workplace after her child is born, she is likely to feel less fulfilled, underutilized, or unappreciated. At this point, she probably scales her ambitions back even further since she no longer believes that she can get to the top.

There are many powerful reasons to exit the workforce. No one should pass judgment on these highly personal decisions. My point is that the time for a woman to scale back is when a break is needed or a child arrives—not before, and certainly not years in advance. For those who even have a choice, choosing to leave a child in someone else's care and return to work is a hard decision. Anyone who has made this decision—myself included—knows how heartwrenching this can be. Only a compelling, challenging and rewarding job will begin to make that choice a fair contest.

Success and Likability

In 2003, Columbia Business School professor Frank Flynn and New York University professor Cameron Anderson ran an experiment. They started with a Harvard Business School case study about a real-life entrepreneur named Heidi Roizen. It described how Roizen became a successful venture capitalist by using her "outgoing personality … and vast personal and professional network … [which] included many of the most powerful business leaders in the technology sector." Half the students in the experiment were assigned to read Heidi's story. The other half got the same story with just one difference—the name was changed from Heidi to Howard.

When students were polled, they rated Heidi and Howard as equally competent. But Howard came across as a more appealing colleague. Heidi was seen as selfish and not "the type of person you would want to hire or work for." This experiment supports what research has already clearly shown: success and likability are positively correlated for men and negatively correlated for women. When a man is successful, he is liked by both men and women. When a woman is successful, people of both genders like her less.

I believe this bias is at the very core of why women are held back. It is also at the very core of why women hold themselves back. When a woman excels at her job, both men and women will comment that she is accomplishing a lot but is "not as well liked by her peers." She is probably also "too aggressive," "not a team player," "a bit political"; she "can't be trusted," or is "difficult." Those are all things that have been said about me and almost every senior woman I know.

The solution is making sure everyone is aware of the penalty women pay for success. Recently at Facebook, a manager received feedback that a woman who reported to him was "too aggressive." Before including this in her review, he decided to dig deeper. He went back to the people who gave the feedback and asked what aggressive actions she had taken. After they answered, he asked point-blank, "If a man had done those same things, would you have considered him too aggressive?" They each said no. By showing both men and women how female colleagues are held to different standards, we can start changing attitudes today.

Stop Trying to Have It All

Perhaps the greatest trap ever set for women was the coining of this phrase. No matter what any of us has—and how grateful we are for what we have—no one has it all. Nor can they. The very concept of having it all flies in the face of the basic laws of economics and common sense. Being a working parent means making adjustments, compromises and sacrifices every day.

For most people, sacrifices and hardships are not a choice but a necessity—and tougher than ever because of the expansion of working hours. In 2009, married middle-income parents worked about 8½ hours more per week than in 1979. Just as expectations about work hours have risen dramatically, so have expectations of how much time mothers will spend focused on their children. An employed mom today spends about the same amount of time reading to, feeding, and playing with her children as a nonemployed mother did in 1975.

One of my favorite posters on the walls at Facebook declares in big red letters, "Done is better than perfect." I have tried to embrace this motto and let go of unattainable standards. My first six months at Facebook were really hard. A lot of my colleagues followed Mark Zuckerberg's lead and worked night-owl engineering hours. I worried that leaving too early would make me stand out like a sore—and old—thumb. I missed dinner after dinner with my kids. I realized that if I didn't take control of the situation, my new job would prove unsustainable. I started forcing myself to leave the office at 5:30. Every competitive, type-A fiber of my being was screaming at me to stay, but unless I had a critical meeting, I walked out that door. And once I did it, I learned that I could.

I do not have the answers on how to make the right choices for myself, much less for anyone else. I do know that I can too easily spend time focusing on what I am not doing. When I remember that no one can do it all and identify my real priorities at home and at work, I feel better—and I am more productive in the office and probably a better mother as well. Instead of perfect, we should aim for sustainable and fulfilling.

I believe that if more women lean in, we can change the power structure of our world and expand opportunities. Shared experience forms the basis of empathy and, in turn, can spark the institutional changes we need. More female leadership will lead to fairer treatment for all women. We also need men to lean into their families more, especially since research has consistently found that children with involved and loving fathers have higher levels of psychological well-being and better cognitive abilities.

The hard work of generations before us means that equality is within our reach. We can close the leadership gap now. Each individual's success can make success a little easier for the next. We can do this—for ourselves, for one another, for our daughters, and for our sons. If we push hard now, this next wave can be the last wave. In the future there will be no female leaders. There will just be leaders.

Credit _____
Sandberg, Sheryl. "Why I Want Women to Lean In." *Time* 7 March 2013. Print.

(Rethinking) Gender

Debra Rosenberg

Debra Rosenberg is a freelance writer and editor and has served as a deputy editor of Newsweek. *Her coverage focuses on health, environment, education, and social issues, and she has been a speaker on NBC, Fox News, CNN, and NPR. In 2007, her article "(Rethinking) Gender" was published on* Newsweek's *website. Joining a broader conversation concerning gender identity, Rosenberg urges readers to re-examine traditional gender roles. She provides a brief historical exploration of gender and gender identity, examines cultural shifts, and gives multiple examples of people who have transitioned.*

CR80CR80CR80

A growing number of Americans are taking their private struggles with their identities into the public realm. How those who believe they were born with the wrong bodies are forcing us to re-examine what it means to be male and female.

CR80CR80CR80

Growing up in Corinth, Miss., J. T. Hayes had a legacy to attend to. His dad was a well-known race-car driver and Hayes spent much of his childhood tinkering in the family's greasy garage, learning how to design and build cars. By the age of 10, he had started racing in his own right. Eventually Hayes won more than 500 regional and national championships in go-kart, midget and sprint racing, even making it to the NASCAR Winston Cup in the early '90s. But behind the trophies and the swagger of the racing circuit, Hayes was harboring a painful secret: he had always believed he was a woman. He had feminine features and a slight frame—at 5 feet 6 and 118 pounds he was downright dainty—and had always felt, psychologically, like a girl. Only his anatomy got in the way. Since childhood he'd wrestled with what to do about it. He'd slip on "girl clothes" he hid under the mattress and try his hand with makeup. But he knew he'd find little support in his conservative hometown.

In 1991, Hayes had a moment of truth. He was driving a sprint car on a dirt track in Little Rock when the car flipped end over end. "I was trapped upside down, engine throttle stuck, fuel running all over the racetrack and me," Hayes recalls. "The accident didn't scare me, but the thought that I hadn't lived life to its full potential just ran chill bumps up and down my body." That night he vowed to complete the transition to womanhood. Hayes kept racing while he sought therapy and started hormone treatments, hiding his growing breasts under an Ace bandage and baggy T shirts.

Finally, in 1994, at 30, Hayes raced on a Saturday night in Memphis, then drove to Colorado the next day for sex-reassignment surgery, selling his prized race car to pay the tab. Hayes chose the name Terri O'Connell and began a new life as a woman who figured her racing days were over. But she had no idea what else to do. Eventually, O'Connell got a job at the mall selling women's handbags for $8 an hour. O'Connell still hopes to race again, but she knows the odds are long: "Transgendered and professional motor sports just don't go together."

To most of us, gender comes as naturally as breathing. We have no quarrel with the "M" or the "F" on our birth certificates. And, crash diets aside, we've made peace with how we want the world to see us—pants or skirt, boa or blazer, spiky heels or sneakers. But to those who consider themselves transgender, there's a disconnect between the sex they were assigned at birth and the way they see or express themselves. Though their numbers are relatively few—the most generous estimate from the National Center for Transgender Equality is between 750,000 and 3 million Americans (fewer than 1 percent)—many of them are taking their intimate struggles public for the first time. In April, *L.A. Times* sportswriter Mike Penner announced in his column that when he returned from vacation, he would do so as a woman, Christine Daniels. Nine states plus Washington, D.C., have enacted antidiscrimination laws that protect transgender people—and an additional three states have legislation pending, according to the Human Rights Campaign. And this month the U.S. House of Representatives passed a hate-crimes prevention bill that included "gender identity." Today's transgender Americans go far beyond the old stereotypes (think "Rocky Horror Picture Show"). They are soccer moms, ministers, teachers, politicians, even young children. Their push for tolerance and acceptance is reshaping businesses, sports, schools and families. It's also raising new questions about just what makes us male or female.

What is gender anyway? It is certainly more than physical details of what's between our legs. History and science suggest that gender is more subtle and more complicated than anatomy. (It's separate from sexual orientation, too, which determines which sex we're attracted to.) Gender helps us organize the world into two boxes, his and hers, and gives us a way of quickly sizing up every person we see on the street. "Gender is a way of making the world secure," says feminist scholar Judith Butler, a rhetoric professor at University of California, Berkeley. Though some scholars like Butler consider gender largely a social construct, others increasingly see it as a complex interplay of biology, genes, hormones, and culture.

Genesis set up the initial dichotomy: "Male and female he created them." And historically, the differences between men and women in this country were thought to be distinct. Men, fueled by testosterone, were the providers, the fighters, the strong and silent types who brought home dinner. Women, hopped up on estrogen (not to mention the mothering hormone oxytocin), were the nuturers, the communicators, the soft, emotional ones who got that dinner on the table. But as society changed, the stereotypes faded. Now even discussing gender differences can be fraught. (Just ask former Harvard president Larry Summers, who unleashed a wave of criticism when he suggested, in 2005, that women might have less natural aptitude for math and science.) Still, even the most diehard feminist would likely agree that, even apart from genitalia, we are not exactly alike. In many cases, our habits, our posture, and even cultural identifiers like the way we dress set us apart.

Now, as transgender people become more visible and challenge the old boundaries, they've given voice to another debate—whether gender comes in just two flavors. "The old categories that everybody's either biologically male or female, that there are two distinct categories and there's no overlap, that's beginning to break down," says Michael Kimmel, a sociology professor at SUNY-Stony Brook. "All of those old categories seem to be more fluid." Just the terminology can get confusing. "Transsexual" is an older term that usually refers to someone who wants to use hormones or surgery to change their sex. "Transvestites," now more politely called "cross-dressers," occasionally wear clothes of the opposite sex. "Transgender" is an umbrella term that includes anyone whose gender identity or expression differs from the sex of their birth—whether they have surgery or not.

Gender identity first becomes an issue in early childhood, as any parent who's watched a toddler lunge for a truck or a doll can tell you. That's also when some kids may become aware that their bodies and brains don't quite match up. Jona Rose, a 6-year-old kindergartner in northern California, seems like a girl in nearly every way—she wears dresses, loves pink and purple, and bestowed female names on all her stuffed animals. But Jona, who was born Jonah, also has a penis. When she was 4, her mom, Pam, offered to buy Jona a dress, and she was so excited she nearly hyperventilated. She began wearing dresses every day to preschool and no one seemed to mind. It wasn't easy at first. "We wrung our hands about this every night," says her dad, Joel. But finally he and Pam decided to let their son live as a girl. They chose a private kindergarten where Jona wouldn't have to hide the fact that he was born a boy, but could comfortably dress like a girl and even use the girls' bathroom. "She has been pretty adamant from the get-go: 'I am a girl'," says Joel.

Male or female, we all start life looking pretty much the same. Genes determine whether a particular human embryo will develop as a male or female. But each individual embryo is equipped to be either one—each possesses the Mullerian ducts that become the female reproductive system as well as the Wolffian ducts that become the male one. Around eight weeks of development, through a complex genetic relay race, the X and the male's Y chromosomes kick into gear, directing the structures to become testes or ovaries. (In most cases, the unneeded extra structures simply break down.) The ovaries and the testes are soon pumping out estrogen and testosterone, bathing the developing fetus in hormones. Meanwhile, the brain begins to form, complete with receptors—wired differently in men and women—that will later determine how both estrogen and testosterone are used in the body.

After birth, the changes keep coming. In many species, male newborns experience a hormone surge that may "organize" sexual and behavioral traits, says Nirao Shah, a neuroscientist at UCSF. In rats, testosterone given in the first week of life can cause female babies to behave more like males once they reach adulthood. "These changes are thought to be irreversible," says Shah. Between 1 and 5 months, male human babies also experience a hormone surge. It's still unclear exactly what effect that surge has on the human brain, but it happens just when parents are oohing and aahing over their new arrivals.

Here's where culture comes in. Studies have shown that parents treat boys and girls very differently—breast-feeding boys longer but talking more to girls. That's going on while the baby's brain is engaged in a massive growth spurt. "The brain doubles in size in the first five years after birth, and the connectivity between the cells goes up hundreds of orders of magnitude," says Anne Fausto-Sterling, a biologist and feminist at Brown University who is currently investigating whether subtle differences in parental behavior could influence gender identity in very young children. "The brain is interacting with culture from day one."

So what's different in transgender people? Scientists don't know for certain. Though their hormone levels seem to be the same as non-trans levels, some scientists speculate that their brains react differently to the hormones, just as men's differ from women's. But that could take decades of further research to prove. One 1997 study tantalizingly suggested structural differences between male, and female and transsexual brains, but it has yet to be successfully replicated. Some transgender people blame the environment, citing studies that show pollutants have disrupted reproduction in frogs and other animals. But those links are so far not proved in humans. For now, transgender issues are classified as "Gender Identity Disorder" in the psychiatric manual DSM-IV. That's controversial, too—gay-rights activists spent years campaigning to have homosexuality removed from the manual.

Gender fluidity hasn't always seemed shocking. Cross-dressing was common in ancient Greece and Rome, as well as among Native Americans and many other indigenous societies, according to Deborah Rudacille, author of "The Riddle of Gender." Court records from the Jamestown settlement in 1629 describe the case of Thomas Hall, who claimed to be both a man and a woman. Of course, what's considered masculine or feminine has long been a moving target. Our Founding Fathers wouldn't be surprised to see men today with long hair or earrings, but they might be puzzled by women in pants.

Transgender opponents have often turned to the Bible for support. Deut. 22:5 says: "The woman shall not wear that which pertaineth unto a man, neither shall a man put on a woman's garment: for all that do so are abomination unto the Lord thy God." When word leaked in February that Steve Stanton, the Largo, Fla., city manager for 14 years, was planning to transition to life as a woman, the community erupted. At a public meeting over whether Stanton should be fired, one of many critics, Ron Sanders, pastor of the Lighthouse Baptist Church, insisted that Jesus would "want him terminated." (Stanton did lose his job and this week will appear as Susan Stanton on Capitol Hill to lobby for antidiscrimination laws.) Equating gender change with homosexualtiy, Sanders says that "it's an abomination, which means that it's utterly disgusting."

Not all people of faith would agree. Baptist minister John Nemecek, 56, was surfing the Web one weekend in 2003, when his wife was at a baby shower. Desperate for clues to his long-suppressed feelings of femininity, he stumbled across an article about gender-identity disorder on WebMD. The suggested remedy was sex-reassignment surgery—something Nemecek soon thought he had to do. Many families can be ripped apart by such drastic changes, but Nemecek's wife of 33 years stuck by him. His employer of 15 years, Spring Arbor University, a faith-based liberal-arts college in Michigan, did not. Nemecek says the school claimed that transgenderism violated its Christian principles, and when it renewed Nemecek's contract—by then she was taking hormones and using the name Julie—it barred her from dressing as a woman on campus or even wearing earrings. Her workload and pay were cut, too, she says. She filed a discrimination claim, which was later settled through mediation. (The university declined to comment on the case.) Nemecek says she has no trouble squaring her gender change and her faith. "Actively expressing the feminine in me has helped me grow closer to God," she says.

Others have had better luck transitioning. Karen Kopriva, now 49, kept her job teaching high school in Lake Forest, Ill., when she shaved her beard and made the switch from Ken. When Mark Stumpp, a vice president at Prudential Financial, returned to work as Margaret in 2002, she sent a memo to her colleagues (subject: Me) explaining the change. "We all joked about wearing panty hose and whether 'my condition' was contagious," she says. But "when the dust settled, everyone got back to work." Companies like IBM and Kodak now cover trans-related medical care. And 125 Fortune 500 companies now protect transgender employees from job discrimination, up from three in 2000. Discrimination may not be the worst worry for transgender people: they are also at high risk of violence and hate crimes.

☙❧☙❧☙❧

Perhaps no field has wrestled more with the issue of gender than sports. There have long been accusations about male athletes' trying to pass as women, or women's taking testosterone to gain a competitive edge. In the 1960s, would-be female Olympians were required to undergo gender-screening tests Essentially, that meant baring all before a panel of doctors who could verify that an athlete had girl parts. That method was soon scrapped in favor of a genetic test. But that quickly led to confusion over a handful of genetic disorders that give typical-looking women chromosomes other than the usual XX. Finally, the International Olympic Committee ditched mandatory lab-based screening, too. "We found there is no scientifically sound lab-based technique that can differentiate between man and woman," says Arne Ljungqvist, chair of the IOC's medical commission.

The IOC recently waded into controversy again: in 2004 it issued regulations allowing transsexual athletes to compete in the Olympics if they've had sex-reassignment surgery and have taken hormones for two years. After convening a panel of experts, the IOC decided that the surgery and hormones would compensate for any hormonal or muscular advantage a male-to-female transsexual would have. (Female-to-male athletes would be allowed to take testosterone, but only at levels that wouldn't give them a boost.) So far, Ljungqvist doesn't know of any transsexual athletes who've competed. Ironically, Renee Richards, who won a lawsuit in 1977 for the right to play tennis as a woman after her own sex-reassignment surgery, questions the fairness of the IOC rule. She thinks decisions should be made on a case-by-case basis.

Richards and other pioneers reflect the huge cultural shift over a generation of gender change. Now 70, Richards rejects the term transgender along with all the fluidity it conveys. "God didn't put us on this earth to have gender diversity," she says. "I don't like the kids that are experimenting. I didn't want to be something in between. I didn't want to be trans anything. I wanted to be a man or a woman."

But more young people are embracing something we would traditionally consider in between. Because of the expense, invasiveness and mixed results (especially for women becoming men), only 1,000 to 2,000 Americans each year get sex-reassignment surgery—a number that's on the rise, says Mara Keisling of the National Center for Transgender Equality. Mykell Miller, a Northwestern University student born female who now considers himself male, hides his breasts under a special compression vest. Though he one day wants to take hormones and get a mastectomy, he can't yet afford it. But that doesn't affect his self-image. "I challenge the idea that all men were born with male bodies," he says. "I don't go out of my way to be the biggest, strongest guy."

Nowhere is the issue more pressing at the moment than a place that helped give rise to feminist movement a generation ago: Smith College in Northampton, Mass. Though Smith was one of the original Seven Sisters women's colleges, its students have now taken to calling it a "mostly women's college," in part because of a growing number of "transmen" who decide to become male after they've enrolled. In 2004, students voted to remove pronouns from the student government constitution as a gesture to transgender students who no longer identified with "she" or "her." (Smith is also one of 70 schools that has antidiscrimination policies protecting transgender students.) For now, anyone who is enrolled at Smith may graduate, but in order to be admitted in the first place, you must have been born a female. Tobias Davis, class of '03, entered Smith as a woman, but graduated as a "transman." When he first told friends over dinner, "I think I might be a boy," they were instantly behind him, saying "Great! Have you picked a name yet?" Davis passed as male for his junior year abroad in Italy even without taking hormones; he had a mastectomy last fall. Now 25, Davis works at Smith and writes plays about the transgender experience. (His work "The Naked I: Monologues From Beyond the Binary" is a trans take on "The Vagina Monologues.")

As kids at ever-younger ages grapple with issues of gender variance, doctors, psychologists, and parents are weighing how to balance immediate desires and long-term ones. Like Jona Rose, many kids begin questioning gender as toddlers, identifying with the other gender's toys and clothes. Five times as many boys as girls say their gender doesn't match their biological sex, says Dr. Edgardo Menvielle, a psychiatrist who heads a gender-variance outreach program at Children's National Medical Center. (Perhaps that's because it's easier for girls to blend in as tomboys.) Many of these children eventually move on and accept their biological sex, says Menvielle, often when they're exposed to a disapproving larger world or when they're influenced by the hormone surges of puberty. Only about 15 percent continue to show signs of gender-identity problems into adulthood, says Ken Zucker, who heads the Gender Identity Service at the Centre for Addiction and Mental Health in Toronto.

In the past, doctors often advised parents to direct their kids into more gender-appropriate clothing and behavior. Zucker still tells parents of unhappy boys to try more-neutral activities—say chess club instead of football. But now the thinking is that kids should lead the way. If a child persists in wanting to be the other gender, doctors may prescribe hormone "blockers" to keep puberty at bay. (Blockers have no permanent effects.) But they're also increasingly willing to take more lasting steps: Isaak Brown (who started life as Liza) began taking male hormones at 16; at 17 he had a mastectomy.

For parents like Colleen Vincente, 44, following a child's lead seems only natural. Her second child, M. (Vincente asked to use an initial to protect the child's privacy), was born female. But as soon as she could talk, she insisted on wearing boy's clothes. Though M. had plenty of dolls, she gravitated toward "the boy things" and soon wanted to shave off all her hair. "We went along with that," says Vincente. "We figured it was a phase." One day, when she was 2½, M. overheard her parents talking about her using female pronouns. "He said, 'No—I'm a him. You need to call me him'," Vincente recalls. "We were shocked." In his California preschool, M. continued to insist he was a boy and decided to change his name. Vincente and her husband, John, consulted a therapist, who confirmed their instincts to let M. guide them. Now 9, M. lives as a boy, and most people have no idea he was born otherwise. "The most important thing is to realize this is who your child is," Vincente says. That's a big step for a family, but could be an even bigger one for the rest of the world.

*Following this article, there are ten color photographs that are not included.

**A special thanks to the following contributors to this article: Lorraine Ali, Mary Carmichael, Samantha Henig, Raina Kelley, Matthew Philips, Julie Scelfo, Kurt Soller, Karen Springen, and Lynn Waddell.

Credit _____

Rosenberg, Debra, et. al. "(Rethinking) Gender." *Newsweek*: 50–57. Print. From *Newsweek* May 21
© 2007 IBT Media. All rights reserved. Used by permission and protected by the Copyright Laws
of the United States. The printing, copying, redistribution, or retransmission of this Content without
express written permission is prohibited.

Standing Up for the Rights of New Fathers

Tara Siegel Bernard

Tara Siegel Bernard is a personal finance reporter for The New York Times. *She also worked as a news editor at CNBC and contributed to* The Wall Street Journal's *small business columns.* The New York Times *published her article, "Standing Up for the Rights of New Fathers," on November 8, 2013. Entering the controversial discussion pertaining to equal rights between genders, Bernard's article begins with a father's battle with his employer concerning the amount of paid paternity leave available to him. Bernard then examines other American employer paternity leaves, compares policies between mothers, adoptive fathers, and biological fathers, and questions whether or not the policies are discriminatory.*

ᚷ᙭ᚱᚷ᙭ᚱᚷ᙭ᚱ

Josh Levs, father of a new baby girl, emerged from his sleep-deprived stupor last month to take a stand: He is challenging his employer's parental leave policy on the grounds that it discriminates against biological dads.

This was his third child, and this time around, he said he felt compelled to take action. So Mr. Levs, a reporter at CNN, filed a charge with the Equal Employment Opportunity Commission against Time Warner, his employer's parent company.

He took his case public on his Tumblr page, where he laid out his reasoning: Birth mothers are entitled to 10 weeks of paid leave. The same policy applies to both men and women who adopt or have children through a surrogate. Biological fathers, on the other hand, receive only two paid weeks.

He said this left him with two choices: stay home for a longer period of time without pay or go back to work and hire help. "Neither is financially tenable," wrote Mr. Levs, who lives in Atlanta, "and the fact that only biological dads face this choice at this point in a newborn's life is ludicrous."

It was a gutsy move, particularly when there was a new child to feed. Time Warner declined to elaborate on the specifics of the case; though, on the surface, it appears to treat biological fathers as second-class parents compared to their peers. But what's fair and what is discriminatory under the law are two different matters (we'll get to those issues in a minute).

Time Warner's policy does happen to be more generous than that of many American employers, but the bar is pretty low. Most employers don't provide any paid paternity leave (A study conducted by the Society for Human Resource Management that polled human resource professionals found that a mere 15 percent of companies offered paid paternity benefits). Of course, the United States has one of the least civilized policies in the world when it comes to offering paid leave for new mothers. So, it's no surprise that fathers are often treated as an afterthought.

But more workers may be starting to do more than quietly grumble about the policies, according to discrimination lawyers, researchers and legal experts who run a workplace discrimination hotline. More employees—particularly men of the millennial generation, whose oldest members are in their early 30s—are filing legal actions against their employers, these experts say.

"What is happening is the new work-life pioneers are young egalitarian men exactly like this guy," said Joan C. Williams, founding director of the Center for WorkLife Law at the University of California, Hastings College of the Law. "In many ways, these younger men are acting in ways that mothers have always acted: 'I have family responsibilities that aren't going away and either you accommodate them or there is going to be a fight against it.' In many ways, this is economic contraction fueling gender equality."

There aren't any federal laws that explicitly prohibit discrimination against workers with family responsibilities, but some states and municipalities have more specific protections. The type of claim filed by Mr. Levs is brought under Title VII of the Civil Rights Act of 1964, enforced by the E.E.O.C., which prohibits employment discrimination based on sex. Mothers who claim they were treated differently from men with children file claims under the law, and so do fathers who say they were denied leave or benefits available to female caregivers.

That's generally what Mr. Levs is contending. "If I gave up my child for adoption, and some other guy at Time Warner adopted her, he would get 10 weeks off, paid, to take care of her," he wrote on his Tumblr page. "I, however, the biological father, can't."

It's hard to predict exactly how the commission will view his claims. But Justine Lisser, an E.E.O.C. lawyer and spokeswoman, offered some insight into what may be considered sex discrimination in a hypothetical situation. It's not necessarily wrong, for instance, if women were given a certain period of paid leave to recover from pregnancy and childbirth, while men (and women) were also entitled to the same period to recover from other medical conditions.

But it would be considered sex discrimination to give women paid time off to care for a newborn, but not give the same time to men. It would also obviously be wrong to have such a policy on the books, but then penalize men for using it. "We see this in some caregiving cases," she said. "Women are presumed to need caregiving time off, but men are presumed not to be invested in their jobs if they want to take the same time for the same reason and are either denied it or demoted after using it."

Mr. Levs's lawyer, A. Lee Parks Jr., a civil rights lawyer in Atlanta, acknowledged that the policies could (and potentially should) be different for men and women. "The bizarre thing here is they give a significant amount of time if you are a certain type of parent," he said. "So, they made a value judgment that, in those situations, that there is really a period where you need to bond."

If you're curious about the legality of your company's policy, legal experts said to look at it as a breakdown of recovery time and bonding time. "Men should get the same bonding time," said Cynthia T. Calvert, a senior adviser on family responsibilities discrimination at the Center for WorkLife Law. She suggests that employers designate six to eight weeks for recovery, and then anything beyond that should be deemed bonding time, and available to all parents.

Workplace experts who read Mr. Levs's blog said he appeared to take the right approach. He started the process two months before the birth of his daughter, followed his company's protocols, and kept the matter confidential. You might start by simply asking your supervisor or human resources department for more information, just to be sure you're understanding the policy correctly. "You don't want to come on too strong, but at the same time, you want to be sure you've done everything in the system before you bring in the lawyers," said Ms. Calvert, who also consults with employers to shape their policies and train their supervisors to avoid discrimination. "Because then, everyone gets their armor on. People don't view you as a team player anymore."

If you have reason to believe your policy could be discriminatory, she said you might ask the human resources department if it considered whether the policy violated Title VII or any state antidiscrimination laws. In many cases, legal experts say, simply nudging employers works. "When we receive calls, we give callers the language they can use, and the employers almost always change their policies," said Ms. Calvert, who oversees a family discrimination hotline at the center. "That's why we don't have a lot of these cases on the books."

Still, men like Mr. Levs may be penalized even more than women when seeking flexibility after the birth of a child because they are stepping outside of their usual gender roles and flouting convention, some researchers found. Several workplace experts report that men still suffer the consequences after taking unpaid leave through the Family and Medical Leave Act of 1993, which requires larger employers and public agencies to provide up to 12 weeks of unpaid leave for the birth or adoption of a child or to care for certain other family members.

"The organizations haven't yet caught up to the attitudinal shift among new dads," said Brad Harrington, executive director of the Boston College Center for Work and Family and a research professor in the Carroll School of Management. "Men who ask for leave time or who are more visibly active and involved in caregiving are experiencing a whole range of negative repercussions as a result of that."

Getting paid leave may do more to change perceptions, some experts say. "Men are supposed to make a living, so if a benefit is not paid, it is not for them," said Eileen Appelbaum, an expert in workplace practices and senior economist at the Center for Economic and Policy Research, who supports a social insurance program that would replace a portion of pay for all workers who need to take leave. "But if it is paid, it changes the culture and expectation inside the organizations."

And when men take time off after the birth of a child, it can have lasting ripple effects. Not only does it help create a connection with the child, but it sets the stage for a more egalitarian division of labor at home over the longer term. It could also help equalize the perception when women take time off. "If it is true that women will not be equal in the workplace until men are equal at home," Ms. Calvert added, "it has greater repercussions as well."

Credit _____

Unit 5

Science and Nature

As humanity steps further away from nature and closer to science and technologies, it is imperative that students of the 21st century not only recognize the shift but also discuss consequences and effects of this growth. Though the scientific community has had many positive breakthroughs and has contributed significantly to society, conversations regarding our relationship to nature and the ethical questions of science and technology must occur. As discussions concerning various issues within science and nature take place, it is important that problems are defined and plausible solutions examined.

Some areas where human interference with nature is problematic include how food is grown and distributed, contamination of oceans and land, and the ramifications of the possible honeybee extinction. Problems such as these illustrate the necessity to analyze conceivable solutions to positively re-shape the future of the earth. Our responsibility to nature warrants investigation, but so does society's intimate relationship with technology and science concerning artificial intelligence and nanotechnologies, eugenics and "designer babies," and the human genome and genetic modifications. The ethical questions these issues raise must be addressed so that we do not lose our humanity in the quest for technological breakthrough.

These conversations are an important step in the journey Cleveland State University students take to become engaged members of a global community. As a community we should concern ourselves with ways to protect natural resources and learn how to preserve those resources. And although there are many serious achievements to applaud in the field of science, there must also be critical discussions of how we are ethically responsible for the implementation of scientific and technological achievements for the well-being of our city and our planet.

The Plight of the Honeybee

Bryan Walsh

Bryan Walsh is an editor at Time *magazine, who handles international news. He has also covered environmental and energy issues for the magazine. In "The Plight of the Honeybee," Walsh argues that the recent, significant death of bee colonies is catastrophic for plant pollination, especially for the world's food sources. He examines the use of pesticides by farmers and bacterial infections as possible culprits in the destruction of bee colonies. He does not believe that the end is near and notes that farmers must make adjustments to the way food is grown if bee colonies are to continue to survive.*

CRSOCREOCREO

You can thank the Apis Mellifera, better known as the Western honeybee, for 1 in every 3 mouthfuls of food you'll eat today. From the almond orchards of central California—where each spring billions of honeybees from across the U.S. arrive to pollinate a multibillion-dollar crop—to the blueberry bogs of Maine, the bees are the unsung, unpaid laborers of the American agricultural system, adding more than $15 billion in value to farming each year. In June, a Whole Foods store in Rhode Island, as part of a campaign to highlight the importance of honeybees, temporarily removed from its produce section all the food that depended on pollinators. Of 453 items, 237 vanished, including apples, lemons and zucchini and other squashes. Honeybees "are the glue that holds our agricultural system together," wrote journalist Hannah Nordhaus in her 2011 book, *The Beekeeper's Lament.*

And now that glue is failing. Around 2006, commercial beekeepers began noticing something disturbing: their honeybees were disappearing. Beekeepers would open their hives and find them full of honeycomb, wax, even honey—but devoid of actual bees. As reports from worried beekeepers rolled in, scientists coined an appropriately apocalyptic term for the mystery malady: colony-collapse disorder (CCD). Suddenly beekeepers found themselves in the media spotlight, the public captivated by the horror-movie mystery of CCD. Seven years later, honeybees are still dying on a scale rarely seen before, and the reasons remain mysterious. One-third of U.S. honeybee colonies died or disappeared during the past winter, a 42% increase over the year before and well above the 10% to 15% losses beekeepers used to experience in normal winters.

Though beekeepers can replenish dead hives over time, the high rates of colony loss are putting intense pressure on the industry and on agriculture. There were just barely enough viable honeybees in the U.S. to service this spring's vital almond pollination in California, putting a product worth nearly $4 billion at risk. Almonds are a big deal—they're the Golden State's most valuable agricultural export, worth more than twice as much as its iconic wine grapes. And almonds, totally dependent on honeybees, are a bellwether of the larger problem. For fruits and vegetables as diverse as cantaloupes, cranberries and cucumbers, pollination can be a farmer's only chance to increase maximum yield. Eliminate the honeybee and agriculture would be permanently diminished. "The take-home message is that we are very close to the edge," says Jeff Pettis, the research leader at the U.S. Department of Agriculture's Bee Research Laboratory. "It's a roll of the dice now."

That's why scientists like Pettis are working hard to figure out what's bugging the bees. Agricultural pesticides were an obvious suspect—specifically a popular new class of chemicals known as neonicotinoids, which seem to affect bees and other insects even at what should be safe doses. Other researchers focused on bee-killing pests like the accurately named Varroa destructor, a parasitic mite that has ravaged honeybee colonies since it was accidentally introduced into the U.S. in the 1980s. Others still have looked at bacterial and viral diseases. The lack of a clear culprit only deepened the mystery and the fear, heralding what some greens call a "second silent spring," a reference to Rachel Carson's breakthrough 1962 book, which is widely credited with helping launch the environmental movement. A quote that's often attributed to Albert Einstein became a slogan: "If the bee disappears from the surface of the globe, man would have no more than four years to live."

One problem: experts doubt that Einstein ever said those words, but the misattribution is characteristic of the confusion that surrounds the disappearance of the bees, the sense that we're inadvertently killing a species that we've tended and depended on for thousands of years. The loss of the honeybees would leave the planet poorer and hungrier, but what's really scary is the fear that bees may be a sign of what's to come, a symbol that something is deeply wrong with the world around us. "If we don't make some changes soon, we're going to see disaster," says Tom Theobald, a beekeeper in Colorado. "The bees are just the beginning."

Sublethal Effects

If the honeybee is a victim of natural menaces like viruses and unnatural ones like pesticides, it's worth remembering that the bee itself is not a natural resident of the continent. It was imported to North America in the 17th century, and it thrived until recently because it found a perfect niche in a food system that demands crops at ever cheaper prices and in ever greater quantities. That's a man-made, mercantile ecosystem that not only has been good for the bees and beekeepers but also has meant steady business and big revenue for supermarkets and grocery stores.

Jim Doan has been keeping bees since the age of 5, but the apiary genes in his family go back even further. Doan's father paid his way to college with the proceeds of his part-time beekeeping, and in 1973 he left the bond business to tend bees full time. Bees are even in the Doan family's English coat of arms. Although Jim went to college with the aim of becoming an agriculture teacher, the pull of the beekeeping business was too great.

For a long time, that business was very good. The family built up its operation in the town of Hamlin, in western New York, making money from honey and from pollination contracts with farmers. At the peak of his business, Doan estimates he was responsible for pollinating 1 out of 10 apples grown in New York, running nearly 6,000 hives, one of the biggest such operations in the state. He didn't mind the inevitable stings—"you have to be willing to be punished"—and he could endure the early hours. "We made a lot of honey, and we made a lot of money," he says.

All that ended in 2006, the year CCD hit the mainstream, and Doan's hives weren't spared. That winter, when he popped the covers to check on his bees—tipped off by a fellow beekeeper who experienced one of the first documented cases of CCD—Doan found nothing. "There were hundreds of hives in the backyard and no bees in them," he says. In the years since, he has experienced repeated losses, his bees growing sick and dying. To replace lost hives, Doan needs to buy new queens and split his remaining colonies, which reduces honey production and puts more pressure on his few remaining healthy bees. Eventually it all became unsustainable. In 2013, after decades in the business, Doan gave up. He sold the 112 acres (45 hectares) he owns—land he had been saving to sell after his retirement—and plans to sell his beekeeping equipment as well, provided he can find someone to buy it. Doan is still keeping some bees in the meantime, maintaining a revenue stream while considering his options. Those options include a job at Walmart.

Doan and I walk through his backyard, which is piled high with bee boxes that would resemble filing cabinets, if filing cabinets hummed and vibrated. Doan lends me a protective jacket and a bee veil that covers my face. He walks slowly among the boxes—partly because he's a big guy and partly because bees don't appreciate fast moves—and he spreads smoke in advance, which masks the bees' alarm pheromones and keeps them calm. He opens each box and removes a few frames—the narrowly spaced scaffolds on which the bees build their honeycombs—checking to see how a new population he imported from Florida is doing. Some frames are choked with crawling bees, flowing honey and healthy brood cells, each of which contains an infant bee. But other frames seem abandoned, even the wax in the honeycomb crumbling. Doan lays these boxes—known as dead-outs—on their side.

He used to love checking on his bees. "Now it's gotten to the point where I look at the bees every few weeks, and it scares me," he says. "Will it be a good day, will they be alive, or will I just find a whole lot of junk? It depresses the hell out of me."

Doan's not alone in walking away from such unhappy work. The number of commercial beekeepers has dropped by some three-quarters over the past 15 years, and while all of them may agree that the struggle is just not worth it anymore, they differ on which of the possible causes is most to blame. Doan has settled on the neonicotinoid pesticides—and there's a strong case to be made against them.

The chemicals are used on more than 140 different crops as well as in home gardens, meaning endless chances of exposure for any insect that alights on the treated plants. Doan shows me studies of pollen samples taken from his hives that indicate the presence of dozens of chemicals, including the neonicotinoids. He has testified before Congress about the danger the chemicals pose and is involved in a lawsuit with other beekeepers and with green groups that calls on the Environmental Protection Agency (EPA) to suspend a pair of pesticides in the neonicotinoid class. "The impacts [from the pesticides] are not marginal, and they're not academic," says Peter Jenkins, a lawyer for the Center for Food Safety and a lead counsel in the suit. "They pose real threats to the viability of pollinators."

American farmers have been dousing their fields with pesticides for decades, meaning that honeybees—which can fly as far as 5 miles (8 km) in search of forage—have been exposed to toxins since well before the dawn of CCD. But neonicotinoids, which were introduced in the mid-1990s and became widespread in the years that followed, are different. The chemicals are known as systematics, which means that seeds are soaked in them before they're planted. Traces of the chemicals are eventually passed on to every part of the mature plant—including the pollen and nectar a bee might come into contact with—and can remain for much longer than other pesticides do. There's really no way to prevent bees from being exposed to some level of neonicotinoids if the pesticides have been used nearby. "We have growing evidence that neonicotinoids can have dangerous effects, especially in conjunction with other pathogens," says Peter Neumann, head of the Institute of Bee Health at the University of Bern in Switzerland.

Ironically, neonicotinoids are actually safer for farmworkers because they can be applied more precisely than older classes of pesticides, which disperse into the air. Bees, however, seem uniquely sensitive to the chemicals. Studies have shown that neonicotinoids attack their nervous system, interfering with their flying and navigation abilities without killing them immediately. "The scientific literature is exploding now with work on sublethal impacts on bees," says James Frazier, an entomologist at Penn State University. The delayed but cumulative effects of repeated exposure might explain why colonies keep dying off year after year despite beekeepers' best efforts. It's as if the bees were being poisoned very slowly.

It's undeniably attractive to blame the honeybee crisis on neonicotinoids. The widespread adoption of these pesticides roughly corresponds to the spike in colony loss, and neonicotinoids are, after all, meant to kill insects. Chemicals are ubiquitous—a recent study found that honeybee pollen was contaminated, on average, with nine different pesticides and fungicides. Best of all, if the problem is neonicotinoids, the solution is simple: ban them. That's what the European Commission decided to do this year, putting a two-year restriction on the use of some neonicotinoids. But while the EPA is planning to review neonicotinoids, a European-style ban is unlikely—in part because the evidence is still unclear. Beekeepers in Australia have been largely spared from CCD even though neonicotinoids are used there, while France has continued to suffer bee losses despite restricting the use of the pesticides since 1999. Pesticide makers argue that actual levels of neonicotinoid exposure in the field are too low to be the main culprit in colony loss. "We've dealt with insecticides for a long time," says Randy Oliver, a beekeeper who has done independent research on CCD. "I'm not thoroughly convinced this is a major issue."

Hostile Terrain

Even if pesticides are a big part of the bee-death mystery, there are other suspects. Beekeepers have always had to protect their charges from dangers such as the American foulbrood—a bacterial disease that kills developing bees—and the small hive beetle, a pest that can infiltrate and contaminate colonies. Bloodiest of all is the multidecade war against the Varroa destructor, a microscopic mite that burrows into the brood cells that host baby bees. The mites are equipped with a sharp, two-pronged tongue that can pierce a bee's exoskeleton and suck its hemolymph—the fluid that serves as blood in bees. And since the Varroa can also spread a number of other diseases—they're the bee equivalent of a dirty hypodermic needle—an uncontrolled mite infestation can quickly lead to a dying hive.

The Varroa first surfaced in the U.S. in 1987—likely from infected bees imported from South America—and it has killed billions of bees since. Countermeasures used by beekeepers, including chemical miticides, have proved only partly effective. "When the Varroa mite made its way in, it changed what we had to do," says Jerry Hayes, who heads Monsanto's commercial bee work. "It's not easy to try to kill a little bug on a big bug."

Other researchers have pointed a finger at fungal infections like the parasite Nosema ceranae, possibly in league with a pathogen like the invertebrate iridescent virus. But again, the evidence isn't conclusive: some CCD-afflicted hives show evidence of fungi or mites or viruses, and others don't. Some beekeepers are skeptical that there's an underlying problem at all, preferring to blame CCD on what they call PPB—piss-poor beekeeping, a failure of beekeepers to stay on top of colony health. But while not every major beekeeper has suffered catastrophic loss, colony failures have been widespread for long enough that it seems perverse to blame the human victims. "I've been keeping bees for decades," says Doan. "It's not like I suddenly forgot how to do it in 2006."

There's also the simple fact that beekeepers live in a country that is becoming inhospitable to honeybees. To survive, bees need forage, which means flowers and wild spaces. Our industrialized agricultural system has conspired against that, transforming the countryside into vast stretches of crop monocultures—factory fields of corn or soybeans that are little more than a desert for honeybees starved of pollen and nectar. Under the Conservation Reserve Program (CRP), the government rents land from farmers and sets it aside, taking it out of production to conserve soil and preserve wildlife. But as prices of commodity crops like corn and soybeans have skyrocketed, farmers have found that they can make much more money planting on even marginal land than they can from the CRP rentals. This year, just 25.3 million acres (10.2 million hectares) will be held in the CRP, down by one-third from the peak in 2007 and the smallest area in reserve since 1988.

Lonely Spring

For all the enemies that are massing against honeybees, a bee-pocalypse isn't quite upon us yet. Even with the high rates of annual loss, the number of managed honeybee colonies in the U.S. has stayed stable over the past 15 years, at about 2.5 million. That's still significantly down from the 5.8 million colonies that were kept in 1946, but that shift had more to do with competition from cheap imported honey and the general rural depopulation of the U.S. over the past half-century. (The number of farms in the U.S. fell from a peak of 6.8 million in 1935 to just 2.2 million today, even as food production has ballooned.) Honeybees have a remarkable ability to regenerate, and year after year the beekeepers who remain have been able to regrow their stocks after a bad loss. But the burden on beekeepers is becoming unbearable. Since 2006 an estimated 10 million beehives have been lost, at a cost of some $2 billion. "We can replace the bees, but we can't replace beekeepers with 40 years of experience," says Tim Tucker, the vice president of the American Beekeeping Federation.

As valuable as honeybees are, the food system wouldn't collapse without them. The backbone of the world's diet—grains like corn, wheat and rice—is self-pollinating. But our dinner plates would be far less colorful, not to mention far less nutritious, without blueberries, cherries, watermelons, lettuce and the scores of other plants that would be challenging to raise commercially without honeybee pollination. There could be replacements. In southwest China, where wild bees have all but died out thanks to massive pesticide use, farmers laboriously hand-pollinate pear and apple trees with brushes. Scientists at Harvard are experimenting with tiny robobees that might one day be able to pollinate autonomously. But right now, neither solution is technically or economically feasible. The government could do its part by placing tighter regulations on the use of all pesticides, especially during planting season. There needs to be more support for the CRP too to break up the crop monocultures that are suffocating honeybees. One way we can all help is by planting bee-friendly flowers in backyard gardens and keeping them free of pesticides. The country, says Dennis vanEngelsdorp, a research scientist at the University of Maryland who has studied CCD since it first emerged, is suffering from a "nature deficit disorder"—and the bees are paying the price.

But the reality is that barring a major change in the way the U.S. grows food, the pressure on honeybees won't subside. There are more than 1,200 pesticides currently registered for use in the U.S.; nobody pretends that number will be coming down by a lot. Instead, the honeybee and its various pests are more likely to be changed to fit into the existing agricultural system. Monsanto is working on an RNA-interference technology that can kill the Varroa mite by disrupting the way its genes are expressed. The result would be a species-specific self-destruct mechanism—a much better alternative than the toxic and often ineffective miticides beekeepers have been forced to use. Meanwhile, researchers at Washington State University are developing what will probably be the world's smallest sperm bank—a bee-genome repository that will be used to crossbreed a more resilient honeybee from the 28 recognized subspecies of the insect around the world.

Already, commercial beekeepers have adjusted to the threats facing their charges by spending more to provide supplemental feed to their colonies. Supplemental feed raises costs, and some scientists worry that replacing honey with sugar or corn syrup can leave bees less capable of fighting off infections. But beekeepers living adrift in a nutritional wasteland have little choice. The beekeeping business may well begin to resemble the industrial farming industry it works with: fewer beekeepers running larger operations that produce enough revenue to pay for the equipment and technologies needed to stay ahead of an increasingly hostile environment. "Bees may end up managed like cattle, pigs and chicken, where we put them in confinement and bring the food to them," says Oliver, the beekeeper and independent researcher. "You could do feedlot beekeeping."

That's something no one in the beekeeping world wants to see. But it may be the only way to keep honeybees going. And as long as there are almonds, apples, apricots and scores of other fruits and vegetables that need pollinating—and farmers willing to pay for the service—beekeepers will find a way.

So if the honeybee survives, it likely won't resemble what we've known for centuries. But it could be worse. For all the recent attention on the commercial honeybee, wild bees are in far worse shape. In June, after a landscaping company sprayed insecticide on trees, 50,000 wild bumblebees in Oregon were killed—the largest such mass poisoning on record. Unlike the honeybee, the bumblebee has no human caretakers. Globally, up to 100,000 animal species die off each year—nearly every one of them without fanfare or notice. This is what happens when one species—that would be us—becomes so widespread and so dominant that it crowds out almost everything else. It won't be a second silent spring that dawns; we'll still have the buzz of the feedlot honeybee in our ears. But humans and our handful of preferred species may find that all of our seasons have become lonelier ones.

Our Oceans Are Turning into Plastic ... Are You?

A vast swath of the Pacific twice the size of Texas is full of plastic stew that is entering the food chain. Scientists say it's causing obesity, infertility ... and worse.

Photographs by Gregg Segal
Susan Casey

Plastic Plague: (left) A jellyfish whose tentacles became entangled in plastic line; (right) A sample of the North Pacific gyre—a virtual trash dump where plastic outweighs plankton by a ratio of 6 to 1.

Susan Casey is the author of The Devil's Teeth: A True Story of Obsession and Survival Among America's Great White Sharks, *a New York Times bestseller. She also supported the efforts behind the publications of the bestselling books* Into Thin Air *and* The Perfect Storm. *Casey is also the editor-in-chief of* O, the Oprah Magazine. *In "Our Oceans Are Turning into Plastic ... Are You?" Casey argues that the significant amount of plastic products in the oceans is affecting the esthetics of the natural world. Even more significantly, Casey asserts that these plastics are wreaking havoc on the food chain because of the chemicals contained in them and the chemical toxins that are leaching into the habitat of ocean species, which not only affects the reproduction of these species but also will soon begin to affect human health.*

Man in the Plastic Bubble: Captain Charles Moore shows off a sample of our plastic ocean aboard the *Alguita* on his 2002 voyage to the gyre.

Fate can take strange forms, and so perhaps it does not seem unusual that Captain Charles Moore found his life's purpose in a nightmare. Unfortunately, he was awake at the time, and 800 miles north of Hawaii in the Pacific Ocean. It happened on August 3, 1997, a lovely day, at least in the beginning: Sunny. Little wind. Water the color of sapphires. Moore and the crew of *Alguita*, his 50-foot aluminum-hulled catamaran, sliced through the sea.

Returning to Southern California from Hawaii after a sailing race, Moore had altered *Alguita's* course, veering slightly north. He had the time and the curiosity to try a new route, one that would lead the vessel through the eastern corner of a 10-million-square-mile oval known as the North Pacific subtropical gyre. This was an odd stretch of ocean, a place most boats purposely avoided. For one thing, it was becalmed. "The doldrums," sailors called it, and they steered clear. So did the ocean's top predators: the tuna, sharks, and other large fish that required livelier waters, flush with prey. The gyre was more like a desert—a slow, deep, clockwise-swirling vortex of air and water caused by a mountain of high-pressure air that lingered above it.

The area's reputation didn't deter Moore. He had grown up in Long Beach, 40 miles south of L.A., the Pacific literally in his front yard, and he possessed an impressive aquatic résumé: deckhand, able seaman, sailor, scuba diver, surfer, and finally captain. Moore had spent countless hours in the ocean, fascinated by its vast trove of secrets and terrors. He'd seen a lot of things out there, things that were glorious and grand; things that were ferocious and humbling. But he had never seen anything nearly as chilling as what lay ahead of him in the gyre.

It began with a line of plastic bags ghosting the surface, followed by an ugly tangle of junk: nets and ropes and bottles, motor oil jugs and cracked bath toys, a mangled tarp. Tires. A traffic cone. Moore could not believe his eyes. Out here in this desolate place, the water was a stew of plastic crap. It was as though someone had taken the pristine seascape of his youth and swapped it for a landfill.

How did all the plastic end up here? How did this trash tsunami begin? What did it mean? If the questions seemed overwhelming, Moore would soon learn that the answers were even more so, and that his discovery had dire implications for human—and planetary—health. As *Alguita* glided through the area that scientists now refer to as the "Eastern Garbage Patch," Moore realized that the trail of plastic went on for hundreds of miles. Depressed and stunned, he sailed for a week through bobbing, toxic debris trapped in a purgatory of circling currents. To his horror, he had stumbled across the 21st century Leviathan. It had no head, no tail. Just an endless body.

CR&ED

"Everybody's plastic, but I love plastic. I want to be plastic." This Andy Warhol quote is emblazoned on a six-foot-long magenta and yellow banner that hangs—with extreme irony—in the solar-powered workshop in Moore's Long Beach home. The workshop is surrounded by a crazy Eden of trees, bushes, flowers, and fruits, as well as vegetables ranging from the prosaic (tomatoes) to the exotic (cherimoyas, guavas, chocolate persimmons, white figs the size of

Plastic Bullets: An albatross on Kure Atoll that mistook too many floating plastic particles for baitfish.

baseballs). This is the house in which Moore, 59, was raised, and it has a kind of open-air earthiness that reflects his sixties-activist roots, which included a stint in a Berkeley commune. Composting and organic gardening are serious business here—you can practically smell the humus—but there is also a kidney-shaped hot tub surrounded by palm trees. Two wet suits hang drying on a clothesline above it.

This afternoon, Moore strides the grounds. "How about a nice, fresh boysenberry?" he asks, and plucks one off a bush. He's a striking man wearing no-nonsense black trousers and a shirt with official-looking epaulettes. A thick brush of salt-and-pepper hair frames his intense blue eyes and serious face. But the first thing you notice about Moore is his voice, a deep, bemused drawl that becomes animated and sardonic when the subject turns to plastic pollution. This problem is Moore's calling, a passion he inherited from his father, an industrial chemist who studied waste management as a hobby. On family vacations, Moore recalls, part of the agenda would be to see what the locals threw out. "We could be in paradise, but we would go to the dump," he says, with a shrug. "That's what we wanted to see."

Since his first encounter with the Garbage Patch nine years ago, Moore has been on a mission to learn exactly what's going on out there. Leaving behind a 25-year career running a furniture-restoration business, he has created Algalita Marine Research Foundation to spread the word of his findings. He has resumed his science studies, which he'd set aside when his attention swerved from pursuing a university degree to protesting the Vietnam War. His tireless effort has placed him on the front lines of this new, more abstract battle. After enlisting scientists such as Steven B. Weisberg, Ph.D. (director of the Southern California Coastal Water Research Project and an expert in marine environmental monitoring), to develop methods for analyzing the gyre's contents, Moore has sailed *Alguita* back to the Garbage Patch several times. On each trip, the volume of plastic has grown alarmingly. The area in which it accumulates is now twice the size of Texas.

At the same time, all over the globe, there are signs that plastic pollution is doing more than blighting the scenery; that it is also making its way into the food chain. Some of the most obvious victims are the dead seabirds that have been washing ashore in startling numbers, their bodies packed with plastic: things like bottle caps, cigarette lighters, tampon applicators, and colored scraps that, to a foraging bird, resemble baitfish. (One animal dissected by Dutch researchers contained 1,603 pieces of plastic.) And the birds aren't alone. All sea creatures are threatened by floating plastic, from whales down to zooplankton. There's basic moral horror in seeing the pictures: a sea turtle with a plastic band strangling its shell into an hourglass shape; a humpback towing plastic nets that cut into its flesh and make it impossible for the animal to hunt. More than a million seabirds, 100,000 marine mammals, and countless fish die in the North Pacific each year, either from mistakenly eating this junk or from being ensnared in it and drowning.

Plastic Bullets: A turtle that grew in to an hourglass shape after swimming through a plastic ring.

Bad enough. But Moore soon learned that the big, tentacled balls of trash were only the most visible signs of the problem; others were far less obvious, and far more evil. Dragging a fine-meshed net known as a manta trawl, he discovered minuscule pieces of plastic, some barely visible to the eye, swirling like fish food throughout the water. He and his researchers parsed, measured, and sorted their samples and arrived at the following conclusion: By weight, this swath of sea contains six times as much plastic as it does plankton.

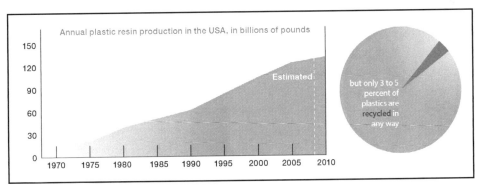

This statistic is grim—for marine animals, of course, but even more so for humans. The more invisible and ubiquitous the pollution, the more likely it will end up inside us. And there's growing—and disturbing—proof that we're ingesting plastic toxins constantly, and that even slight doses of these substances can severely disrupt gene activity. "Every one of us has this huge body burden," Moore says. "You could take your serum to a lab now, and they'd find at least 100 industrial chemicals that weren't around in 1950." The fact that these toxins don't cause violent and immediate reactions does not mean they're benign: Scientists are just beginning to research the long-term ways in which the chemicals used to make plastic interact with our own biochemistry.

CR80

In simple terms, plastic is a petroleum-based mix of monomers that become polymers, to which additional chemicals—such as di (2-ethylhexyl) phthalate (DEHP) and polybrominated biphenyls (PBBs)—are added for suppleness, inflammability, and other qualities. When it comes to these substances, even the syllables are scary. For instance, if you're thinking that perfluorooctanoic acid (PFOA) isn't something you want to sprinkle on your microwave popcorn, you're right. Recently, the Science Advisory Board of the Environmental Protection Agency (EPA) voted PFOA a likely carcinogen. And yet when your butter deluxe meets your superheated microwave oven, so much PFOA leaches into the popcorn oil from the product packaging that a single serving spikes the amount of this poison in your blood.

How toxins enter your body

TOXIC	Nalgene bottles (marked #7)	Plastic food wrap (marked #3)	Polystyrene cups and clamshell take-out containers (marked #6)	Pizza boxes and french-fry containers (with waxy lining)	Polyvinyl chloride (PVC), used in vinyl flooring, shower curtains, and car interiors
DANGER	Bisphenol A (BPA), a synthetic estrogen, can leach into contents	Phthalates, a probable human carcinogen and known endocrine disruptor, can migrate into food (especially fatty foods, such as deli meats and cheeses)	Styrene, a possible human carcinogen, can leach into contents	Perfluorooctanoic acid (PFOA), the grease-repelling chemical found in fluorinated telomers and a possible human carcinogen, can migrate from the waxy plastic coating onto the food inside, especially at high temperatures	Vinyl chloride is a known human carcinogen and off-gases into the surrounding air; it is inhaled instead of ingested
LINKED TO	Lowered sperm count; reproductive-organ abnormalities; prostate cancer in preliminary animal studies	Reproductive-organ damage (such as undescended testes); lowered sperm count in preliminary animal studies	Cancer	Cancer; lung and kidney damage in preliminary studies	Cancer; liver damage
ACCORDING TO	Researchers at the University of Missouri, the University of Chicago, and the University of Cincinnati	Researchers at the University of Rochester	The EPA's Office of Research and Development, and the World Health Organization's International Agency for Research on Cancer	The EPA Science Advisory Board and the Environmental Working Group	The EPA and the Center for Health, Environment and Justice
NONTOXIC SUBSTITUTE	Stainless-steel water bottles (kleankanteen. com)	Waxed paper	Paper cups (without wax lining); ceramic or glass dishes	Sit-down restaurant instead of drive-thru or delivery	Ceramic tile; hemp shower curtains, open car windows

Other nasty chemical additives are the flame retardants known as polybrominated diphenyl ethers (PBDEs). These chemicals have been shown to cause liver and thyroid toxicity, reproductive problems, and memory loss in preliminary animal studies. In vehicle interiors, PBDEs—used in moldings and floor coverings, among other things—combine with another group called phthalates to create that much-vaunted "new-car smell." Leave your new wheels in the hot sun for a few hours, and these substances can "off-gas" at an accelerated rate, releasing noxious byproducts.

It's not fair, however, to single out fast food and new cars. PBDEs, to take just one example, are used in many products, incuding computers, carpeting, and paint. As for phthalates, we deploy about a billion pounds of them a year worldwide despite the fact that California recently listed this as a chemical known to be toxic to our reproductive systems. Used to make plastic soft and pliable, phthalates leach easily from millions of products—food, cosmetics, varnishes, the coatings of timed-release pharmaceuticals—into our blood, urine, saliva, seminal fluid, breast milk, and amniotic fluid. In food containers and plastic bottles, phthalates are now found with another compound called bisphenol A (BPA), which scientists are now discovering can wreak stunning havoc in the body. We produce 6 billion pounds of that each year, and it shows: BPA has been found in nearly every human who has been tested in the United States. We're eating these plasticizing additives, drinking them, breathing them, and absorbing them through our skin every single day.

Most alarming, these chemicals may disrupt the endocrine system—the delicately balanced set of hormones and glands that affect virtually every organ and cell—by mimicking the female hormone estrogen. In marine environments, excess estrogen has led to *Twilight Zone*-esque discoveries of male fish and seagulls that have sprouted female sex organs.

On land, things are equally gruesome. "Fertility rates have been declining for quite some time now, and exposure to synthetic estrogen—especially from the chemicals found in plastic products—can have an adverse effect," says Marc Goldstein, M.D., director of the Cornell Institute for Reproductive Medicine. Dr. Goldstein also notes that pregnant women are particularly vulnerable: "Prenatal exposure, even in very low doses, can cause irreversible damage in an unborn baby's reproductive organs." And after the baby is born, he or she is hardly out of the woods. Frederick vom Saal, Ph.D., a professor at the University of Missouri at Columbia who specifically studies estrogenic chemicals in plastics, warns parents to "steer clear of polycarbonate baby bottles. They're particularly dangerous for newborns whose brains, immune systems, and gonads are still developing." Vom Saal's research spurred him to throw out every polycarbonate plastic item in his house, and to stop buying plastic-wrapped food and canned goods (cans are plastic-lined) at the grocery store. "We now know that BPA causes prostate cancer in mice and rats, and abnormalities in the prostate's stem cell, which is the cell implicated in human prostate cancer," he says. "That's enough to scare the hell out of me." At Tufts University, Ana M. Soto, M.D., a professor of anatomy and cellular biology, has also found connections between these chemicals and breast cancer.

As if the potential for cancer and mutation weren't enough, Dr. Vom Saal says "prenatal exposure to very low doses of BPA increases the rate of postnatal growth in mice and rats." In other words, BPA made rodents fat. Their insulin output surged wildly and then crashed into a state of resistance—the virtual definition of diabetes. They produced bigger fat cells, and more of them. A recent scientific paper Dr. Vom Saal coauthored contains this chilling sentence: "These findings suggest that developmental exposure to BPA is contributing to the obesity epidemic that has occurred during the last two decades in the developed world, associated with the dramatic increase in the amount of plastic being produced each year." Given this, it is perhaps not entirely coincidental that America's dramatic rise in diabetes—a 735 percent increase since 1935—follows the same arc.

CRSO

Such news is depressing enough to make a person reach for the bottle. Glass, at least, is easily recyclable. You can take one tequila bottle, melt it down, and make another tequila bottle. With plastic, recycling is more complicated. Unfortunately, that promising-looking triangle of arrows that appears on products doesn't signify endless reuse; it merely identifies which type of plastic the item is made from. And of the seven different plastics in common use, only two of them—PET (#1, used in soda bottles) and HDPE (#2, used in milk jugs)—have much of an aftermarket. So no matter how virtuously you toss your chip bags and shampoo bottles into your blue bin, few of them will escape the landfill—only 3 to 5 percent of plastics are recycled in any way.

"There's no legal way to recycle a milk container into another milk container without adding a new virgin layer of plastic," Moore says, pointing out that because plastic melts at low temperatures, it retains pollutants and the tainted residue of its former contents. Turn up the heat to sear these off, and some plastics release deadly vapors.

So the reclaimed stuff is mostly used to make entirely different products, things that don't go anywhere near our mouths, such as fleece jackets and carpeting. Therefore, unlike glass, metal, or paper, recycling plastic doesn't always result in less use of virgin material. It also doesn't help that fresh-made plastic is far cheaper.

Moore routinely finds half-melted blobs of plastic in the ocean, as though the person doing the burning realized partway through the process that this was a bad idea, and stopped (or passed out from the fumes). "That's a concern as plastic proliferates worldwide, and people run out of room for trash and start burning plastic—you're producing some of the most toxic gases known," he says. The color-coded bin system may be alive and well in Marin County, but it is somewhat less effective in subequatorial Africa or rural Peru.

"Except for the small amount that's been incinerated—and it's a very small amount—every bit of plastic ever made still exists," Moore says, describing how the material's molecular structure resists biodegradation. Instead, plastic crumbles into ever-tinier fragments as it's exposed to sunlight and the elements. And none of these untold gazillions of fragments is disappearing anytime soon: Even when plastic is broken down to a single molecule, it remains too tough for biodegradation.

Truth is, no one knows how long it will take for plastic to biodegrade, or return to its carbon and hydrogen elements. We only invented the stuff 144 years ago, and science's best guess is that its natural disappearance will take several more centuries. Meanwhile, every year, we churn out 60 billion tons of it, much of which becomes disposable products meant only for a single use. Set aside the question of why we're creating ketchup bottles and six–pack rings that last for half a millennium, and consider the implications of it: *Plastic never really goes away.*

ಚಿಞಚಿಞಚಿಞ

Ask a group of people to name an overwhelming global problem, and you'll hear about climate change, the Middle East, or AIDS. No one, it is guaranteed, will cite the sloppy transport of nurdles as a concern. And yet nurdles, lentil–size pellets of plastic in its rawest form, are especially effective couriers of waste chemicals called persistent organic pollutants, or POPs, which include known carcinogens such as DDT and PCBs. The United States banned these poisons in the 1970s, but they remain stubbornly at large in the environment, where they latch on to plastic because of its molecular tendency to attract oils.

The word itself—*nurdles*—sounds cuddly and harmless, like a cartoon character or a pasta for kids, but the thing that it refers to is most certainly not. Absorbing up to a million times the level of POP pollution in their surrounding waters, nurdles become supersaturated poison pills. They're light enough to blow around like dust, to spill out of shipping containers, and to wash into harbors, storm drains, and creeks. In the ocean, nurdles are easily mistaken for fish eggs by creatures that would very much like to have such a snack. And once inside the body of a bigeye tuna or a king salmon, these tenacious chemicals are headed directly to your dinner table.

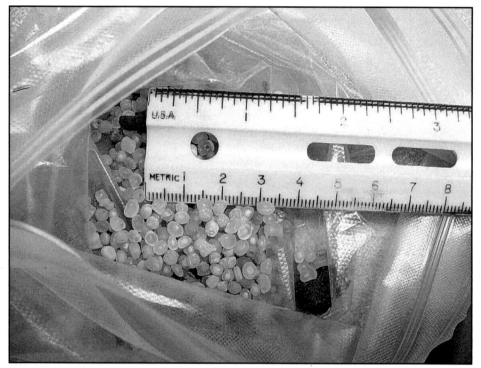

Poison Pellets: Plastic pellets known as nurdles soak up toxins like DDT and can now be found mixed in with beach sand around the world.

One study sponsored by the California Water Resources Control Board estimated that nurdles now account for 10 percent of plastic ocean debris. And once they're scattered in the environment, they're diabolically hard to clean up (think wayward confetti). At places as remote as Rarotonga, in the Cook Islands, 2,100 miles northeast of New Zealand and a 12-hour flight from L.A., they're commonly found mixed with beach sand. In 2004, Moore received a $500,000 grant from the state of California to investigate the myriad ways in which nurdles go astray during the plastic manufacturing process. On a visit to a polyvinyl chloride (PVC) pipe factory, as he walked through an area where railcars unloaded ground-up nurdles, he noticed that his pant cuffs were filled with a fine plastic dust. Turning a corner, he saw windblown drifts of nurdles piled against a fence. Talking about the experience, Moore's voice becomes strained and his words pour out in an urgent tumble: "It's not the big trash on the beach. It's the fact that the whole biosphere is becoming mixed with these plastic particles. What are they doing to us? We're breathing them, the fish are eating them, they're in our hair, they're in our skin."

Though marine dumping is part of the problem, escaped nurdles and other plastic litter migrate to the gyre largely from land. That polystyrene cup you saw floating in the creek, if it doesn't get picked up and specifically taken to a landfill, will eventually be washed out to sea. Once there, it will have plenty of places to go: The North Pacific gyre is only one of five such high-pressure zones in the oceans. There are similar areas in the South Pacific, the North and South Atlantic, and the Indian Ocean. Each of these gyres has its own version of the Garbage Patch, as plastic gathers in the currents. Together, these areas cover 40 percent of the sea. "That corresponds to a quarter of the earth's surface," Moore says. "So twenty-five percent of our planet is a toilet that never flushes."

CRUCRUCRU

It wasn't supposed to be this way. In 1865, a few years after Alexander Parkes unveiled the first man-made plastic, a scientist named John W. Hyatt set out to make a synthetic replacement for ivory billiard balls. He had the best of intentions: Save the elephants! After some tinkering, he created celluloid. From then on, each year brought a miraculous recipe: rayon in 1891, Teflon in 1938, Velcro in 1957. Durable, cheap, versatile—plastic seemed like a miracle. And in many ways, it was. Plastic has given us bulletproof vests, credit cards, slinky spandex pants. It has led to breakthroughs in medicine, aerospace engineering, and computer science. And who among us doesn't own a Frisbee?

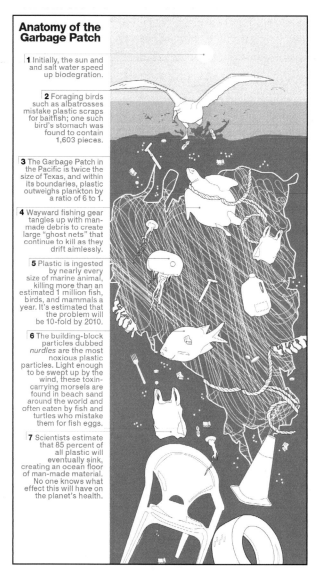

Anatomy of the Garbage Patch

1 Initially, the sun and and salt water speed up biodegration.

2 Foraging birds such as albatrosses mistake plastic scraps for baitfish; one such bird's stomach was found to contain 1,603 pieces.

3 The Garbage Patch in the Pacific is twice the size of Texas, and within its boundaries, plastic outweighs plankton by a ratio of 6 to 1.

4 Wayward fishing gear tangles up with man-made debris to create large "ghost nets" that continue to kill as they drift aimlessly.

5 Plastic is ingested by nearly every size of marine animal, killing more than an estimated 1 million fish, birds, and mammals a year. It's estimated that the problem will be 10-fold by 2010.

6 The building-block particles dubbed *nurdles* are the most noxious plastic particles. Light enough to be swept up by the wind, these toxin-carrying morsels are found in beach sand around the world and often eaten by fish and turtles who mistake them for fish eggs.

7 Scientists estimate that 85 percent of all plastic will eventually sink, creating an ocean floor of man-made material. No one knows what effect this will have on the planet's health.

That plastic has benefits, no one would deny. Few of us, however, are as enthusiastic as the American Plastics Council. One of its recent press releases, titled "Plastic Bags—A Family's Trusted Companion," reads: "Very few people remember what life was like before plastic bags became an icon of convenience and practicality—and now art. Remember the 'beautiful' [sic] swirling, floating bag in *American Beauty*?"

Alas, the same ephemeral quality that allows bags to dance gracefully across the big screen also lands them in many less desirable places. Twenty-three countries, including Germany, South Africa, and Australia, have banned, taxed, or restricted the use of plastic bags because they clog sewers and lodge in the throats of livestock. Like pernicious Kleenex, these flimsy sacks end up snagged in trees and snarled in fences, blighting the scenery. They also trap rainwater, creating perfect little breeding ponds for disease-carrying mosquitoes.

In the face of public outrage over pictures of dolphins choking on "a family's trusted companion," the American Plastics Council takes a defensive stance, sounding not unlike the NRA: Plastics don't pollute, people do.

It has a point. Each of us tosses about 185 pounds of plastic per year. We could certainly reduce that. And yet—do our products have to be quite so lethal? Must a discarded flip-flop remain with us until the end of time? Aren't disposable razors and foam packing peanuts a poor consolation prize for the destruction of the world's oceans, not to mention our own bodies and the health of future generations? "If 'more is better' and that's the only mantra we have, we're doomed," Moore says, summing it up.

Oceanographer Curtis Ebbesmeyer, Ph.D., an expert on marine debris, agrees. "If you could fast-forward 10,000 years and do an archaeological dig … you'd find a little line of plastic," he told *The Seattle Times* last April. "What happened to those people? Well, they ate their own plastic and disrupted their genetic structure and weren't able to reproduce. They didn't last very long because they killed themselves."

Wrist-slittingly depressing, yes, but there are glimmers of hope on the horizon. Green architect and designer William McDonough has become an influential voice, not only in environmental circles but among Fortune 500 CEOs. McDonough proposes a standard known as "cradle to cradle" in which all manufactured things must be reusable, poison-free, and beneficial over the long haul. His outrage is obvious when he holds up a rubber ducky, a common child's bath toy. The duck is made of phthalate-laden PVC and bears a warning about cancer and reproductive harm. "What kind of people are we that we would design like this?" McDonough asks. In the United States, it's commonly accepted that children's teething rings, cosmetics, food wrappers, cars, and textiles will be made from toxic materials. Other countries—and many individual companies—seem to be reconsidering. Currently, McDonough is working with the Chinese government to build seven cities using "the building materials of the future," including a fabric that is safe enough to eat and a new, nontoxic polystyrene.

Thanks to people like Moore and McDonough, and media hits such as Al Gore's *An Inconvenient Truth*, awareness of just how hard we've bitch-slapped the planet is skyrocketing. After all, unless we're planning to colonize Mars soon, this is where we live, and none of us would choose to live in a toxic wasteland or to spend our days getting pumped full of drugs to deal with our haywire endocrine systems and runaway cancer.

None of plastic's problems can be fixed overnight, but the more we learn, the more likely that, eventually, wisdom will trump convenience and cheap disposability. In the meantime, let the cleanup begin: The National Oceanographic & Atmospheric Administration (NOAA) is aggressively using satellites to identify and remove "ghost nets," abandoned plastic fishing gear that never stops killing. (A single net recently hauled up off the Florida coast contained more than 1,000 dead fish, sharks, and one loggerhead turtle.) New biodegradable starch- and corn-based plastics have arrived, and Wal-Mart has signed on as a customer. A consumer rebellion against dumb and excessive packaging is afoot. And in August 2006, Moore was invited to speak about "marine debris and hormone disruption" at a meeting in Sicily convened by the science advisor to the Vatican. This annual gathering, called the International Seminars on Planetary Emergencies, brings scientists together to discuss mankind's worst threats. Past topics have included nuclear holocaust and terrorism.

Ghost Killers: The *Alguita's* crew deploys a tracking buoy on fishing gear that was either discarded or lost at sea and has now amassed with other wayward debris.

CR80

The gray plastic kayak floats next to Moore's catamaran, *Alguita*, which lives in a slip across from his house. It is not a lovely kayak; in fact, it looks pretty rough. But it's floating, a sturdy, eight-foot-long two-seater. Moore stands on *Alguita*'s deck, hands on hips, staring down at it. On the sailboat next to him, his neighbor, Cass Bastain, does the same. He has just informed Moore that he came across the abandoned craft yesterday, floating 3 yards offshore. The two men shake their heads in bewilderment. "That's probably a six-hundred-dollar kayak," Moore says, adding, "I don't even shop anymore. Anything I need will just float by." (In his opinion, the movie *Cast Away* was a joke—Tom Hanks could've built a village with the crap that would've washed ashore during a storm.)

Watching the kayak bobbing disconsolately, it is hard not to wonder what will become of it. The world is full of cooler, sexier kayaks. It is also full of cheap plastic kayaks that come in more attractive colors than battleship gray. The ownerless kayak is a lummox of a boat, 50 pounds of nurdles extruded into an object that nobody wants but that'll be around for centuries longer than we will.

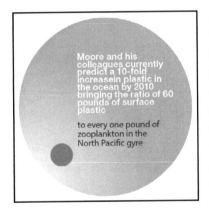

Moore and his colleagues currently predict a 10-fold increase in plastic in the ocean by 2010 bringing the ratio of 60 pounds of surface plastic

to every one pound of zooplankton in the North Pacific gyre

And as Moore stands on deck looking into the water, it is easy to imagine him doing the same thing 800 miles west, in the gyre. You can see his silhouette in the silvering light, caught between ocean and sky. You can see the mercurial surface of the most majestic body of water on earth. And then below, you can see the half-submerged madhouse of forgotten and discarded things. As Moore looks over the side of the boat, you can see the seabirds sweeping overhead, dipping, and skimming the water. One of the journeying birds, sleek as a fighter plane, carries a scrap of something yellow in its beak. The bird dives low and then boomerangs over the horizon. Gone.

Credit ——————————————————————————————
Casey, Susan. "Plastic Ocean." *Best Life Magazine* 20 Feb. 2007. Print. Reproduced with permission of Rodale via Copyright Clearance Center.

Building Baby from the Genes Up

Ronald M. Green

Ronald M. Green is Professor Emeritus of Religion and of Ethics and Human Values at Dartmouth College, as well as the director of its Institute for the Study of Applied and Professional Ethics. He has written over 80 articles on ethics, covering such subtopics as theory, religion, medicine, and business. Originally written for The Washington Post, *"Building Baby from the Genes Up" explores the possible outcomes of using therapeutic gene therapy. Green understands the risks but believes that what can be discovered about the human gene will not only become commonplace but also will allow humanity to utilize its benefits.*

CRROCRROCRRO

The two British couples no doubt thought that their appeal for medical help in conceiving a child was entirely reasonable. Over several generations, many female members of their families had died of breast cancer. One or both spouses in each couple had probably inherited the genetic mutations for the disease, and they wanted to use in-vitro fertilization and preimplantation genetic diagnosis (PGD) to select only the healthy embryos for implantation. Their goal was to eradicate breast cancer from their family lines once and for all.

In the United States, this combination of reproductive and genetic medicine—what one scientist has dubbed "reprogenetics"—remains largely unregulated, but Britain has a formal agency, the Human Fertilization and Embryology Authority (HFEA), that must approve all requests for PGD. In July 2007, after considerable deliberation, the HFEA approved the procedure for both families. The concern was not about the use of PGD to avoid genetic disease, since embryo screening for serious disorders is commonplace now on both sides of the Atlantic. What troubled the HFEA was the fact that an embryo carrying the cancer mutation could go on to live for 40 or 50 years before ever developing cancer, and there was a chance it might never develop. Did this warrant selecting and discarding embryos? To its critics, the HFEA, in approving this request, crossed a bright line separating legitimate medical genetics from the quest for "the perfect baby."

Like it or not, that decision is a sign of things to come—and not necessarily a bad sign. Since the completion of the Human Genome Project in 2003, our understanding of the genetic bases of human disease and non-disease traits has been growing almost exponentially. The National Institutes of Health has initiated a quest for the "$1,000 genome," a 10-year program to develop machines that could identify all the genetic letters in anyone's genome at low cost (it took more than $3 billion to sequence the first human genome). With this technology, which some believe may be just four or five years away, we could not only scan an individual's—or embryo's—genome, we could also rapidly compare thousands of people and pinpoint those DNA sequences or combinations that underlie the variations that contribute to our biological differences.

With knowledge comes power. If we understand the genetic causes of obesity, for example, we can intervene by means of embryo selection to produce a child with a reduced genetic likelihood of getting fat. Eventually, without discarding embryos at all, we could use gene-targeting techniques to tweak fetal DNA sequences. No child would have to face a lifetime of dieting or experience the health and cosmetic problems associated with obesity. The same is true for cognitive problems such as dyslexia. Geneticists have already identified some of the mutations that contribute to this disorder. Why should a child struggle with reading difficulties when we could alter the genes responsible for the problem?

Many people are horrified at the thought of such uses of genetics, seeing echoes of the 1997 science-fiction film *Gattaca*, which depicted a world where parents choose their children's traits. Human weakness has been eliminated through genetic engineering, and the few parents who opt for a "natural" conception run the risk of producing offspring—"invalids" or "degenerates"—who become members of a despised underclass. Gattaca's world is clean and efficient, but its eugenic obsessions have all but extinguished human love and compassion.

These fears aren't limited to fiction. Over the past few years, many bioethicists have spoken out against genetic manipulations. The critics tend to voice at least four major concerns. First, they worry about the effect of genetic selection on parenting. Will our ability to choose our children's biological inheritance lead parents to replace unconditional love with a consumerist mentality that seeks perfection?

Second, they ask whether gene manipulations will diminish our freedom by making us creatures of our genes or our parents' whims. In his book *Enough*, the techno-critic Bill McKibben asks: "If I am a world-class runner, but my parents inserted the 'Sweatworks2010 GenePack' in my genome, can I really feel pride in my accomplishments? Worse, if I refuse to use my costly genetic endowments, will I face relentless pressure to live up to my parents' expectations?"

Third, many critics fear that reproductive genetics will widen our social divisions as the affluent "buy" more competitive abilities for their offspring. Will we eventually see "speciation," the emergence of two or more human populations so different that they no longer even breed with one another? Will we re-create the horrors of eugenics that led, in Europe, Asia and the United States, to the sterilization of tens of thousands of people declared to be "unfit" and that in Nazi Germany paved the way for the Holocaust?

Finally, some worry about the religious implications of this technology. Does it amount to a forbidden and prideful "playing God"?

To many, the answers to these questions are clear. Not long ago, when I asked a large class at Dartmouth Medical School whether they thought that we should move in the direction of human genetic engineering, more than 80 percent said no. This squares with public opinion polls that show a similar degree of opposition. Nevertheless, "babies by design" are probably in our future—but I think that the critics' concerns may be less troublesome than they first appear.

Will critical scrutiny replace parental love? Not likely. Even today, parents who hope for a healthy child but have one born with disabilities tend to love that child ferociously. The very intensity of parental love is the best protection against its erosion by genetic technologies. Will a child somehow feel less free because parents have helped select his or her traits? The fact is that a child is already remarkably influenced by the genes she inherits. The difference is that we haven't taken control of the process. Yet.

Knowing more about our genes may actually increase our freedom by helping us understand the biological obstacles—and opportunities—we have to work with. Take the case of Tiger Woods. His father, Earl, is said to have handed him a golf club when he was still in the playpen. Earl probably also gave Tiger the genes for some of the traits that help make him a champion golfer. Genes and upbringing worked together to inspire excellence. Does Tiger feel less free because of his inherited abilities? Did he feel pressured by his parents? I doubt it. Of course, his story could have gone the other way, with overbearing parents forcing a child into their mold. But the problem in that case wouldn't be genetics, but bad parenting.

Granted, the social effects of reproductive genetics are worrisome. The risks of producing a "genobility," genetic overlords ruling a vast genetic underclass, are real. But genetics could also become a tool for reducing the class divide. Will we see the day when perhaps all youngsters are genetically vaccinated against dyslexia? And how might this contribute to everyone's social betterment?

As for the question of intruding on God's domain, the answer is less clear than the critics believe. The use of genetic medicine to cure or prevent disease is widely accepted by religious traditions, even those that oppose discarding embryos. Speaking in 1982 at the Pontifical Academy of Sciences, Pope John Paul II observed that modern biological research "can ameliorate the condition of those who are affected by chromosomic diseases," and he lauded this as helping to cure "the smallest and weakest of human beings … during their intrauterine life or in the period immediately after birth." For Catholicism and some other traditions, it is one thing to cure disease, but another to create children who are faster runners, longer-lived or smarter.

But why should we think that the human genome is a once-and-for-all-finished, untamperable product? All of the biblically derived faiths permit human beings to improve on nature using technology, from agriculture to aviation. Why not improve our genome? I have no doubt that most people considering these questions for the first time are certain that human genetic improvement is a bad idea, but I'd like to shake up that certainty.

Genomic science is racing toward a future in which foreseeable improvements include reduced susceptibility to a host of diseases, increased life span, better cognitive functioning and maybe even cosmetic enhancements such as whiter, straighter teeth. Yes, genetic orthodontics may be in our future. The challenge is to see that we don't also unleash the demons of discrimination and oppression. Although I acknowledge the risks, I believe that we can and will incorporate gene technology into the ongoing human adventure.

Credit _____

Green, Ronald M. "Building Baby from the Genes up." *Washington Post*, Opinions 13 Apr. 2008. Reproduced with permission of Washington Post Co. via Copyright Clearance Center.

Genetically Modified Humans? No Thanks.

Richard Hayes

Richard Hayes is a visiting scholar at the University of California at Berkeley in the College of Natural Resources/Energy and Resources Group. He holds a Ph.D. in Energy and Resources from that same university and has addressed the United Nations about banning human cloning worldwide. In "Genetically Modified Humans? No Thanks," he argues against using genetic therapy in human research because of the risks to human rights, which, he believes, could likely result in the escalation of social inequality. His article is a direct response to Ronald M. Green's.

⊙⊱⊙⊰⊱⊙⊰⊱⊙

In an essay[1] in Sunday's Outlook section, Dartmouth ethics professor Ronald Green asks us to consider a neo-eugenic future of "designer babies," with parents assembling their children quite literally from genes selected from a catalogue. Distancing himself from the compulsory, state-sponsored eugenics that darkened the first half of the last century, Green instead celebrates the advent of a libertarian, consumer-driven eugenics motivated by the free play of human desire, technology and markets. He argues that this vision of the human future is desirable and very likely inevitable.

To put it mildly: I disagree. Granted, new human genetic technologies have real potential to help prevent or cure many terrible diseases, and I support research directed towards that end. But these same technologies also have the potential for real harm. If misapplied, they would exacerbate existing inequalities and reinforce existing modes of discrimination. If more widely abused, they could undermine the foundations of civil and human rights. In the worst case, they could undermine our experience of being part of a single human community with a common human future.

Once we begin genetically modifying our children, where do we stop? If it's acceptable to modify one gene, why not two, or 20 or 200? At what point do children become artifacts designed to someone's specifications rather than members of a family to be nurtured?

Given what we know about human nature, the development and commercial marketing of human genetic modification would likely spark a techno-eugenic rat-race. Even parents opposed to manipulating their children's genes would feel compelled to participate in this race, lest their offspring be left behind.

Green proposes that eugenic technologies could be used to reduce "the class divide." But nowhere in his essay does he suggest how such a proposal might ever be made practicable in the real world.

The danger of genetic misuse is equally threatening at the international level. What happens when some rogue country announces an ambitious program to "improve the genetic stock" of its citizens? In a world still barely able to contain the forces of nationalism, ethnocentrism, and militarism, the last thing we need to worry about is a high-tech eugenic arms race.

In his essay, Green doesn't distinguish clearly between different uses of genetic technology—and the distinctions are critical. It's one thing to enable a couple to avoid passing on a devastating genetic condition, such as Tay-Sachs.[2] But it's a different thing altogether to create children with a host of "enhanced" athletic, cosmetic and cognitive traits that could be passed to their own children, who in turn could further genetically modify their children, who in turn … you get the picture. It's this second use of gene technology (the technical term is "heritable genetic enhancement") that Green most fervently wants us to embrace.

In this position, Green is well outside the growing national and international consensus on the proper use of human genetic science and technology. To his credit, he acknowledges that 80 percent of the medical school students he surveyed said they were against such forms of human genetic engineering, and that public opinion polls show equally dramatic opposition. He could have noted, as well, that nearly 40 countries[3]—including Brazil, Canada, France, Germany, India, Japan, and South Africa—have adopted socially responsible policies regulating the new human genetic technologies. They allow genetic research (including stem cell research) for medical applications, but prohibit its use for heritable genetic modification and reproductive human cloning.

In the face of this consensus, Green blithely announces his confidence that humanity "can and will" incorporate heritable genetic enhancement into the "ongoing human adventure."

Well, it's certainly possible. Our desires for good looks, good brains, wealth, and long lives, for ourselves and for our children, are strong and enduring. If the gene-tech entrepreneurs are able to convince us that we can satisfy these desires by buying into genetic modification, perhaps we'll bite. Green certainly seems eager to encourage us to do so.

But he would be wise to listen to what medical students, the great majority of Americans and the international community appear to be saying: We want all these things, yes, and genetic technology might help us attain them, but we don't want to run the huge risks to the human community and the human future that would come with altering the genetic basis of our common human nature.

Notes

1   Ronald M. Green, "Building Baby from the Genes Up," *The Washington Post,* April 13, 2008, http://www.washingtonpost.com/wp-dyn/content/article/2008/04/11/AR2008041103330.html.

2   "Tay-Sachs Disease Information Page," *National Institute of Neurological Disorders,* http://www.ninds.nih.gov/disorders/taysachs/taysachs.htm.

3   "National Polices on Human Genetic Modification: A Preliminary Survey," *Center for Genetics and Society,* November 15, 2007, http://www.geneticsandsociety.org/article.php?id=304.

Creating "Companions" for Children: The Ethics of Designing Esthetic Features for Robots

Yvette Pearson and Jason Borenstein

Yvette Pearson is an Associate Professor and chair of the Philosophy and Religious Studies Department at Old Dominion University in Norfolk, Virginia, and is an expert in Bioethics. Jason Borenstein is the Director of Graduate Research Ethics Program at Georgia Tech. In "The Ethics of Designing Esthetic Features for Robots," they examine their shared interest in the ethics of employing robots in everyday life, specifically as attendants for children. The authors also discuss whether robots should resemble and act like humans and whether gender should be assigned to them. Pearson and Borenstein argue that robot design is crucial, but that more investigation and discussion must be done in the area of robots and their relationships with children, as their use might affect both short and long-term development of children.

⊰౸◌ C౸◌ C౸◌

1. Introduction

This article examines the ethical aspects of robots that function as friends, caregivers, assistive devices, or toys for children. The increased use of robots is intended to affect various facets of human life, including individual welfare, decision-making, and relationships among humans. In addition to anticipating and addressing basic safety issues, roboticists should also grapple with ethical questions generated by design decisions that have no obvious safety-related implications. While it is important to minimize the probability of harmful malfunction, the focus of this article will be on risks emerging from properly functioning robots. More specifically, we will discuss the relative importance of a robot companion's esthetic features, including whether it should be gendered. Our hope is that continued examination of design decisions will promote children's well-being and contribute to positive transformations of social institutions.

2. Background and Rationale

Contemporary societies are moving away from robots operating in isolation from human beings to an era of pervasive human–robot interaction (HRI). Regarding the increasing prevalence of HRI, the International Federation of Robotics (IFR) quotes a "robot expert" who states that "as technological improvements resulting in more intelligent robot systems with better sensors enable closer interaction between human workers and robots, it will become a reality" (IFR 2011a, p. 31). Though the development of robots outside of military and industrial contexts is still in its early stages, the rate of advance in robotics is accelerating. Robots designed for therapeutic or educational purposes are increasingly being used in experimental settings. Moreover, according to *World Robotics 2011,* "about 2.2 million service robots for personal and domestic use were sold," marking an increase of 35% over 2009 sales (IFR 2011b, XIV). The report also projected that this number would increase significantly between 2011 and 2014 to 14.4 million "units of service robots for personal use" (IFR 2011b, XV). Rather than waiting until various social or personal robots become common, we prefer a proactive approach that identifies potential design-related ethical problems and aims to prevent or mitigate them.

Using the capabilities approach as our primary theoretical foundation, our previous work emphasized the importance of incorporating robots into society in ways that promote human flourishing (Borenstein and Pearson 2010). Mere "avoidance of harm," while a worthy goal, does not go far enough. The integration of robots into society should involve the careful examination of existing institutions and practices. We should aim to avoid simply integrating robots into our lives in ways that perpetuate problematic practices and instead use their introduction as an opportunity to question longstanding social institutions and interpersonal interactions. Among other things, we will consider whether robots should be designed to be humanlike and, if so, how closely and in what ways they should resemble humans. Even if designing humanlike robots turns out to be an ethically sound course of action, it does not follow that other design pathways should be off-limits. It may be acceptable, or even preferable, for practical or moral reasons to design robots that are zoomorphic or even abstract—bearing no resemblance to any living animal, human, or non-human (e.g., e-puck; Mondada et al. 2009).

Though the focus here will be on the design and use of robots *for children,* we recognize that there is great variation among children, according to their age group as well as other factors affecting their development. This means that the design and use of a robot that promotes the welfare of one group of children (e.g., toddlers) may be deficient in achieving this aim with another group of children (e.g., 6-year-olds). Because of the wide variation in the abilities of children as they move through the stages of development, the recommendations we provide here will be general enough to apply to a plurality of categories of children without being so general that they fail to provide practical guidance.

Capurro maintains that it is important to understand *why* we are trying to realize certain values via robots. He claims that we "redefine ourselves in comparison with robots … as we redefine ourselves in comparison with animals or gods" and that doing so has "far reaching economic, ethical, and cultural implications" (2009, p. 120). Additionally, some scholars suggest that interaction with emerging technologies can generate new ways of understanding the world and ourselves. For example, though not referring to the context of robotics, Hausman (1995) explains that "new developments in technology make new discursive situations possible, open up new subject positions" (14). In a similar vein, Fior et al. (2010) suggest that children interacting with robots over time will develop "a new system or schema of understanding and subsequent vocabulary to articulate their sense of friendship with a robot that is likely distinct from their friendships with children" (p. 15). The transformative power of increased HRI combined with society's obligation to protect children from harm requires us to implement proactive measures that will promote the flourishing of developing children and avoid inadvertently cutting off their "right to an open future."

3. Types of Robots

Many different types of companion robots have been, or are in the process of being, created to fulfill a wide range of functions. For purposes of this paper, we are using the term "companion" in a broad sense to include not only robots that interact in "friendly" ways (e.g., playing games with people), but also more passive robots that simply keep a person company without necessarily responding to the persons specific actions or commands. Included in this definition are robotic pets such as *Paro*, a robotic seal, and *Aibo*, a robotic dog. More recently, *MyKeepon* was introduced to the public; it is a robotic toy first used in research aimed at helping autistic children (Ceceri 2011). Another robot, *Wakamaru*, is supposed to offer a higher level of engagement and provide companionship, and *CareBot* is touted as being able to monitor care recipients. MIT's Personal Robotics Group is in the process of creating a series of socially assistive robots that will be able to interact with people in a variety of contexts. Our definition of a "companion" includes socially assistive and other types of robots intended to be used by an individual person, typically outside of military or industrial contexts.

Of course, the ethical dimensions associated with the design of each kind of robot might overlap, but there are subtleties that distinguish different categories of robots. In general, the ethical concerns relating to robots tend to grow and intensify as the amount of "responsibility" delegated to them for a child's care increases. For example, Prazak et al. (2004) draw a distinction between robotic toys and robots that assist children while they play with a toy. Users should reasonably expect more from a robotic assistant than they would from a toy, since the former is intentionally designed to take on a caregiving or educational role. Yet, as the field of robotics advances, users will likely demand and expect more from all types of robots.

4. The Importance of Context-Sensitive Design

For HRI to promote the welfare of children effectively, some degree of bonding between the robot and child will have to occur. It is necessary, however, to determine which esthetic features are more conducive to a robot's ability to fulfill this function. For example, Walters et al. (2008) note how the appearance of a robotic tour-guide may vary sharply from a companion robot; the former is supposed to instruct groups of people while the latter can be tailored to the demands of an individual person. At first glance, the appearance of a robot intended to be a child's companion might be more crucial than if the robot is merely performing mundane tasks such as cleaning the child's room. This is not to say that esthetics is unimportant in the latter case, but it is a matter of degree. Certain esthetic features will be determined according to the frequency and duration of the interactions between the robot and the child, which overlaps with the child's expectations of what the robot can provide. For instance, Turkle notes, children often believe a robot is alive if it can move on its own; also, it has become common during the digital age that a child thinks an electronic toy is "alive" if it can "think" (2006). Taking this kind of psychological finding into account, designers could make it rather obvious that a robot is thinking by mimicking human behavior (e.g., placing a hand on its chin). Assessing the appropriateness of this sort of design strategy hinges on a number of considerations; this includes whether eliciting a less than accurate understanding of reality is ethically problematic.

Design features must be integrated so that they are compatible with how a robot will be used. To minimize confusion, disappointment, or other negative emotional responses, Feil-Seifer and Mataric (2011) astutely point out that users should be provided with a clear explanation of the robot's role, abilities, and limitations. They cite recent studies that show that people "quickly form mental models of robots … based on what they know best: other people" (p. 27). Since a human caregiver's behaviors can amplify this tendency and promote gross misunderstandings of the robot's actual abilities and limitations, designers and users must exercise caution not only when making decisions about the robot's size, but also how a robot is "dressed and accessorized." For example, Feil-Seifer and Mataric (2011) note that a robot may be mistakenly viewed as medically competent if it is "dressed in a lab coat and wearing a stethoscope" (p. 27). In short, design choices generate expectations, perhaps some of which are erroneous, about the abilities that a robot possesses (Goetz et al. 2003).

A high priority is anticipating and avoiding design features likely to frighten children, such as an overwhelmingly large size or a "creepy" appearance. For example, Movellan recalls the reaction that toddlers had when he brought *Robovie*, a social robot, into his son's classroom; it caused them to be distressed (Tucker, 2009). In contrast, Movellan suggests that another robot, *RUBI*, may have helped children to learn vocabulary words. Besides warding off negative emotional reactions in children, Salter et al. (2008) remind us that it is equally important to avoid boring children. Whether a robot's features will elicit a negative reaction from a child will depend in large part on the child's developmental level and the context in which the child's interaction with the robot occurs.

A number of variables make it difficult to generalize about how children will respond to particular design features. For instance, the existence of countless forms of animation and art seems to imply that there are many standards for what is considered esthetically appealing. It follows that there will be at least some variability in people's responses to esthetic features. With the expansion of global communication, it is an open question whether apparent cultural differences in taste may become less striking and more homogenized.

Reber et al.'s (2004) review of literature from social psychology, cognitive psychology, and experimental esthetics indicates that esthetic judgment is affected by "objective" or "core" features (e.g., quantity of information, figure-ground contrast, and clarity) as well as a perceiver's prior experience with certain kinds of stimuli. Further, it is possible that some preferences are "hardwired" into human psychology. For instance, Brown et al. (2008) argue that for evolutionary reasons, symmetry is integrally connected to whether someone is deemed to be attractive. Hence, how stimuli are processed is not solely a function of the features of the object perceived but also the present state and previous experiences of the perceiver and the perceiver's psychological make-up. This suggests that in addition to integrating "core" esthetic features into the design of robots, the manner in which individuals are socialized is a key variable. While far from conclusive, Ho et al. (2008) observe that "anecdotal evidence indicates that the eeriness of a human-looking robot habituates with exposure" (p. 170); in other words, people tend to adapt to a robot whose appearance initially repels them. Presumably, those who have greater exposure to robots may respond more positively, at least to certain types of robots, and those who are exposed to a broad array of robot types may respond rather favorably to them.

Because esthetic judgments and corresponding affective responses are partially a function of fluency, which can develop over time, designers of robots for children should incorporate certain of the aforementioned "core" esthetic features into a robot's design if they hope to promote its acceptance. "Clarity" is one example of a core feature, and this seems to be what Breazeal (2002) identifies when she refers to readability of facial expressions as an important element in the design of sociable robots. In other words, if the manner in which a robot tries to convey an emotion is too vague or ambiguous, the design pathway could fail. Along these lines, if the tone of voice does not match the emotional content of what is being said, it could be unsettling to the user. For example, Nass and Yen (2010) devised a scenario that involved a "male" synthetic voice telling two stories (one happy and one sad), and the voice could sound happy or sad. They state that "... when the emotion of the content and the voice matched, the emotional message was clear and strong. On the other hand, mismatching the tone of voice muddled the emotion of the content" (p. 128). In a later section, the connection between this type of issue and the uncanny valley hypothesis will be explored.

Roboticists will not be able to control fully how users respond to robots (nor perhaps should they). Yet the robotics community should make a concerted effort to predict problematic uses and user reactions to robots. Both policy makers and consumers should be made aware of the true capabilities of companion robots and be provided with guidance about how to avoid negative consequences from their use. For example, if a child believes that a robot is caring and can be trusted (e.g., "The robot can protect me") but it cannot fulfill these expectations, this can be highly problematic (Sharkey and Sharkey 2010). Of greater concern, perhaps, is that adults entrusted with the welfare of children will expect too much of robots and assign them far greater responsibility for children than is warranted by the robot's actual abilities. Belpaeme and Morse (2010) argue that growing more accustomed to robots "... will more than counter this tendency to over-attribute the abilities of robots" (p. 194). Yet it is not clear that their far-reaching optimism is warranted especially considering how willing many parents already are to surrender portions of their caregiving responsibilities to technology (e.g., using a television or an electronic game system as a babysitter). Hence, it will be necessary to tread carefully when considering which beliefs might be affected by HRI and how various modifications to children's beliefs will impact their view of themselves and others.

5. Cultural Factors

In addition to contemplating the possible basis for individual esthetic judgments, it is also worthwhile to consider the collective esthetic preferences attributed to a particular culture. For example, Japanese people are commonly viewed as being technophiles, while Americans are often considered to be less enamored with robotic technology or downright fearful of it (e.g., *Terminator*; Kaplan 2004). Yet MacDorman et al. (2009) argue that the perception of Japan as a "robot-loving" culture is overstated. Their study, which surveyed U.S. and Japanese faculty, found significant agreement between both groups in attitudes toward robots even though Japan does not seem to have as many cultural or religious reservations about technology. Arguably, Japan's widespread use of robots for non-military applications is grounded in practical considerations, such as predicted labor shortages, rather than a mere fondness for artificial beings.

Along similar lines, Wagner (2009) believes that it is a mistake to view Japanese culture as a whole as naturally inclined to interact with robots because external forces pushed robots into various facets of domestic life in Japan. For example, she points out that "the development of mechanical dolls … was caused by [an edict] of the Japanese military rulers … who prohibited in 1649 any further research and development of new technological products in the fear of riots" and the rise of a potent technological rival (p. 511). Hence, a plausible explanation is that a military edict, not the "national character" of the Japanese people, contributed to the creation and use of mechanical dolls in domestic settings. Wagner also discusses the claim that Japan may have been trying to exert its own technological prowess in response to allegations that the country was stealing ideas from the West (p. 511).

Nishida (2009) draws similar conclusions, suggesting that the interest of Japanese young people in robot contests may be due to their excitement about the prospect of winning high-tech products and "opportunities for enhancing collaborative learning" (pp. 111–112). He offers reasons that do not seem culture specific even though these practices may evoke the "robot-loving" stereotype. For example, Nishida explains that the use of industrial robots or sushi robots is just a way to improve efficiency and lower costs. He also alleges that Japanese people are no more eager to replicate humans than people in other countries. This assertion, however, is at odds with other research indicating that xenophobia may be a motivating factor behind the drive to increase the use of robot caregivers (Parks 2010) and at least one empirical study that alleges that there is significant anti-immigrant sentiment in Japan (Richey 2010). Ironically, Parks (2010) observes that many Japanese are more comfortable with robots than humans even though they desire robots that are "as authentically human as possible" (104). Regardless of the nature and extent of difference in attitudes toward robots between the United States and Japan, Melson (2010) notes that the increased use of mediated interactions in the United States is paving the way for "receptivity to robots in children's lives" (p. 229). Robots might not "invade" as many facets of human life in the United States as in Japan, but interaction with children is one area where significant HRI is likely to emerge. Interestingly, children in a study by Fior et al. (2010) were inclined to view a robotic arm as a social being despite its relative lack of sophistication. They concluded that "children will readily accept these types of devices as companions or friends even when they exhibit minimal emotional cues" (p. 16).

Despite apparent cultural differences in attitudes toward robots, the recognition of similarities across human beings can guide at least some design decisions. The esthetic features of a robot are ethically salient in part because they can influence the kinds of characteristics that children will attribute to the robot. It is equally important to consider robot behavior and its impact on HRI. According to Woods et al. (2006) "... many designers focus predominantly on the different types of facial features and expressions needed for a robot while ignoring robot movement and body shape" (p. 1412). Children's perceptions of a robot's behavioral intentions are not only affected by whether a robot appears machinelike or humanlike, but also by factors like the robot's means of locomotion. Woods and colleagues acknowledge, however, that further study is necessary to evaluate the relative importance of behavioral and esthetic features of robots in promoting positive responses to the technology.

6. Humanlike Appearance and the Uncanny Valley

A major design consideration is whether and to what degree robots should be humanlike. A useful starting point is to distinguish between humanoid robots and androids. MacDorman and Ishiguro (2006) explain that while androids are designed to be indistinguishable from humans, humanoid robots are humanlike only in the sense that their "gross morphology" resembles that of a human (p. 322). Yet androids are designed to resemble humans in many ways beyond gross morphology; for example, an android's skin texture, gestures, and other behaviors should be designed to mimic a human's features. One example of an android is Ishiguro's *Repliee Q1Expo*, which has been described in the following terms: "She has flexible silicone for skin rather than hard plastic ... She can flutter her eyelids and move her hands like a human. She even appears to breathe" (Whitehouse 2005). Though MacDorman and Ishiguro's distinction does not appear to be universally embraced in the robotics literature (Halpern and Katz 2012), it is useful for the present discussion.

Discussions about the physical appearance of robots usually include cautionary words about the "uncanny valley" hypothesis put forth by Mori (1970/2012). Mori claimed that there is a "valley" of great discomfort when we interact with a robot or other entity that looks human but lacks key attributes that we would normally expect to accompany a certain (human) appearance. For example, Woods et al. (2006) note that children in their study became "more comfortable" as a robot's appearance approached the uncanny valley. However, they also observed that the children's attitudes toward humanlike robots, at least up to a certain point, were more positive than toward machinelike or animallike robots. When the robots started to seem too humanlike, the children tended to attribute negative character traits to the robots (e.g., bossy, aggressive, angry; p. 1409).

Doubts about the validity of the uncanny valley hypothesis continue to emerge. According to Hanson et al. (2005), worries about the uncanny valley are overstated and that humanlike robots "will serve as an unparalleled tool for investigating human social perception and cognition" (p. 31). Bartneck et al. (2009) claim that empirical evidence in support of Mori's hypothesis has been minimal. Participants in their study were asked to rate the likeability of humans as compared to "highly realistic androids" (p. 270). Real human beings were found to be more humanlike than androids, but the likability ratings of the humans versus androids were fairly similar (p. 274). A potential limitation of the study is that the researchers did not measure differences in the likeability of androids with differing levels of anthropomorphism (i.e., human likeness).

While avoiding the uncanny valley may still be a desirable goal, it is possible that cultural changes over the past several decades may render this concern somewhat less relevant today. Not only have various technologies been more fully integrated into our lives (e.g., realistic-looking animation), but also social attitudes and behaviors toward people with impairments have shifted. Though things were beginning to change during the time of Mori's research, a tendency to institutionalize individuals with cognitive or physical impairments persisted. It was therefore less common to either see or interact with individuals whose appearance or behavior was unfamiliar. On a related note, Bartneck et al. (2009), referencing Nancy Etcoff's *Survival of the Prettiest: The Science of Beauty*, point out that "Sick or injured people are generally perceived as disturbing ..." (p. 272). In a society where it is rare to see people with severe impairments or using assistive medical devices to interface with their environment, encountering an individual who is clearly human but appears or behaves in a way that is not well understood can cause an "uncanny valley" type of experience. Many societies have begun to at least question practices that marginalize people with cognitive and physical impairments or otherwise cause them to be treated poorly. In short, ongoing changes in prevailing social practices or shifts in individual comfort levels might diminish the impact of the uncanny valley.

More frequent exposure to humans with physical or cognitive impairments may put people more at ease while they are in the company of individuals whose appearance or behavior does not match their expectations. Yet this may not entirely resolve the uncanny valley problem if there are other significant contributors to that experience. As Mitchell et al. (2011) explain, the feelings of eeriness experienced during HRI may not be due solely to atypical appearances or behavior patterns. Instead, their study indicates that a mismatch between various sense modalities is another factor that can give rise to feelings of eeriness. They showed videos of a robot using a human voice, a robot using a synthetic voice, a human using a human voice, and a human using a synthetic voice (Mitchell et al. 2011). Study participants were asked to rate the humanness, eeriness, and warmth of the characters viewed on the video screen.

They found that the eeriness rating was highest for the human figure—synthetic voice and robot figure—human voice conditions. Mitchell and colleagues conclude that there should be a match between the degree of human likeness of the voice and visual elements. They did not seem to detect a significant difference in the results in terms of the participants' age or gender.

Even though a perceived mismatch appears to generate feelings of eeriness, Ho et al. (2008) point out that there is at least anecdotal evidence indicating that people can become reasonably comfortable with a humanlike robot over time even if an initial encounter with it gives them "the creeps." What remains unclear, however, is whether there are other relevant phenomena that could generate similar feelings of eeriness. As mentioned previously, a mismatch among sense modalities can cause greater discomfort, but this may not be the source, or at least not the only eeriness-generating factor. The public has now been exposed for decades to Stephen Hawking's mechanical voice, and this experience might make it less likely that the human figure–mechanical voice pairing will be viewed as disturbing to people today as it might have been viewed when such devices were first used (e.g., for those who had their vocal cords removed). Whether the mismatches that adults found disturbing are likely to translate to children is something that should not be assumed a priori. It is possible, for example, that a child's reactions will correspond more closely to Ho et al.'s (2008) finding that "older people were more willing to overlook defects in a robot" when rating whether it looks "humanlike" (p. 175).

Ho et al. (2008) consider other possible sources that may contribute to feelings of eeriness. They mention the possibility that these feelings may arise depending on the extent to which robots elicit feelings of fear, especially fear of death or fear of losing bodily control. They give examples of human-looking robots eliciting a fear of being replaced or threatening a deeply held metaphysical assumption that humans have souls and are not simply "soulless machines" (Ho et al. 2008, 170). While their study does not rule out the possibility of associations between the uncanny valley and either fear of mortality or disgust "as an evolved mechanism for pathogen avoidance" (175), they point out that further research is needed to identify the aspects of a robot's appearance or behavior that prompts such reactions from humans. Where children, particularly very young children, are concerned, it seems unlikely that views about human mortality will play a significant role in how they react to robots. Moreover, it is possible that children's interaction with robots will render moot some of the concerns raised here. For example, if an individual is accustomed to robots from early childhood, she will presumably not find encounters with robots as unusual or as jarring as an adult who has not interacted with them before.

Briefly stated, additional empirical evidence is needed to answer questions regarding what precisely might be called for in terms of a robot's appearance. The etiology or manifestation of uncanny valley-type experiences in adults may not necessarily translate to the case of children. A standardized approach (e.g., making them look "humanlike") is neither necessary nor desirable. At this early stage of the robotic era, it is preferable to have a plurality of design strategies until there is greater clarity regarding which ones are most conducive to promoting human well-being. The varied tastes and preferences of children in their selection of toys, television programs, etc. indicate that convergence may be unwise. Walters et al. (2008) suggest in their study that a person's personality type might give some indication of how that individual will respond to a robot. For example, they claim that introverted humans prefer a more mechanical-looking robot, whereas extroverts prefer a more human-looking robot (p. 175). Considering the benefits of animal-assisted therapy, there are compelling reasons to continue creating at least some robots that look like non-human animals. The fact that the benefits of robotic animals have already been substantiated to some degree only serves to reinforce this point (Banks et al. 2008).

7. Gender

One underexplored area within robot ethics is the relationship between gender stereotypes and decisions about the design and use of robots. A key issue to consider is whether robots should be gendered and exactly what it would mean for a robot to be gendered. For example, would this require having a certain body type or merely a "feminine" or "masculine" voice? Further, if a robot does not display clear signs of a particular gender (i.e., it looks "too androgynous"), will this elicit an "uncanny valley" type of reaction? Of course, there are other gender-related matters surrounding robot design. These include whether robots should be designed to recognize the gender of an individual and, if so, whether the robot should respond differently according to the gender of the person that it encounters. Understanding whether and how gender differences affect an individual's responses to robots is also salient.

A related matter is whether gendering should depend on the particular type of robot. For example, gendering toy robots might have a different impact than gendering a caregiver robot. Whether toys are gender-specific may be less of an issue, because it appears that the tendency to select same-gender toys is influenced heavily by parent/caregiver biases (Fine 2010). In contrast to a robotic *toy*, a gendered robot *caregiver or playmate* might strongly influence beliefs about gender roles in the way that human caregivers and peers do. Gender features are sometimes integrated into technology unconsciously, and this is a pattern likely to persist with robots (e.g., creating a robotic kindergarten teacher that looks "female"). It is also possible that designers might decide to integrate gender features deliberately. One reason for this is to facilitate bonding. Within the context of HRI, Woods et al. (2006) observe that a "female gender was associated with positive robot traits such as happiness and friendliness" (p. 1412). Yet, as Carpenter et al. (2009) explain, gendering humanoid robots is likely to perpetuate stereotypes that persist in interpersonal interaction. Along these lines, referring to the Japanese roboticist Tomotaka Takahashi, Robertson (2010) states that "Technical difficulties aside, Takahashi—and my research suggests that he is representative of Japanese roboticists in general—invokes, in no uncertain terms, his common-sense view that an attribution of female gender requires an interiorized, slender body, and male gender an exteriorized, stocky body" (p. 19). Such tendencies can have the unfortunate consequence of reinforcing rigid views of how individuals of a particular gender should present themselves or behave.

Not only could gendering a robot perpetuate certain problematic stereotypes, but also it can influence how users interact with the technology. Nass and Yen (2010) claim that a group of German males were unwilling to take instructions from a female-sounding navigation system in their automobiles. Similarly, if a robot has a "masculine" or "feminine" tone of voice, this will likely affect how humans respond to it (Sigel et al. 2009). For example, Crowell et al. (2009) claim that women viewed a female-sounding synthetic voice as more likeable and trustworthy and were "more persuaded in a choice-making task" by such a voice (p. 3736). According to Coeckelbergh (2011), "… we can expect that a person's response to gender differences in relations with robots will resemble that person's response to human gender differences" (p. 199). He offers the example of a cleaning robot and how individuals will respond to the robot if they are told that it is a "lady" (p. 199). Nomura and Tagaki (2011) point out that even if a robot has a gender-neutral appearance, users may assign a particular gender to it based on the specific tasks in which the robot is engaged, especially if those tasks are "strongly related to gender" (p. 28).

Negative stereotypes are objectionable and often destructive. As De Angeli and Brahnam (2006) claim, "the application of negative stereotypes is an important predictor of prejudice, discrimination, and hostility leading to aggression and violence" (p. 1). However, stereotypes can serve a positive function, and arguably, there are times when they are worth perpetuating. For example, a stereotype might be defensible if the by-product is robot behavior that is "appropriately persuasive" (Siegel et al. 2009) and a good outcome follows (e.g., a child accepts a necessary therapeutic intervention). To reiterate, how a robot will be perceived is integrally tied to its appearance and behavior; whether a positive response emerges is apparently affected in part by the preconceptions and assumptions that a person has about the robot because it looks like a particular gender.

Carpenter et al. (2009) found that study participants were more likely to perceive a male robot as being threatening (p. 263). This kind of finding indicates that designing a robot to look female might be preferable in some contexts. If a non-threatening presence more readily elicits cooperation, this could improve an assistive robot's ability to fulfill its function. One could imagine scenarios where a robot with a high, soothing voice could provide comfort, especially since human caregivers commonly modify their voice and make it "higher" in order to calm distressed children. However, a study by Eyssel et al. (2012) indicates that male subjects, for example, felt "psychologically closer to the male voice," and both males and females had a stronger tendency to anthropomorphize voices that corresponded to their own gender (p. 126). Crowell et al. (2009) conclude that people "resonate more with a gendered voice that matches their own" (p. 3736). Yet they also distinguish between people's perceptions of the trustworthiness of embodied versus disembodied voices and maintain that more research is needed before drawing definitive conclusions about the "highly complex" interactions between gendered robots and humans (p. 3741). At a minimum, the varying hypotheses about the impact of gendered voices and robots has on humans remind us of the importance of attending closely to the context in which these elements are introduced as well as whether their use is aimed at achieving ethically sound goals.

Young children, especially boys, tend to play with gender-typed toys, but this tendency appears to vary across individuals and can be significantly modified by relatively minor interventions, e.g., reading a counter-stereotypical story to a child (Green et al. 2004). Whether children choose gender-typed/typical toys seems to depend significantly on the reinforcement they receive from adults and peers in their environments. Green et al. (2004) suggest that boys are more rigidly locked into playing with "masculine" toys because of the harsher treatment they endure when they show interest in "feminine" toys. Fine (2010) observes that "four-year-old children will play for three times as long with a xylophone or balloon if it is labeled as for their own sex rather than for children of the other sex" (p. 230). She also explains that as early as 10 months, children begin to recognize what counts as gender-appropriate behavior, dress, and so on. These very young children are purportedly "gender detectives" who sort people and objects into gender categories.

Inquiry within the domain of robots and gender should force us to reexamine current social attitudes and practices. This is one way in which robots might help us to move forward and become increasingly sensitized to gender issues. In general, design and use decisions that reinforce gender stereotypes remain ethically questionable. Roboticists presumably would respond by arguing that gendering robots is defensible in at least some situations; this may include that female children might be more willing to interact with a "female" robot, and a similar phenomenon might be witnessed with male children and "male" robots. While comforting children is a noble goal, we should not assume that reinforcing gender stereotypes is part of an appropriate means to achieve that end. For instance, a cautious approach would require that we avoid reinforcing beliefs such as "all and only females are capable of nurturing others" or "females naturally derive immense joy from menial household chores."

8. Conclusion

Designing robots for children in a way that will allow them to flourish requires us to pay close attention to the many ways in which particular design features might affect both their short- and long-term development. Because HRI has the potential to alter not only children's development but also their interactions with other humans, design decisions must be made in ways that are likely to promote their physical, psychological, and emotional health. We questioned whether concerns about the uncanny valley hypothesis are as relevant today, primarily in the context of designing robots for children. We also delved into the underexplored area of gendering robots. Additional research will be necessary to investigate whether, beyond that which is insinuated by mere appearance, certain types of robot behaviors are ethically permissible.

There are many ethically salient aspects to a robot's design, and our hope is that roboticists will continue to examine a growing catalog of ethical issues. Focusing on the intersection of robotics, esthetics, and ethics should ideally promote careful re-examination of certain assumptions about the appropriateness of a particular design pathway. As this process continues, it may lend additional insight into the nature and appropriateness of existing human interactions and institutions. This may offer a profound opportunity to re-examine and, when necessary, revise current social practices and institutions.

Works Cited

Banks MR, Willoughby LM, Banks WA (2008) "Animal-Assisted Therapy and Loneliness in Nursing Homes: Use of Robotic Versus Living Dogs." *J Am Med Dir Assoc* 9(3):173–177.

Bartneck C, Kanda T, Ishiguro H, Hagita N (2009) "My Robot Doppelganger: A Critical Look at the Uncanny Valley." *Robot and Human Interactive Communication RO-MAN.*

Belpaeme T, Morse A (2010) "Time Will Tell—Why it is too Early to Worry." *Interact Stud* 11(2):191–195.

Borenstein J, Pearson Y (2010) "Robot Caregivers: Harbingers of Expanded Freedom for All?" *Ethics Inf Technol* 12(3): 277–288.

Breazeal C (2002) *Designing Sociable Robots.* MIT Press, Cambridge.

Brown WM, Price ME, Kang J, Pound N, Zhao Y, Yu H (2008) "Fluctuating Asymmetry and Preferences for Sex-Typical Bodily Characteristics." *PNAS* 105(35):12938–43.

Capurro R (2009) "Ethics and Robotics. In: Nagenborg M, Capurro R (Eds)" *Ethics and Robotics.* IOS Press, Heidelberg, 117–123.

Carpenter J, Davis JM, Erwin-Stewart N, Lee TR, Bransford JD, Vye N (2009) "Gender Representation and Humanoid Robots Designed for Domestic Use." *Int J Soc Robot* 1:261–265.

Ceceri K (2011) "My Keepon Dances Into Stores in October!" *Wired Magazine.* http://www.wired.com/geekdad/2011/10/my-keepon-dances-into-stores-in-october/. Accessed 9 Oct 2011.

Coeckelbergh M (2011) "Humans, Animals, and Robots: A Phenomenological Approach to Human–Robot Relations." *Int J Soc Rob* 3(2):197–204.

Crowell CR, Scheutz M, Schemerhorn P, Villano M (2009) "Gendered Voice and Robotic Entities: Perceptions and Reactions of Male and Female Subjects." In: IEEE/RSJ international conference on intelligent robots and systems (October), 3735–41.

De Angeli A, Brahnam S (2006) "Sex Stereotypes and Conversational Agents." In: Proceedings of the AVI 2006 workshop on gender and interaction: real and virtual women in a male world, Venice, Italy. http://sherylbrahnam.com/papers/EN2033.pdf. Accessed 30 May 2012.

Eyssel F, Kuchenbrandt D, Bobinger S, de Ruiter L, Hegel F (2012) "'If You Sound Like Me, You Must Be More Human': On the Interplay of Robot and User Features on Human–Robot Acceptance and Anthropomorphism *Hri'12.*" In: Proceedings of the 7th annual ACM/IEEE international conference on human–robot interaction pages (March), 125–26.

Feil-Seifer D, Mataric MJ (2011) "Socially Assistive Robotics: Ethical Issues Related to Technology." IEEE Rob Autom 18(1):24–31.

Fine C (2010) *Delusions of Gender: How our Minds, Society, and Neurosexism Create a Difference.* W W Norton and Company, New York.

Fior M, Nugent S, Beran TN, Ramirez-Serrano A, Kuzyk R (2010) "Children's Relationships With Robots: Robot is Child's New Friend." *J Phys Agents* 4(3):9–17.

Goetz J, Kiesler S, Powers A (2003) "Matching Robot Appearance and Behavior to Tasks to Improve Human–Robot Cooperation." In: Proceedings of the 12th IEEE international workshop on robot and human interactive communication (RO-MAN 2003). Milbrae, 55–60.

Green VA, Bigler R, Catherwood D (2004) "The Variability and Flexibility of Gender-Typed Toy Play: A Close Look at Children's Behavioral Responses to Counterstereotypic Models." *Sex Roles* 51 (7–8): 371–386.

Halpern D, Katz JE (2012) "Unveiling Robotophobia and Cyberdystopianism: The Role of Gender, Technology and Religion on Attitudes Towards Robots *Hri'12.*" In: Proceedings of the 7th annual ACM/IEEE international conference on human–robot interaction pages (March), 139–140.

Hanson D, Olney A, Prilliman S, Mathews E, Zielke M, Hammons D, Fernandez R, Stephanou H (2005) "Upending the Uncanny Valley." In: Cohn A (ed) Proceedings of the 20th national conference on artificial intelligence 4 (AAAI'05). AAAI Press, 1728–29.

Hausman BL (1995) *Changing Sex: Transsexualsim, Technology, and the Idea of Gender.* Duke University Press, Durham.

Ho C–C, MacDorman KF, Dwi Pramono ZAD (2008) "Human Emotion and the Uncanny Valley: A Glm, Mds, and Isoma Analysis of Robot Video Ratings." In: Proceedings of the 3rd ACM/IEEE international conference on human robot interaction (HRI '08). ACM, New York, 169–176.

International Federation of Robotics (IFR) (2011a) "Positive Impact of Industrial Robots on Employment." http://www.ifr.org/uploads/media/Metra_Martech_Study_on_robots_02.pdf. Accessed 18 June 2012.

International Federation of Robotics (IFR) (2011b) "World Robotics 2011 (Executive Summary)." http://www.worldrobotics.org/uploads/media/2011_Executive_Summary.pdf. Accessed 31 May 2012.

Kaplan F (2004) "Who is Afraid of the Humanoid? Investigating Cultural Differences in the Acceptance of Robots." *Int J Humanoid Rob* 1(3):1–16.

MacDorman KF, Ishiguro H (2006) "The Uncanny Advantage of Using Androids in Social and Cognitive Science Research." *Interact Stud* 7(3):297–337.

MacDorman KF, Vasudevan SK, Ho C (2009) "Does Japan Really Have Robot Mania? Comparing Attitudes by Implicit and Explicit Measure." *AI & Soc* 23(4):485–510.

Melson GF (2010) "Child Development Robots: Social Forces, Children's Perspectives." *Interact Stud* 11(2):227–232.

Mitchell WJ, Szerszen KA, Lu AS, Schermerhorn PW, Scheutz M, MacDorman KF (2011) "A Mismatch in the Human Realism of Face and Voice Produces an Uncanny Valley." *i-Perception* 2(1):10–12.

Mondada F, Bonani M, Raemy X, Pugh J, Cianci C, Klaptocz A, Magnenat S, Zufferey J-C, Floreano D, Martinoli A (2009) "The E-Puck, A Robot Designed for Education in Engineering." In: Proceedings of the 9th conference on autonomous robot systems and competitions, vol 1, no 1, 59–65.

Mori M (2012) "The Uncanny Valley" (KF MacDorman and N Kageki, Trans.) *IEEE Robotics and Automation,* 19(2):98–100 (Original work published in 1970). doi:10.1109/MRA.2012.2192811. http://spectrum.ieee.org/automaton/robotics/humanoids/the-uncanny-valley. Accessed 18 June 2012.

Nass C, Yen C (2010) *The Man Who Lied to His Laptop: What Machines Teach Us About Human Relationships.* Penguin Group, New York.

Nishida T (2009) "Towards Robots With Good Will." In: Capurro R, Nagenborg M (eds) *Ethics and robotics.* IOS Press, Heidelberg, 105–116.

Nomura T, Tagaki S (2011) "Exploring Effects of Educational Backgrounds and Gender in Human Robot Interaction." In: International conference on user science and engineering (i-USEr), 24–29.

Parks JA (2010) "Lifting the Burden of Women's Care Work: Should Robots Replace the Human Touch?" *Hypatia* 25(1):100–120.

Prazak B, Kronreif G, Hochgatterer A, Furst M (2004) "A Toy Robot for Physically Disabled Children." *Technol Disabil* 16:131–136.

Reber R, Schwarz N, Winkielman P (2004) "Processing Fluency and Aesthetic Pleasure: Is Beauty in the Perceiver's Processing Experience." *Pers Soc Psychol Rev* 8(4):364–382.

Richey S (2010) "The Impact of Anti-Assimilationist Beliefs on Attitudes Toward Immigration." *Int Stud Q* 54:197–212.

Robertson J (2010) "Gendering Humanoid Robots: Robo-Sexism in Japan." *Body Soc* 16(2)1–36.

Salter T, Werry I, Michaud F (2008) "Going into the Wild in Child–Robot Interaction Studies: Issues in Social Robotic Development." *Intel Serv Robot* 1(2):93–108.

Sharkey N, Sharkey A (2010) "The Crying Shame of Robot Nannies: An Ethical Appraisal." *Interact Stud* 11(2):161–190.

Siegel M, Breazeal C, Norton MI (2009) "Persuasive Robotics: The Influence of Robot Gender on Human Behavior." In: IEEE/RSJ international conference on intelligent robots and systems, 2563–68.

Tucker A (2009) "Robot Babies." *Smithsonian Magazine* (July):56–65. http://www.smithsonianmag.com/science-nature/Birth-of-a-Robot.html. Accessed 8 Oct 2011.

Turkle S (2006) "A Nascent Robotics Culture: New Complicities for Companionship." AAAI technical report series (July).

Wagner C (2009) "'The Japanese Way of Robotics': Interacting 'Naturally' With Robots as a National Character?" In: The 18th IEEE international symposium on robot and human interactive communication (September), 510–515.

Walters ML, Syrdal S, Dautenhahn K, Boekhorst R, Koay KL (2008) "Avoiding the Uncanny Valley: Robot Appearance, Personality, and Consistency of Behavior in an Attention-Seeking Home Scenario for a Robot Companion." *Auton Robot* 24:159–178.

Whitehouse D (2005) "Japanese Develop 'Female' Android." *BBC News,* July 27, http://news.bb.co.uk/2/hi/science/nature/4714135.stm. Accessed 5 May 2012.

Woods S, Dautenhahn K, Schulz J (2006) "Exploring the Design of Space Roots: Children's Perspectives." *Interact Comput* 1(5–6):1390–1418.

Credit